"A true story about three friends trying to bring a bit of decency to some of the most savage and indecent spots on our planet. On that level alone the book succeeds. Just as important, it is also a reminder that flesh-and-blood human beings are out there doing God's work in this bloody, bloody world . . . I was enthralled."

—Tim O'Brien

"For decades, television has been looking for another, more modern *M.A.S.H.*, the comedy series that drew the sting from death and war. Maybe this book is it. In these "True Stories from a War Zone," it's the early 1990's and three young, good-looking civilians working for the UN and the Red Cross first meet in Cambodia. For a decade, they operate in the bloody theatres of Rwanda, Bosnia, Somalia, Haiti and Liberia. These three voices from the world's front line are personal, these three characters from the global ground zero are fallible; their youth and idealism, faults and failures, and triumphs and tears, all work to humanise recent history and bring it home for a reckoning."

—*The Times of London*

"A riveting read that vividly dramatizes the many contradictions of the world it moves through."

—*The Guardian*

"Vividly told . . . this book is all the more engaging because its perspective is personal before it is political."

—*Daily Mail*

"The real beauty of *Emergency Sex* is that it's one of those rare books that is as wonderfully written as it is controversial . . . impossible to put down."

—*The Sunday Telegraph*

"Riveting but excruciating."

—*Santa-Cruz Sentinel*

"This is a unique and rewarding book, a mix of memoir, history, travel, and personal analysis."

—*Booklist*

"Powerfully written . . ."

"This engaging account . . . may also be a great recruiting tool. The motto: See Life, See Death, Have Sex."

"Despite the horrors that these three young people witness, their book is often funny, romantic and giddy . . . the writing is frequently beautiful. And even if it weren't, the book would be worth reading for its harrowing reporting from the front lines."

"A remarkable new book. The stories of what they did and saw and felt will make your hair stand on end . . . the end of illusions about doing good and the deep anger about what grotesque atrocities we human beings are capable of. The book is both an extraordinary testament to the nature of friendship and a searing exposé of what can go wrong when politicians and bureaucrats get scared."

"Vivid and intimate . . . "

"Serious, beautifully composed and aggressively honest. Weaving the authors' three distinct narratives, it's uniquely able to show how various peacekeeping and intervention efforts in the post-Cold War 1990's completely fell apart after Somalia."

"This three-dimensional approach is both entertaining and intellectually stimulating. . . . *Emergency Sex* is not for the faint of heart. But neither is humanitarian work."

"This is what it feels like—the heat, the anxiety, the satisfaction—to hang your hide on the Edge for reasons bigger than any of us. Yet the miracle of the book is its grit, its pounding pace. The voices linger in the air after the page is turned."

EMERGENCY SEX
And Other Desperate Measures:

❖ ❖ ❖

A True Story from Hell on Earth

Kenneth Cain, Heidi Postlewait
and
Andrew Thomson

miramax books

HYPERION

NEW YORK

The publisher and authors would like to thank Anvil Press Poetry for permission to reprint the poem Posthumous Rehabilitation from Tadeusz Rozewicz: They Came to See A Poet translated by Adam Czerniawski, 1991

"Mama, You've Got A Daughter" written by John Lee Hooker. Copyright 1958, 1986 KING OF BOOGIE MUSIC (BMI)/Administered by BUG. All Rights Reserved. Used by Permission.

"September 1, 1939" copyright 1940 & renewed 1968 by W.H. Auden, from COLLECTED POEMS by W.H. Auden. Used by permission of Random House, Inc.

In Your Eyes (Peter Gabriel, Real World Music, Ltd.) Used with permission of Lipservices Music Publishing, Brooklyn, NY. All Rights Reserved.

TWO PRINCES Copyright 1991 Sony/ATV LLC, Mow, B'Jow Music, Inc. and Troubadour 12 Music. All rights administered by Sony/ATV Music Publishing, 8 Music Square West, Nashville, TN 37203. All rights reserved. Used by permission.

ISBN 1-4013-5966-3

First Paperback Edition
10 9 8 7 6 5 4 3 2 1

To the Memories of
Marc-Arthur and Kai

And to our parents

NOTE TO THE READER

Everything in these pages is true as we experienced it, perceived it, and remember it. The book does not, however, pretend to be about the nuances of international politics, and we are not claiming objective historical, journalistic, or academic accuracy. The work is derived from our official memos, personal diaries, letters home, and memories—some many years after the fact. These pages therefore include all the subjective distortions and revisions we told ourselves, our friends, and our bosses. We have changed the names and identities of lovers, acquaintances, and colleagues. We have telescoped time, adjusted the sequence of events, and altered minor facts in some passages to help render the progression of our lives and missions more understandable. We have not artificially re-created dialogue; instead we have simply reported conversations as we remember them. Dialogue that does appear in quotes indicates a more distinct recollection of specific words and phrases.

EMERGENCY SECURITY DESIGNATIONS

United Nations peacekeeping operations in the 1990s used a security threat designation system proceeding in descending order from Condition Alpha to Bravo, Charlie, Delta, and Echo. Condition Alpha is "All Clear"; Bravo means that some caution is warranted, no immediate threat but follow normal security protocols; Charlie indicates a direct threat, either seek shelter at your duty station or relocate in an orderly manner away from danger; Delta signifies a substantial deterioration, all activities suspended, lockdown wherever you are, only movements necessary to stay alive are advised; and Echo is the end of the line, evacuate urgently to save your life. Return to Normal means the threat has subsided.

CONTENTS

CONDITION ALPHA
December 1990–February 1991

Now, we can see a new world coming into view. A world in which there is the very real prospect of a new world order. In the words of Winston Churchill, a world order in which "the principles of justice and fair play protect the weak against the strong. . . ." A world where the United Nations, freed from Cold War stalemate, is poised to fulfill the historic vision of its founders. A world in which freedom and respect for human rights find a home among all nations. The Gulf War put this new world to its first test. And, my fellow Americans, we passed that test.

—President George H. W. Bush, address to Joint Session of Congress, at the end of the Gulf War, March 6, 1991.

Heidi, December 1990
Christmas in New York

My husband's colleagues don't believe he has a wife since I never show up at any of their events. He's an agent, represents models, and there's always a party somewhere. He's been cheerfully making the rounds of holiday celebrations around town, solo and without much complaint, but I know he'd like me to join him. So, in a gesture of goodwill, I agree to attend the agency's annual Christmas party.

I started dragging myself up and down the avenues of New York City a month ago, abhorring every minute of my search for the perfect little black fuck-me dress. I don't want to stand out at the party like the Bowery social worker I am. I figure if I'm dressed like the models, I can at least blend in. Little black dresses are camouflage in that world.

The salespeople were good sports about it. They looked me over in my old jeans, muddy boots, and ski parka, and took it on as a challenge. "A little makeup, honey, and you'll look dynamite." My mother says the same thing.

It pains me now to slip this tiny, slinky dress over my head and wiggle it down over my hips. I struggle to get my panty hose on straight and without a snag, and then spend an hour in the bathroom, applying and reapplying makeup until in the end I just wash it all off and decide on a little Vaseline for my lips. I don't even attempt to do anything with my hair; I just use a scissor to cut the rubber band out and smooth it down with some hand lotion.

I check the mirror for the hundredth time. I look good. Tallish, lots of curves, decent legs. I'm not crazy about my body, but I don't loathe it either. Whatever its imperfections, men still pay me enough attention.

I step out of the cab, take a deep breath, and stride confidently, special invitation in hand, toward the large man behind the velvet rope. He checks my name, nods, and opens the door wide.

Beyond, a long hallway opens onto a cavernous room full of beautiful people. But the only little black dress in the room is on me. The models are all wearing designer jeans and T-shirts. I don't even step in. I tell the doorman I forgot to buy cigarettes and make a dash around the corner, where I throw myself against the wall and vow to hate my husband till death do us part for not cluing me in to the secret dress code of the tall and beautiful. Even when I try, I can't fit into his life.

I return to the club only after strange men on the street start propositioning me. I circle the crowd, forcing myself to smile up into the faces of the six-foot-tall models. They're young, make a lot of money, and date TV stars and NBA players. They call my husband in the middle of the night whenever they get into a jam. I think of him as their babysitter.

Across the room my husband is busy entertaining the producer of the David Letterman show. Their conversation is animated, full of laughter, drawing in the people around them. He's well liked and I'm proud of him. I wonder what they're talking about. He and I seem to have nothing left to say to each other when we're alone.

I know I should be over there at his side, laughing and joining in the conversation. He's a good man—handsome and smart and funny and exactly what every woman is supposed to want. We met at the tail end of our teenage years and have been together since, best friends, practically siblings now. But he needs someone who's supportive and caring, someone who lets him shine. I should at least pretend to be a good wife, but I just don't have the energy to fake it anymore. Somehow, I've lost control. Or maybe I never had it and I'm only realizing that now. I'm living on the periphery of my husband's world and I'm powerless.

The room is filled with photographers busy documenting this terribly insignificant moment in history to be forgotten by morning. It's dark and the camera flashes illuminate the powder on the guests' noses and the bartender hands me a shot of something and I down it and the vibration from a nearby speaker is making me nauseated. I think I'm going to be sick.

I'm thirty years old and my life is over.

Ken, December 1990
Harvard Law School

The law library is fed by old oak staircases, borne by polished marble floors, monitored by oil portraits of scholars and patriots who studied here, the men who built this country, we're told. A marble carving overhead reads NOT UNDER MAN BUT UNDER GOD AND THE LAW. I'm due to graduate in the spring and we need to commit soon to prospective employers. So I sit in the reading room and write and rewrite lists of options. Each list brings me more and more apprehension, but no closer to an insight.

A gaggle of students stands nearby, in a circle, chatting. They ignore me, but I observe them closely. There's one woman in particular I like to watch. At thirty-second intervals in the conversation, she clenches her jaw, inhales deeply through her nose, strains the tendons in her neck tautly, and says "rrriiigghht". She then throws her head back and laughs assuredly, smugly, mirthlessly. That tight clench in the jaw and neck travels all the way to the other end of her digestive tract, surely.

Morton Melkin holds forth in the center of the circle. He's a pudgy little pink man but he's impressive in class. His comments are always humane and articulate. I stopped him after seminar once to ask about his career plan. "Corporate tax law," he squealed, leaning forward, gleefully wagging his chubby little finger in my face, "tax law is where the money is." No one has ever been more certain of anything than Morton Melkin is about a future in corporate tax law. What a colossal waste of talent.

But that talent is for sale and there are buyers. Wall Street is overflowing with cash right now and corporate law firms are recruiting Harvard students by offering a New York "fantasy night"—$1,000, but you have to blow it all in Manhattan and all in one night. Some people rent helicopters, others drink vintage wines. It's a hell of a night for a student and I'm tempted.

The downside is you have to spend thirteen hours a day for the rest of your life trapped in an office with a lawyer-man in a yellow polka-dotted tie telling you what to do, then itemize what you did in six-minute intervals to bill the client. But it's worth it for ninety percent of my classmates because it provides shelter for all that mirthless self-confidence. They know which firms are suitably elite, which pedigrees are appropriate to marry, which suburbs are worthy of their presence, which schools are deserving of their kids. They are members of an exclusive club in which certainty is the condition for membership; they recognize it in each other and revel in it together.

My attention turns from my classmates when Archibald Cox walks by my table, ramrod straight. He was the special prosecutor who sued Nixon over the Watergate tapes. Professor Cox's integrity brought down a president: he's a cousin to those giants on the wall. My parents are both academics at the University of Michigan, and they take this kind of intellectual idealism deadly seriously. When they dropped me off here for my first year, they recognized Professor Cox and were so proud I'd have the opportunity to study with such a man.

As Professor Cox passes my table, the memory of my parents' hopes for what I might do with this education passes through my body like an electrical current. Fantasy night is just that, I resolve. I don't need a list of alternatives, I know what to do. It's thesis season: I need to find a way onto an unconventional career track, and an unconventional third-year thesis project is my best chance to get started.

I need a hero—and a thesis supervisor. The best thing about Harvard is that when you need an intellectual hero, you can find one in the flesh and blood, you just have to choose. My choice is Alan Dershowitz. He's not for sale to the corporate machine, he's the best defense lawyer in the country, and he never stops fighting if he thinks he's right.

So I go see the Dersh.

The Cold War is ending and democratic revolutions are erupting everywhere; the most inspiring to me is in South Africa, where the African National Congress is finally vanquishing apartheid. So I propose a thesis paper that requires field research in Johannesburg: "The Courage of Your Convictions—Jewish Opposition to Apartheid and the Legacy of the Holocaust." It's not a normal thesis topic, Professor Dershowitz says, it's not legal enough. I beg. He has hate letters from neo-Nazis plastered all over his office and the remains of a burned Israeli flag on the door. I tell him that no other professor at the law school will understand why this subject is so important to me, at this moment in history. The world is changing as we speak, I say. We have an historical obligation and enormous power to fulfill it now. "Never again" can mean something in the real world at last. I came to law school for this, not corporate tax law.

He looks at me intently and is silent for a while. Finally he nods, more to himself than to me, like he's reminding himself of something important—what it feels like to be young? He snaps up the form and signs his approval.

Andrew, December 1990
A Red Cross Hospital in Cambodia

I'm sweltering in the hammock, under a tropical sun that won't descend, waiting for a breeze I know won't come. The generator is broken again. I've wired the fan to a car battery but it just stirs up more hot air and agitates the mosquitoes. Soon I'll concede defeat, retreat to the Land Cruiser, and burn all my diesel with the air-con on full.

I can see from a distance it's a serious case when a motorcycle-drawn cart bounces off the highway and into the dusty hospital compound. There's a lumpy form motionless in the back, covered with a green army tarpaulin. Empty glass infusion bottles swing forlornly from a bamboo pole. Chances are it's either cerebral malaria or a landmine victim.

I know it's the latter when the motorcycle and cart rattle straight past the general medical ward to the operating block. I grab my stethoscope and run over.

It's a young man. He stepped on a landmine in the Khmer Rouge–controlled forest where only soldiers and woodcutters go. It's taken him more than a day to get here, carried without morphine to the nearest road in a hammock slung from a bamboo pole, then the long bumpy ride to the hospital. His left leg is shattered and jagged bone ends protrude where his foot used to be. Gravel and red soil from the upward force of the explosion have punctured the once smooth brown flesh of his calf. From the fetid odor of gangrene, I know I'm going to have to take his leg off above the knee, and even then it will be touch and go. He must have been in agony after the explosion, but he's not conscious enough to feel anything now.

Someone pays the motorcycle driver with a handful of worthless Cambodian banknotes as I help lift the inert body onto the operating table. I insert a wide-gauge drip into his right arm and hang the first of many bags of plasma, watching as it flows smoothly into his depleted veins. After he's anesthetized, I slice away the dead muscle and then use a wire bone saw to grind through his femur. When the bleeding slows, I partially close the wound, bandage the stump down hard, and toss the useless limb into a black plastic rubbish bag for incineration. Forty-five minutes and it's done, another name in the surgical logbook. I've saved his life but ruined his future.

Heidi, January 1991
At Work on the Bowery

The fluorescent lights of the ten-story men's shelter cast a glow across Bowery. The weak winter sun hasn't yet risen but the building's inhabitants are already standing aimlessly on the sidewalk in front. A wheelchair ramp leads into a long, brightly lit hallway smelling of ammonia and fried food. I punch the time clock and head back to the cafeteria for coffee.

The voices of men of all ages and races fill the space, competing with the clatter of breakfast dishes. The men greet me as I pass among their tables. Some of them have lived here over a decade and consider me part of their family.

One of the security guards comes looking for me, trailed by officers from the NYPD. A few guys slip quietly out of the cafeteria and a few others look down into their plates, their heads turned at an angle away from the cops. But it's me the police are looking for. I've gained a reputation with the local precinct for my work in crisis intervention, so they come here often, asking me to check up on some wretched soul who's crawled down into a subway tunnel, hiding like a cat when it's ready to die.

At the Broadway-Lafayette station, the woman in the token booth is expecting me and buzzes me through the service entrance. At the end of the platform, waiting passengers watch with curiosity as I step behind the railing marked DANGER and disappear into the tunnel.

Fifteen feet in, the walkway widens into small utility rooms. The only light comes from red hazard bulbs behind wire cages. I stop and listen for sounds, smell the air. And there it is, the familiar stench of gangrene.

I hear a rustle and call out into the darkness. I know most of the homeless on the Lower East Side from my Friday night volunteer stints on the food service truck, handing out hot meals and oranges to people lined up a block long at designated areas. It's Heidi, I say. I brought you a sandwich and some hot coffee. This guy's sick and fearful. I need to be able to convince him that I'm different from all the other doctors, nurses, and social workers who've treated him like shit. He needs to believe that I care about him.

Then I see him bundled up in the corner, an older white man. It looks like he has three or four coats on and a couple of knit caps. I set my sack down and pretend I'm adjusting my scarf and coat collar, to buy some time. I don't want to get too close too fast. I need to act nonchalant, confident, and in control of the situation. You lose everything in these moments if you let any apprehension show. I just keep talking. What's your name? Where're you from? I've been to Georgia. What made you come up to this cold weather? I kneel down over my sack and take the thermos out. Coffee? I ask, as if he's a guest in my home.

An icy draft pokes its head into the room and stirs yellowed newspapers. Rusty water leaks from a pipe above and drips down the wall into a fetid pool. Rats squeak in the silence left between passing trains. I imagine my husband down here with me, watching me do this job I love. I owe him

8

for this. My income as a social worker is around poverty level; without his lucrative salary, I couldn't support myself. He spends his days selling the faces of the nineties—beautiful, young women with the world at their feet. But I still want him to understand where his wife spends her days.

The man and I talk for hours. He wants to know if I'm married, if I have kids. They're always sad when they find out I have none, as if they've discovered some personal tragedy in my life. Don't worry, they say, one day you'll have some. Their fatherly concern makes them feel stronger.

Do you have a fever? I ask the man, moving closer to place my wrist against his forehead. He's burning up and my hand comes away damp with his sweat. Let me go with you to see a doctor, I say. He refuses and I understand why. At least one of his legs is rotting away and he's afraid they'll cut it off. We have guys at the shelter who try to hide their gangrenous legs from us out of the same fear of amputation, but there's no hiding that smell. I tell him that I know he's got an infection in his leg and we can get him on antibiotics to clear it up. You can stay at the shelter, I say, and I'll see you every day.

So what do you say? Let's go to the hospital and get that leg looked at. Okay, he finally says, and climbs awkwardly to his feet. I take his hand and we leave the dark room, climb back around the guardrail, and go upstairs toward daylight. As we pass by the token booth, the woman inside gives me a thumbs-up sign and smiles.

Ken, January 1991
Research in Johannesburg

I'm introduced to David Bruce, a young, white South African recently released from prison for refusing to serve in the South African Army. He is one of South Africa's most famous conscientious objectors. We sit in a funky café on the edge of Johannesburg. He's polite and casual in jeans and a T-shirt. He seems a typical suburban Jewish grad student, like the guys I go to law school with. Until he starts to speak.

He says his mother escaped the Nazis to South Africa in 1939. Ten members of her family stayed behind and were killed. Jews condemn the Nazis, he says, but for me to say that what happened in Germany was wrong, I have to show by my actions that if I had been a German citizen, I would have risked my life and fought the regime; I am a hypocrite if my action does not match my belief.

9

He was twenty-four when he showed up at the recruitment center and announced his objection to conscription into apartheid's army. He could have easily avoided the authorities and quietly dodged the draft. Instead he chose to expose himself to danger, to break permanently with suburban safety and comfort. He was sentenced to six years in a South African prison. He knew he would be, he asked for it.

But now a New World Order is forming. Nelson Mandela is finally free. So they cut David's sentence to time served and set him free too. As he celebrates the death throes of apartheid a free man in a Johannesburg café, he looks at me with an intensity I've never seen before in a contemporary and says he's conscious of the historical moment he is not only living and feeling on his skin but actually affecting.

I'm conscious of the historical moment I've been watching on CNN.

He ends the interview with a line he's obviously recited before—to himself, the judge, the press: "The legacy of the Holocaust must be applied to other forms of oppression. I feel I have a duty as a Jew not to be silenced by fear, a moral duty to fight racism, to defy apartheid."

As a kid I was obsessed by the Holocaust. I'd lie awake in bed at night and try to picture what I would have done if I had been a German Jew. Died passively? Found a way to survive? Fought back? I leave the café with my head spinning. No idea I've articulated has had the impact on another person that David Bruce's idea is having on me—let alone any action I've taken. In fact, I'm twenty-five and I've never done anything of moral significance in my life.

Desert Storm is raging in Iraq. Tel Aviv got hit again last night, the third Scud to hit its target this week. Tomorrow I'm on a plane to Israel. I can't afford to reroute a new ticket home just to avoid the danger, it would cost thousands. And half the interviews I need to do for my thesis are South African Jews who fled to Israel after they were drafted. I have to go.

But the truth is that this is the first time in my life I have been implicated in anything bigger than myself. I want to go.

Andrew, January 1991
The Hospital, Cambodia

The nurse barges into the recovery room and tells me there's another emergency. The single sheet of paper on the clipboard she hands me says the patient is thirty years old and her name is Sofany. I bend over the stretcher and shout that pretty name inches from her right ear, but she doesn't respond. I grind my knuckles across her sternum, but there's no sign of pain. Her pupils react sluggishly to light: she's in a coma.

My heart races, like it did the very first time I treated a cardiac arrest. Amputations are straightforward, but I'm neither experienced enough nor properly equipped to deal with a deeply unconscious patient out here on my own. Back home in New Zealand, I'd have sent her straight to intensive care.

She'll get no care at all unless I can get a drip into her. I fail three times in the collapsed veins of her forearms. The needles puncture her flesh and spread hemorrhage under the skin. So I'm forced to go for her neck, where the external jugular is pulsing weakly. Sweat runs into my eyes, stinging. A nurse inserts a catheter into Sofany's bladder, and a few drops of blood-stained urine trickle down the clear plastic tubing. I send blood to the laboratory, but there's no time to wait for the result. If this is cerebral malaria, she needs treatment now. I snap open glass vials of quinine and inject them into a bag of dextrose solution, then hang the bag from a hook above her head. The late afternoon sun slants through the wooden shutters, throwing amber light across her washed-out cotton sarong.

Her husband wipes sweat and spittle off her face. He tells me his name is Rithy. As I fill in the chart, I leave the family history blank; I just don't have the heart to ask about children. Rithy squats with the cheeks of his ass pressing the backs of his heels, his arms stretched out over his knees for balance. Cambodians can remain like that for hours, watching the world go by. It looked comfortable until I tried it and my legs went numb. So I sit on the cool concrete floor. Rithy watches me as I watch Sofany's chest rise and fall.

The lab technician arrives with the results. They're bad. It's malaria, and at the maximum concentration. I bend down and shake her urine bag. Nothing. I've little choice now but to give her a shot of diuretic and turn up the fluids before her kidneys fail, but if I overdo it, that fluid will end up in her lungs and she'll drown.

I gamble and put up extra bags of fluid.

Rithy keeps staring at me, waiting for me to do more. But all I can do now is wait for the quinine to do its work. If it doesn't act fast enough, she'll be dead by sunup.

I can't bear to watch, so I leave Sofany's side and cross the courtyard, with its empty fountain and stray dogs and cow shit, to the post-op ward. Another amputee, recovering from surgery this morning, is lying on his back staring at the ceiling, flyblown stump hanging in the air on a sling. I leave before he catches my eye. I hope no more of these come in today; it's just too hot to think straight, let alone amputate.

I make for the hammock in my bungalow. Six months ago I was working at Auckland Hospital in New Zealand. I had entered medical school at seventeen, graduated at twenty-three, and then worked as a resident for three years. Back home I'd be filling in my time sheet, handing over to the next shift, and heading for the elevator to the basement car park. Mind lighter, tension easing, putting distance between the patients and me. Here the distance to my bungalow is fifty yards. There's no one to hand over to and the tension never eases.

But I'm relieved to be far from academic medicine, with its rigid hierarchy, where demigod professors in white coats hold forth and terrorize medical students at the bedsides of hapless patients. They could have been mentors but they had it backward, with medicine as the end and patients the means. I chafed under their yoke for almost a decade before I grabbed this opportunity to throw away my white coat and be a true doctor. Out here there's no pretense, just dust and heat and life and death.

I wake suddenly to find a nurse shaking my arm. She tells me I'm needed over at the medical ward. It can only be about Sofany, either to approve morphine for her last hours of life or to sign her death certificate. There will be another body to burn. When the family can't afford a funeral, we wrap the corpse in white sheets and incinerate it out back in the rice fields. I unfold myself from the hammock, wishing someone else could do this part of the job.

As I enter the medical ward, I pause to ask one of the nurses whether we have any burial sheets left. Then I notice something's not right. A man who looks like Rithy is gently spooning rice gruel through a Cambodian woman's cracked lips, and there's a bag full of clear urine on the floor. I blink several times and close my eyes. When I open them she's still there. It's Sofany. I'm here to sign her death certificate and she's sitting up, eating. I smile at her, but she just stares at me blankly through bloodshot eyes. Then I realize she's never seen me before. Rithy puts down the rice bowl, bends very low, takes both my hands in his, and begins to slowly rock back and forth, chanting quietly in Khmer. I'm embarrassed when he doesn't let go. Then I think of Sofany's body being incinerated and I look down at him and then back to her and I have to pull away. I turn my face to the wall, but Rithy sees and hands me his handkerchief.

12

Heidi, January 1991
Manhattan

Two thirty in the afternoon, I'm home from work. Winter. Nothing to do. I flip through the channels, nothing but soap operas. I have to fight the urge to climb into bed, afraid I may never get up again. This ennui has taken human form and, with its dusty, white hands around my throat, has me gasping for breath. My mother tells me it's how most people live. You get up, go to work, pay the bills. Cook, clean, do the laundry. If you're lucky, you take a vacation once in a while. You get old, retire, and die. That's life. But all the questions can't be answered already; there's got to be something more. Maybe it's time to get pregnant, buy a house, adopt a dog.

There's a break in programming, a special news alert. Like an unwanted guest, the television shouts out the latest news from the Persian Gulf. I watch as streaks of white light slash across the screen through the dark night. In Israel they're passing out gas masks.

Ashamed, I find myself envying the Iraqis and the Israelis. There seems nothing false about war. Loyalties are strong. The enemy is known. There are none of the subtleties and nuances of ordinary life; you're at the core of every feeling. Nothing else matters but to stay alive. And that's how I want to feel.

I've been numb for so long, but suddenly I have this urgent feeling of emotional clarity: I need to be true to myself, and to do that, I need to leave my marriage.

Ken, January 1991
Tel Aviv, Israel

I have a list of people to call for a place to stay while I'm in Israel—distant cousins, a roommate's girlfriend, friends from my last trip here, and Tali. Each choice is laid out in front of me like a string, leading somewhere different. I just have to choose one.

I choose Tali. I've never met her but she's a friend of a friend and I have a standing invitation.

"Hi, it's Kenneth. I just arrived at the airport."

"Yeh, I hear you coming. You have place to stay not Tel Aviv?"

"No," I lie.

"Okay, I alone now, you stay with me in Tel Aviv, if you not scared."

I'm scared and I'm staying with you.

13

The road to Tel Aviv from the airport is almost empty; it's eerie. But there's an exodus of cars and buses heading out of town as the day gets old and the same sun starts to set over Baghdad.

I find the apartment block, a collection of ugly ice-cube-tray apartments with little balconies. It looks like a grungy neighborhood in Miami. She buzzes me up, the door opens and reveals Tali. She's brown and compact and erect and a woman and she scares me somehow. I enter and look to the right, a small messy bedroom with girl smells and an unmade bed, straight ahead a cramped living room with a battered couch. On the wall hangs a framed photo of a smiling soldier with a machine gun, a purple beret, and a big smile. Boyfriend?

We chat as I settle in. Her English is hilarious. It's more or less fluent, she can express everything, but all the tenses and verb constructions are wrong. After a few minutes, she puts her hand on my arm, and says, "Listen, Kenny"—nobody has called me that since I was a kid, she turns it into an Israeli name, sings it, with an emphasis on the *y* at the end—"I must to take you out a bit, have good café close by, Terminal Café we call her, you want to go out?"

The Terminal Café sits across from the Mediterranean, a coffee bar inside, a patio outside opening to an expansive view of the sea. Young Israelis lounge in defiant composure as they sit and wait for the next Scud missile. Tali sits across from me—jeans, T-shirt, sandals, sunglasses—looking like she was born in this café, it would be impossible to appear more comfortable and in place. I'm still trying to absorb what she looks like. Israelis are a mix of North African, Levantine, and Eastern European, which inflames the politics but does amazing things for the women. She has long, untamed curly black hair, pulled up and back. Large, jet-black almond eyes, her lips wide and dark. She has black eyebrows flowing up and out from the bridge of her nose all the way, more and more sparsely, to her hairline.

I can hear the guys at law school snickering about unacceptable facial hair. They talk a lot about finding an "appropriate" girlfriend. It means education, money, status, waxed eyebrows. I probably wouldn't be interested in Tali in the company of those friends. But I think I am learning something important here today at the Terminal Café: fuck those guys. This is an imperfect woman, not an appropriate girl, and I desperately want her to want me.

Her mouth seems never to close, just forms an endless array of judgments and emotions. The chin juts out accusingly. Her most striking feature is not a feature at all, it's a direct wave of affect, shooting out from her eyes and mouth. She leans intently into me when she wants to know something, her hand goes from my arm to my leg with the intensity of her questions, then she recedes back into herself when my response is unsatisfying.

She doesn't discuss career or money or fish for hints of social class, the currency of social intercourse at Harvard. Her look is decadent and flippant but the conversation is not—West Bank settlements, the Intifada, Arab culture, Saddam Hussein, American Patriot missiles: "What you think? The Patriot work good? America to protect Israel? You were in the army?"

All Israelis serve in the army, including women. No one I know serves at home. All I have are ideas and opinions. I'm vaguely aware that we've deployed Patriot missiles here to shoot down the Scuds. I'm proud of the projection of American military power all the way to the Terminal Café. But I've not lived these things. She has. Professor Dershowitz can't help me here.

It starts to get late, the mood and sky darken, and it's time to go home.

She absently kicks the front door into place behind us with her foot, her back to it. The force is just right; it doesn't slam but the bolt engages in a ringing clank. We're alone.

She puts a cassette in a little boom box; it sounds Arabic. I turn it up but she says no, turn it down. Then she turns the radio on, but there's no sound. She says the army has a special station, called *gal sheket*, the quiet station. It's always silent except when it announces an attack. We have to keep it on all night.

How many other security protocols are there that I can't even conceive of?

She goes into the bedroom, the door is only half closed, I can see clothes swaying and her shadow bobbing. She comes back out in sweats and a tank top, dripping in coffee-colored skin, black hair everywhere. That girl smell wafts toward me again, it almost hurts. I get up to go to the bathroom, not because I have to but because I want to avoid facing her on the couch.

I go to my bag, digging for my toothbrush, *beep beep beep beep*—from the radio not the boom box. It's the quiet station. The announcer repeats two words in Hebrew over and over again, *Nachash tsefa*. "What does that mean?" I ask, I hope not too hysterically. She puts her hand on my shoul-

15

der and says, "Dey attack us, it a code from the army. *Nachash tsefa* mean poison snake, you must to take your mask gas, we go up to sealed room." A siren starts to wail outside.

The quiet station is loud now. The announcer is repeating messages in Hebrew, Arabic, English, Russian, and Amharic for the Ethiopians. He says, "Citizens of Israel, a missile attack has been launched against us. You are requested to enter your sealed room calmly, put on your gas masks, bring radio batteries and water with you."

This isn't a story on CNN, this is real: I'm with Tali in Tel Aviv and "dey attack us."

Okay, okay, just follow her lead.

I unpack the gas mask the army handed me as soon as I arrived at the airport. She takes my hand and we go upstairs. There's a room completely sealed in nylon sheeting. She says, "This the sealed room. We wait here after the Scud come, but maybe we go on the porch to see him first, sometimes we also to see the Patriot missile. You want?" She nods yes.

Fuck no I don't, I want to curl up in the sealed room and lay my head in your lap.

"Yeah, okay, good," I say. "Let's go on the porch, I want to see."

We put on the masks, walk out to the porch, and wait. The mask makes her look like a monster with a huge ugly black nose. When we talk it's muffled and echoes. It's hot and the strap hurts. She points to where the Scuds usually come, from the east, she says, the direction of Jerusalem. Amman. Baghdad. Then she points again, "Dare, dare, you see, the Scud, a red light over dare." I follow her little smooth brown finger, and there's a red trail hanging in the sky far off. It's not moving fast, almost lazy, lobbing down casually. Suddenly I'm conscious of everything. I hear my breathing her breathing the refrigerator humming I feel my blood spurt through my body I see her black eyes through the mask they're wide open. The red light slides steadily lower and lower it's going to hit something eventually it's excruciatingly slow it's not coming at us it's falling far away. I turn to look for the door back to the sealed room, what if it's chemical or gas? The red light hangs lower almost to the ground and flashes orange then flashes again and it's gone, like the sun setting into the sea.

I just watched a missile land, and people died. They're bleeding and burning right now. That Scud hit and killed people. I keep repeating it all in my mind, to make it real.

The phone rings downstairs, my heart jumps, for a second I think it's my parents, but they have no idea where I am. Tali takes her gas mask off

16

and says the Scud landed far away this time, we can wait downstairs for the All Clear code word on the quiet station. What about the sealed room, I ask, what if it was a chemical or gas attack? She says, "If it chemical or gas the army to tell us, please, you sit inside if you scared of chemical, no problem, I go down to talk to my friend."

I'm alone on the porch. I take the mask half off but go sit in the sealed room. She's laughing on the phone downstairs. At me? I feel like a virgin deflowered and abandoned. Embarrassed, excited, disappointed, proud, I want more and I never want to do it again. I knew that this feeling existed—bombs fall, people die in war—it's horrifying but seems vaguely familiar. I'm sixteen and I'm having sex for the first time. I've pictured it a million times but to really do it? Suddenly it's not a fantasy. Wait I'm not ready yet okay let's do it do I have to now yes I want to but not yet take your pants off. Tears and blood.

This is ridiculous. I'm in a sealed room with the door open and my gas mask half off thinking of adolescent sex. I go downstairs. Tali says her friend from the army called—the one with the smile and the gun?—he said the Scud landed in a field in the West Bank, no one was hurt, they already did the tests and it was conventional, not gas, not chemical.

The announcer on the quiet station reads All Clear messages in five languages with code names that relate to various cities, so the Iraqis won't know where it hit. It's over.

We sit together on the couch and share a beer. She draws her legs up into herself and turns to face me. That moist brown sheath of skin turns pink at her toes, six inches from my hand. Little silver toe ring. A black forest of eyelashes. Her face is right with me but I'm sitting up straight on the couch, at a right angle to her. I feel stiff and formal and unnatural next to her ease. I should just swivel around and into her. I'm dying in my seat. I wish there were another Scud.

There's a mark on her forehead where the gas mask pressed too tight. Maybe I should caress that crease. That would be a nice innocuous start; I could back out of that if I had to. My mind races why am I so nervous she rearranges her legs I'm immobile. I'm an asshole for sitting here like this. I can tell she's waiting, curled up next to me and instead I'm sitting in Constitutional Law class, in a straight-back chair, next to shiny law student corpses. Awkward and falsely smug.

I have to try to kiss her, I'll never forgive myself if I don't. We've stopped talking, there's nothing to say. Okay, okay, I'll count down from ten silently and then do it. What do I say? *Is it all right if I kiss you?* Do you have to ask here? I don't know the rules. You have to ask a Harvard girl. *I've wanted to kiss you all day* . . . fuck it, just do it, coward. But it'll be humiliating if she says no. I'll have to leave. Okay—ten nine eight seven six five four heart racing too fast three two why is this so hard one, "Tali, I . . ." She picks up her beer, it breaks the spell, I'm gonna lose the moment. Do it now, you're a little boy if you don't, you think the soldier in the beret would hesitate? What are you going to do, stare at her eyelashes the rest of the night? She's edible and six inches away, what's wrong with you? Okay five four three two one, "Tali, I've wanted to kiss you for the past five hours"—I hear myself speak like I'm in the audience and it's a bad actor's bad line—"Is it okay if I do?"

She frowns. Hard. Cocks her head quizzically. Shakes her hand vertically, thumb up pinky down, like in the market when you don't offer enough money. It means you're a fool. Fuck. I'm dead, humiliated, I have to go stay with my cousins now.

"Why you don't?" she says, squints, shakes her head in contempt. "Why you don't already?" Maybe she moved her foot or maybe my hand found it, but suddenly I'm cupping that toe with the ring in my palm, those sweats and that tank top and those eyelashes all fold into me at once we are young and we are alive.

Andrew, January 1991
The Hospital, Cambodia

Another journalist is looking for me. I'm sure he wants a quote from the Westerner to complement his article on landmine victims. Sometime during the first beer, he's going to frown and ask me how I ended up working here as a doctor in the middle of a war zone. They all do.

It's eight years ago now but it seems like yesterday. I'm at medical school in New Zealand and the experiment in the physiology lab requires me to skewer a live frog to a wooden board, stick a metal probe through its skull, destroy the brain and dissect out the live calf muscles.

There's an Asian man sitting next to me in lab, quietly dissecting his frog. He's new to our class, looks about ten years older than me, early thirties I'd guess. I recognize him from the front row of the lecture theater, where he usually sits alone paying close attention to the professor. Maybe he has trouble with English.

I can't dissect the calf muscle intact off the bone. It keeps twitching.

Without a word he leans over with his scalpel and forceps and does it for me, with the casual ease of buttoning a shirt.

We look at each other, and he grins. He tells me he used to be a surgeon in Cambodia, during the war. Then the grin fades and he adds, "That was before the genocide."

I didn't go looking for this. I'm worried about final exams and finding money to pay off my new motorcycle. I could have tortured that frog next to someone else, but now I have a choice. I can walk away and pretend I heard nothing about genocide, or rip off the lid and learn everything I can.

I invite him for coffee.

We sit at a plastic table in the cafeteria, next to future doctors playing Space Invaders. He tells me his name is Vary and that the last patient he operated on was his wife. In 1975 his country was being overrun by Pol Pot's Khmer Rouge, and on the day they captured Phnom Penh, he pried the diamond out of her engagement ring, sterilized it, and sewed it into the flesh of her upper arm, concealing it under the vaccination scar. Hours later, victorious soldiers threw doctors and patients out of the hospitals and forcibly evacuated the city. He and his wife survived three and a half years of slave labor in the countryside before escaping to Thailand, where an official from the New Zealand Embassy interviewed them. When they arrived as refugees in Auckland, Vary dissected the diamond out of her arm and sold it to begin their new life.

After some weeks he invites me home to a small house in a rundown neighborhood, where I meet Chandra, his wife. She's svelte and big-eyed and has beautiful skin, except for a one-inch surgical scar on her upper arm.

Vary sits on his sofa, bare-chested, in a sarong. He has scars all over his legs, like a hundred cigarette burns. They're insect bites that wouldn't heal; there was no medicine during the Pol Pot time. Take off your jeans and try a sarong, it's more comfortable, he says.

I feel naked in this skirt, with a disconcerting amount of air between my legs. It slips down my hips when I try to walk, and Chandra giggles.

Then he tells me about his life under the Khmer Rouge—just the facts, chronologically, without emotion. We could be discussing a patient, except the history includes starvation, disease, overwork, and execution. And survival. Vary is one of sixty Cambodian doctors out of six hundred the Khmer Rouge didn't kill. One and a half million Cambodians died. Before I know it, it's three in the morning, so I push my motorcycle into his garage and sleep on the sofa. During the night I hear him screaming.

I devour every book I can find on the Khmer Rouge, and days turn into

weeks in the medical school library. In my study cubicle I hide Pol Pot's bi-
ography under a large anatomy text. What I'm reading makes me want to
scream too. If Pol Pot had been prime minister of New Zealand for three
years, nearly two out of three of us would have died. I sit in the back during
anatomy lectures and look down at Vary in front, and then around me,
thinking, *You're dead and you're dead and you're alive; you're dead and
you're dead and you're like Vary, you somehow survived.*

The more I learn, the less I'm able to grasp the enormity of what they
did. The why keeps slipping through my mind like mercury, so I go looking for answers at our church. I respect our minister and enjoy his ser-
mons, but when I tell him about what happened to Vary, he just shakes his
head and quotes Scripture about evil in the hearts of men. That gets me no
closer to an answer, so I end up spending Sundays hanging out at Vary's
place instead. He becomes my closest friend.

Together we go to the premiere of the film *The Killing Fields*, in which
Vary's Cambodian friend Haing Ngor, another of the sixty doctors to survive, plays the role of journalist Dith Pran. When Pran staggers across
fields of corpses and through the last minefield to look down on the huge
Red Cross hospital tent in the Thai refugee camp below, I have to leave
the theater. Out by the concession stand, as John Lennon's "Imagine"
plays over the credits, I don't imagine or really even decide, I just know
that one day I'll be a Red Cross doctor in a tent somewhere in Cambodia.

Heidi, February 1991
Staten Island, N.Y.

My husband and I spent a weekend sorting through what was his and
what was mine, which was hard to distinguish after ten years together. We
were both sad; he didn't ask many questions. When I left, he insisted I
take one of his ATM cards in case of an emergency.

After studying the rental listings, I concluded Staten Island was the
only affordable location within an hour's commute from my job on the
Bowery. Anxious to get it over with, I signed a lease for the first apartment
I saw. Now I take guilty pleasure in starting my new life.

On my way home from work each day, I like to stand outside at the
front of the Staten Island Ferry, where the spray from the water hits my face
and I can watch the far shore come into view, as the towers of lower Manhattan recede. Behind me, through steamed windows, I catch glimpses of

secretaries returning home from Wall Street. They sit warm and secure, heavy winter coats draped across the long wooden benches, colorful Reebok sneakers lining the aisles.

I watch them on the morning trips to Manhattan, as they stand side by side against the wall-length bathroom mirror, applying their makeup, laughing and gossiping. The eye-watering fume of nail polish fills the air as they touch up their long, manicured nails. They compare engagement rings and share wedding tips. I try to remember when those conversations were of interest to me and I can't.

My biggest worry now is my finances. After taxes, my monthly salary as a social worker is $960. Minus $750 for rent and another $110 to pay the telephone, gas, and electric bills, leaves me with $100 a month for food and entertainment. I buy the store brands of everything, bring left-overs for lunch, and walk instead of taking the subway. Occasionally I take ten or twenty dollars from my husband's account.

At the corner deli, I watch a woman wandering up and down the aisles until she gets the courage up to ask the manager to give her credit for a pack of cigarettes. I can see she feels ashamed, so I turn away. I don't think I could ask, but I don't have to. I have my husband's ATM card in my pocket. But that thought leaves me reeling. I'm being so smug about my independence, and it's a lie. So the first thing I do when I get home is cut the ATM card into a dozen pieces. If things get too bad, I can always call my husband's sister. She works at the UN as a secretary and makes good money. Maybe she can help me get a job there.

Ken, February 1991
Cambridge, Massachusetts

I feel guilty leaving Israel under attack and Tali snuggled under a tattered comforter, but my final semester is starting. I know now I'll never be a lawyer, but I should probably still graduate.

I arrive back home from six weeks of research in what was summer in South Africa and permanent spring in Tel Aviv to the dead of a slushy gray Cambridge winter. The February sun is afraid of New England. My hall-mates are huddled in the dorm common room surrounded by textbooks and class notes; it looks like a scene from *The Paper Chase*. But they're not studying, they're watching the war on CNN. The color of the Scud trail looks different on the replay. It looked more red, less white than it does on TV, and I don't remember it falling as fast as it looks on the screen. It seemed to pause and hang, not shoot like that.

I haven't even put my bag down and they're already lecturing me on the efficacy of Patriot missile intercepts, the details of biological warfare, Saddam Hussein's personality, the nuances of Arab politics and their relation to American military strategy in the Middle East. They master the details bloodlessly, as though war is an arcane point of corporate tax law. The fact that I was just there offers no barrier to their compulsion to display certainty and omniscience.

I've lived in an uneasy truce with this for two and a half years, but it's clear to me now how different my life can be. I'm uncertain about everything, except that I'd rather be sitting with Tali on that beat-up couch listening to the quiet station.

Andrew, February 1991
Pochentong Airport, Phnom Penh

My only real contact with the world outside Cambodia is by shortwave radio. I'm following news of the Gulf War on BBC World Service. Iraq has annexed Kuwait and American aircraft carriers with F-16s, precision bombs, and over half a million GIs are attacking in the Gulf.

This guerrilla war in the rice fields is so different from that air war in the desert. Someone sent me an article about Cambodia from a weekly news magazine, with a detailed analysis of Khmer Rouge military strategy. The troops are supposedly advancing on Phnom Penh and a colorful map illustrates their routes of approach. One of the arrows sweeps straight through this town, tracing out some impending blitzkrieg.

Who writes this nonsense? The Khmer Rouge are confined to the forests and only venture out into open country at night. And the approach road for their grand advance is currently blocked by a herd of water buffalo.

A military jeep pulls into the hospital courtyard, billowing diesel fumes. Sasha and Alexi climb out, hot and dirty. They're officers with Soviet military intelligence. We met a few months ago when we all stopped to watch Cambodian police struggling to extinguish a fire after a car bombing.

Just after we met, glasnost and perestroika hit Phnom Penh, and the officers were given permission to invite me for dinner inside the high-walled Soviet compound. We became unlikely friends behind those walls.

They tell me they're on the way to the airport, they've been recalled

22

home. With the collapse of the Soviet Union, Moscow can no longer afford to bankroll the war here. I'm going to miss them. I'm the only foreigner living in this worn-out town and they've been good company. So I jump into my Red Cross ambulance to see them off.

The Aeroflot jet, its engines warming for Moscow, dwarfs the decrepit Phnom Penh airport terminal. Sasha and Alexi are very despondent and a little drunk. They've been through this before, when the Soviets withdrew from Afghanistan two years ago. They kiss me on both cheeks, their stubble scratching my skin. The jet fuel and the heat send my head spinning as the Russians mount the gangway, where they pause at the top for one last look. There's no martial music or children with bouquets, just defeat. They salute to no one and are gone.

The concrete shudders as their jet takes off and the Soviet tide recedes from Indochina. I walk off the tarmac past two Russian MiG jets rusting impotently in the scorched grass, while thousands of miles from here F-16 jets from an ascendant America are high in the skies pulverizing targets in Iraq.

I'm glad no one can order me to leave. I'm not beholden to a Russian general or other earthly authority. My parents were the same. At my age they served as Anglican missionaries in the Solomon Islands. Some of my earliest memories are of a cappella hymns in South Pacific churches and playing with children whose skins smelled of coconut husks.

From these parents and this religion I grew up taking for granted that contentment in life comes from serving others and not oneself. Now I'm fulfilled by a calling of my own. It's dangerous here, but this conflict gives me the chance to save more lives. I'm staying on to treat the Sofanys and the landmine victims. I was meant to be here, and I'll leave when the war is over.

CONDITION BRAVO
Cambodia, 1993

In the early 1970s, the war in Vietnam spilled over its borders into neighboring Cambodia. In 1975, two weeks before Saigon fell and the United States evacuated Vietnam, a Communist guerrilla group, the Khmer Rouge, marched into Cambodia's capital, Phnom Penh, took power, and decreed Year Zero. During the next four years they killed over a million civilians. With the support of the Soviet Union, the Vietnamese invaded in 1979. They chased the Khmer Rouge to a few isolated bases in the jungle and installed a puppet regime, while the Khmer Rouge continued to conduct sporadic guerrilla operations.

At the end of the Cold War, Vietnam lost its Soviet support and was forced to withdraw. Inspired by the momentum of victory in the Gulf War and the collapse of the Soviet Union, the Western powers funded a massive UN peacekeeping operation in Cambodia. It was the beginning of the New World Order and finally time to conclude the last, lingering conflict of the Vietnam era. Twenty thousand UN soldiers and two thousand civilians arrived to administer national elections, designed to return a legitimate, democratic Cambodian government to the family of nations.

February

Heidi
Phnom Penh

Hotel le Royale sits back a respectable distance from the main road of Phnom Penh amid towering jungle greenery. The cacophony of the market stalls and the din of hundreds of vehicles are only a low, comforting buzz up here in my room on the third floor. I wander over to the balcony and watch the spectacle a block away. I've been traveling for three days but I'm excited and don't want to sleep.

A couple of months ago I returned home to my little apartment in Staten Island to find an eviction notice taped to my door. I was two months behind in the rent and the electricity had been turned off. Even though I had finally left my job on the Bowery and taken a better-paying secretarial post at the UN, I still couldn't make it without my husband's income. I just didn't think it would get that bad that fast.

Then one day I overheard two guys in my office at UN Headquarters talking about signing up for a peacekeeping mission to pay their kids' college tuitions. They were calculating mission per diems in different countries, figuring how much they could save per month, comparing living accommodations, safety, and health risks. Bosnia, Cambodia, Mozambique. I heard "Mozambique" and suddenly the copier room dissolved around me and there I was on a steamy beach in Africa. So I filled out an application and sent it off. I waited two weeks for an answer from the staff selection committee, weeks in which I had already played out every fantasy of starting my life over in Africa, having some cash in hand, leaving the winter wasteland of my life in New York. When the answer finally came, it was a rejection notice. For Mozambique. But there was another letter; I was selected for the election mission in Cambodia. I signed up without a second thought, didn't even know where Cambodia was.

I feel vulnerable and exposed in this other world. I'm reluctant to remove my clothes, as though I might need to flee at any moment. I squat naked in the bath, splashing myself with water dribbling from the tap. This is the first time in my life I'm truly alone and dependent on myself for survival. I don't know a single person in this city—in this country, hell, in Asia for that matter. It's exhilarating. Before me is the opportunity to re-create myself.

My understanding of this election is minimal. Most of what I know about Cambodia is from *The Killing Fields*. I remember a scene from the movie depicting war-happy journalists partying poolside at this very hotel prior to a hasty departure, a run for their lives from the Khmer Rouge. But no parties by the pool now. The halls are silent. I think I'm the only guest.

I spend my first night lying faceup on the narrow cot, listening to the BBC on my shortwave radio, punctuated by the sound of water dripping from the ailing pipes in the bathroom. I slip in and out of a hazy sleep, awakened throughout the night by scratching, scrambling noises on the balcony. Too big to be a rat, too small to be a man. I keep my eyes squeezed shut, afraid of what I will find staring back at me if I open them.

By morning my throat is so dry it hurts to swallow, and the only thing on my mind is finding potable water. Before I left New York, the UN Medical Service convinced me to spend a small fortune on a water-filtering contraption. It's all tubes and hoses and filters, a big box of hardware I lugged halfway around the globe. I sit on the cool tile of the bathroom floor and attempt to assemble the apparatus. The only thing I can clearly understand is that the rubber suction cup should encompass the tap. I'm wedged in, trapped between the sink and the toilet with hoses and tubes surrounding me like tendons and I still have no water. I'm ready to cry.

Fuck it, I have dollars; I'll just buy water. I toss the stupid filter in the trash and I'm off to the street on a mission to find bottled water. Halfway down the stairs, I have this thought of the maid finding the filter and think-ing it's some strange personal hygiene gadget the foreigner has brought along. I run back to the room to hide it in my bag. Swinging open the door, I see a big, mangy monkey scratching himself in the middle of my bed. He's not at all cute like the monkeys on the Discovery Channel. Patches of fur hang off here and there, and when he sees me, he bares big, yellow teeth and hisses. I jump back and close the door softly.

From behind a wooden panel in the hallway, a tiny, hunchbacked Cambodian man appears. "Ummmm, excuse me, sir, there's a monkey on my bed and I don't quite know how to handle this." I babble in English about the occasional stray cat wandering into the house at home but it was usually a neighbor's and we all laughed about it later, but a monkey, well, I never had a stray monkey wander in.

The guy starts screaming at me in Khmer. Not at the monkey, but at me. He dashes into the room, but the monkey has fled for his life out the window. He continues to berate me at the top of his lungs as he slams the tall wooden doors leading to the balcony shut, each time with a bang. As the tiny man storms by me standing mutely in the doorway with my mouth open, I see he's clutching my water filter. Over his shoulder, he grumbles something that sounds like he's spitting but that probably means "stupid American."

The monkey and the water filter both removed from my list of troubles, I head outside. I get to the main road and I just can't cross. Thousands of motorcycles, scooters, and cyclo taxis, and an occasional sedan, swiftly swim and flow within inches of each other. I wait for a break, a hesitancy at least, but it's a raging river of traffic. I know: I'll walk to the corner and wait for the light to change. But at the intersection, there's no little flashing pedestrian symbol, no traffic light, not even a stop sign. From all directions, traffic streams steadily. Like a basket weave, the drivers drift in and out of each other's path without encounter.

A cyclo driver, his head draped in a red-and-white checked headdress and his eyes hidden behind mirrored sunglasses, slows nearby and nods in my direction. I jump in the basket in front of him before he can move on. He adjusts the sun canopy over my head and off we go into the flow of traffic. I signal to the other side of the street and he glares back at me, not understanding. At the curb, he slows and realizes I am getting out already. He's perplexed. I hand him a few dollars and walk away happy. I probably paid him ten times the fare, but it was worth it to get across.

I wander around and find a café. The sole patron is a foreigner; he offers a chair at his table. Serguei is a Russian helicopter pilot who has been in town for months working for the UN. He shows me how to dissect the bread by pulling out the doughy insides and removing the tiny dead wheatworms and fly body parts. We climb into his air-conditioned Land Cruiser and take off on a tour.

Entire families pass by on single motor scooters, toddlers standing in the space between the driver's legs. Live chickens dangle by their legs from a rope tied to the back fender of the bike. *Plunk, plunk, plunk* goes the one with its head caught in the wheel spokes. A naked baby wanders to the curb to squat and defecate. A pile of squirming worms drops to the gutter, with a few left dangling from his bottom. It looks like spaghetti in curry sauce. A man walking by kicks some dirt over the slithering mass.

Cows cruise by like ocean liners, ambling into the sea of traffic. We stop for a Coke and are surrounded by giggling children. One young boy with his face covered inexplicably in Band-Aids clutches a chicken to his breast like a stuffed animal. Suddenly he just tosses it over his shoulder into the air, never even looking back.

We walk around the market. There's a flower stall, and a market to buy toiletries and have a manicure. At the linen market, there's a sudden flourish of bright orange; Buddhist monks, all of them brandishing cigarettes and chatting furiously, toss about robes and sashes the color of sunstruck pumpkins. Gem dealers sort through trays of tiny red rubies and sapphires and amethysts. Marijuana dealers squat on elevated platforms with bowls of weed, rolling fat joint after fat joint—a big bag of fifty for seventy-five cents. Goats stand with their legs hobbled and pigs lie squealing on their backs, unable to move inside the heavy reed baskets woven around their bodies from neck to hock. Cuts of meat lie on every flat surface, crawling with so many flies the cutlets might just lift off and fly away out the gaps in the high ceiling.

I walk away with armloads of stuff I don't need, all of it wrapped in packages of woven palm leaves dyed green and pink, all of it costing pennies. I'm privileged where three days ago I was impoverished, walking down Fifth Avenue among all the women with their designer bags. For once, I'd rather be me.

Ken
Phnom Penh

The space between the walls of my hotel room is only a few feet wider than my bed. I have to twist shoulders and hips to move anywhere. There's a small TV perched on a ledge over the foot of the bed, playing music videos from Hong Kong nonstop. The air-conditioner kicks out cold air and that's what I have—walls, a bed, a TV, and cold air.

I never took the bar exam after law school and I'd been struggling, at length, to figure out how to make constructive use of my degree while avoiding corporate law. Then I ran into a former classmate in a pub in New York. He said in passing he happened to know a human rights group looking for lawyers to send to Cambodia on a subcontract with the UN. Was I interested? I'm not actually a licensed "lawyer" in the U.S., but who's splitting hairs about that in Cambodia? I wrote down the contact name on the coaster under my drink. And after a long night, I forgot about it. Three days later I stuck my hand in my jeans pocket and felt a wad of paper, started to toss it out, saw my writing on the back—and remembered. I called the number, and the director asked me to come to the office immediately; we need to send a body there yesterday, he said. He interviewed me for fifteen minutes, asked when can you leave, I said give me a week. You're hired, he said, get shots, a visa, and on the plane. There's a senior guy there already, he has experience with elections in Asia, he'll be your boss. Just let us know how it's going every couple weeks, he said, as he showed me the door.

That's all? I'd been mulling over this dilemma for years and it's as easy as getting shots and a visa and on the plane?

It's been two weeks now and I'm supposed to call the director to tell him how it's going. Here's how it's going: I hate the boss. He's from some wealthy, high-caste family in India and he calls the Cambodians "buggers," as in, "We're trying to help the buggers and they don't even appreciate it." He arrives at every meeting late, on purpose, but when he is made to wait, he's outraged. We give seminars on the basics of democratic government to Cambodian human rights groups in preparation for the election. They don't speak a word of English and we don't speak Khmer, so we use a translator. But the boss is a proud man and won't be made to wait for a mere translator. So he holds forth with his fake smile and huge gut, and just keeps talking. No one understands a word he's saying, as he sings away in English about the Universal Declaration of Human Rights. The translator smiles, embarrassed, and I hang my head in shame.

Meanwhile I see teams of UN staff racing around town in huge white Land Cruisers. They always seem to be laughing about something uproariously funny. They're young and urbane, all races and nationalities. It looks like the international jet set on vacation. I'd love to know where they're going as I sit suffering under the boss's sneer. It can't all be election work because those UN Land Cruisers line up every night outside restaurants, bars, and massage parlors, sometimes ten deep.

It's a Saturday and I gotta get out of the hotel room. One more minute of TV from Hong Kong and I'll lose my mind. I wander around the market alone, dazed by the expanse of humans, colors, and smells after lifeless hours in my sanitized hotel room.

A flyer catches my eye; something about it reminds me of those overflowing billboards at the student lounge in college. It's a housemate-wanted sign in English:

EMERGENCY SEX AND OTHER DESPERATE MEASURES

ROOM AVAILABLE FOR UN ELECTION STAFF
BIG BEAUTIFUL HOUSE IN DOWNTOWN PHNOM PENH
COOK, MAIDS, WESTERN AMENITIES, CALL CHLOE

I want a room in a big beautiful house, I want a cook, maids, and Western amenities. And I want to meet Chloe.

I run to try to find a phone. I'm desperate to contact this Chloe, just a name on a flyer. Each passing sweaty moment that I don't call, Chloe and the maids and cooks and friendly housemates slip further into distant fantasy. It takes an hour to find a working phone in Phnom Penh's central market, although if you want hubcaps, fried sparrows, dope, or dog meat, you're in luck.

A woman answers and says come right over. She has one of those British public school accents, the kind that takes generations of money and education to get right.

I jump in a cyclo taxi and we rattle to the house. A woman answers the door. She's striking; she has long, straight brown hair and dark eyes, smooth skin; her ethnicity is ambiguous. She smiles a socialite hostess smile, nice but not warm. She looks me over more thoroughly and deliberately than would be polite at the swell parties I imagine she hosts in her villa in some exotic capital. I flash to a scene in the infinity of my future with this woman. I'm entering that villa at that party in that capital, I'm kissing her on both cheeks, she's draped in pearls and silk.

Meanwhile she's coldly interrogating me with her eyes. She's definitely in charge of this house and this moment. This must be Chloe.

She escorts me to a table full of people and presents me. She introduces them briefly. This one's from Morocco, that one from Italy, he's Persian—I'm not exactly sure what that means—this one's from "the UK." They're all in their twenties, poised and dismissive. They don't know or care who I'm supposed to be at home or where I went to school. They're measuring something else I can't see and don't understand.

They nod and turn back to each other. They seem to be waiting for a cue from Chloe to release them from having to feign interest. She introduces herself at substantially more length. Her father is Chinese and her mother is Swiss; she grew up in Hong Kong and "in Europe."

I grew up in Michigan and in Michigan. But she didn't ask.

She shows me the available room, which is simple, but the house is in grand tropical style—rich, oiled wood floors, faded wicker furniture, lazy ceiling fans, corridor after corridor, level after level, patio after patio, all framed by an eruption of flowers. Ripe mangos hang languidly on trees, just out of reach. I walked out of my lonely, sterile hotel room and into a short story from my father's library at home. I've pictured this house a thousand times, in a hundred books. Conrad in Africa, Graham Greene in Asia, Hemingway in Cuba. But it's finally me and it's finally real.

Andrew
Phnom Penh

A blast of chilled air hits me in the face as I enter the gaudy lobby of Phnom Penh's most expensive hotel, the Cambodiana. There's fake marble on the floor and a cheap-looking model of the Angkor Wat temples at reception next to potted palm trees dying of cold. I loathe this place. It's making a mint from new UN arrivals with more dollars than sense who pay exorbitant rates for scarce rooms. It may be the only place in town with hot water, but it's got no warmth. I hate that feeling of sweat cooling in the small of my back.

I pick up my ticket for Sarajevo at the hotel travel agency. The war in Bosnia is getting worse and the Red Cross wants me deployed there as soon as possible. On my way out, I run into a UN official whom I know from my early days at the hospital. He's just been appointed director of human rights for the UN election mission here. It's a big job, and I wish him luck.

I invite him for one last drink on the hotel pool terrace. It overlooks the slow-flowing muddy waters of the Mekong River, where wiry Vietnamese fishermen cast their nets from frail wooden boats on which their families work and eat and sleep.

When our gin and tonics arrive, he tells me that his new job is not going well. The prospect of an election is making the men with the guns nervous. The Khmer Rouge is attacking the UN and the government is attacking the opposition and he's caught right in the middle.

I'm not convinced that it's worth it. How many Cambodians ever asked for a $2 billion election? Ninety percent of them are rice farmers. I lived with them, watched them die at the hospital, and never even heard the word "election" mentioned. That money would repair hundreds of roads and bridges and pay for tons of seed and fertilizer. And clear a lot of landmines.

He says he's got the perfect job for me if I'm willing to stay on and work for him until the election. The UN now has access to Cambodia's jails, where political prisoners and common criminals are dying. The government is officially denying it but privately wants the UN to do something about it as quickly as possible. You know this country and you speak Khmer, he says. I'll support you to do whatever it takes to save lives in there.

The UN's election is a risky gamble with Cambodian lives as the stake and I want no part of it. I've already got more than enough of their blood on my hands. But there's something seductive about his offer. It's the opportunity to exchange my work treating Cambodians at a lone hospital in a single war-torn province for the chance to help bring peace to all Cambodians. He knows which of my buttons to push. Having armed UN peacekeepers behind me to get inside those jails is tempting. A friend of mine has a house near the National Security Prison, and more than once we've heard screams from inside its walls as we drank cocktails on his roof.

I check the small print on my ticket: refundable within seven days of purchase. I tell him if he can get me a UN offer within a week, I'll stay, otherwise I'm Bosnia bound. I'll sleep easier with that decision left to fate and the gods of UN bureaucracy.

The sweat feels good again after that ridiculous icebox as I head to the market for a cold beer and some warm clothes for the winter in Bosnia.

Ken
Phnom Penh

It's the weekend and we're on the roof. Someone brought a rubber kiddie pool back from Bangkok. It's bright blue with yellow lightning bolts shooting along the side. Chloe is in charge of the house but Karim, a Moroccan guy in a Yankees cap, is in charge of the roof. He once played professional soccer in France, knows half a dozen languages, and is the perpetual eye of a social storm.

He's rigged a hose from the sink in his bathroom across the roof to feed the pool. He lets the water run freely, overflowing onto the red roof tiles, cooling them so we can walk barefoot. The top of a mango tree droops nearby, and if you are willing to lean over the ledge far enough that your feet leave the safety of the roof, you can snap a mango right off the tree. You just have to crack the skin and squeeze. Sun-warmed juice and flesh explode out onto your hands, ooze down your wrists, and you lick it up like a melting popsicle.

Karim chops up a block of ice with a huge machete and we make mango daiquiries in the blender until all the ice melts.

It's blistering hot. All the housemates except Chloe are lying in the pool, plus a tan, lithe Swiss girl with long, sun-streaked blond hair, who may or may not be Karim's girlfriend. Daiquiris and mango juice and suntan oil and bodies. Karim smokes joint after massive joint of Cambodian dope. When one gets wet from splashing pool water, he just throws it out and lights another like it's a cheap cigarette. We're on the roof of our mansion in the middle of Indochina, no parents, no boss. Everything everyone does is funny and perfect.

Karim reaches out from the pool, groaning from the exertion, to put a CD into the boom box. It's a Raï singer from Algeria, Khaled. The music sends Karim into a tirade about the Islamic fundamentalists in Algeria who assassinate Raï singers because they represent corrupt Western culture and therefore have to die. He says something indecipherable about how the fundamentalists have to die, and he starts swearing excitedly in Arabic. I think what he's saying might be really interesting and thought provoking if any part of it were comprehensible.

The Swiss girl is wearing one of those revealing European-style bikinis. I can feel the heat of her skin searing in the sun as she rolls around in this tiny, oiled-up kiddie pool. I'm still not sure if she and Karim are together and her writhing right next to me is a little disconcerting. It's all very intimate, but everyone is poised and cool about it. I have to learn how to strike that nonchalant pose they all seem to have down pat.

Karim puts on a House of Pain song, "Jump Around."

It's street music from the States, and I'm the only American on this roof, but they all know the words. Karim is lying flat, splayed out and submerged. He starts to rock his hips rhythmically to the beat and it catches on and then all six of us are thrusting our hips up each time House of Pain chants "Jump." The water starts to form waves in rhythm with the beat of our thrusts and the Swiss girl is beautiful and the pot and rum and music are in charge and then a giant wave forms from a group hip thrust executed in perfect unison and it crashes out of the pool and washes over in a small tidal wave all the way to the electric cable spliced from the generator that's feeding the blender and boom box and everyone stops and waits to die and nothing happens and we're young and immortal and together and drunk and stupid and in Cambodia.

Chloe appears. It's like a parent came home. She's frowning furiously. Is it the music or the dope or the mango mess or the exposed electric cables or the water everywhere or the Swiss girl or is it just that she missed the whole thing?

Lunch is ready, Chloe announces. Heidi the American girl is coming to see the house. She orders us to get dressed to greet this Heidi downstairs. We gather ourselves as best we can—it's useless to oppose the will of the beautiful Chloe creature—and we file downstairs for lunch.

The cook serves *amok,* fresh fish soaked in coconut curry, wrapped in banana leaves, served over fluffy white rice. It's the best fish I've ever tasted. There's ecstasy in the heat of the curry and the rice is sticky white and feathery and who knew rice could taste this good? I'm transfixed by my lunch and then the American girl walks in.

It's an unwelcome interruption. She's dressed like it's a job interview but we're three sheets to the wind and four minutes out of the pool and it doesn't fit. She thrusts her head back and chin up as she strides into the room like she's in a marching band. She stares at us like she wants and expects something from us. Fuck you, I'm making love to my *amok.* She sounds like she's from some exit in New Jersey and the last thing I want is another American here to spoil my gig. I'm in place here and you're not, I can figure this jet-set shit out and you can't and you're going to interfere if you try and I'm voting no. I want an African or a Latin housemate to complete the lineup, go away. I am in love with *amok.* Bye, nice to meet you.

Heidi
Phnom Penh

Since I've been on my own, I spend a lot of time calculating income and expenses, right down to the dollar. I net about $40,000 from my UN salary, plus per diem in Cambodia is $130. Hotel expenses are exorbitant; I need to find a house share fast. If I do, I can save $5,000 a month, pay off all my debt, and six months from now be back at my old job on the Bowery, with $10,000 or $15,000 still left in the bank. No more of this secretary crap.

So I start asking around about rooms. A guy gives me a number for a woman named Chloe. He tells me the house is huge and famous for its

Friday night parties. The room might still be available, he says, but it's probably already taken. Everyone wants to live there, to be a part of that group. There's something evocative about the way he says "that group" that makes me determined to become a member.

I call and speak with Chloe. She schedules me for an interview the following Saturday. Her perfect intercontinental accent is enough to convince me I'm not going to be considered worthy of this room. I spend the ensuing days practicing to be articulate, making sure to clearly pronounce my final consonants. I try my best not to sound like a Dorothy Parker character.

I show up at the house to find six men and women sitting around a long, formal dining room table. As I walk into the room, I pretend that everyone is applauding. I once read somewhere you should do this to gain confidence. I'm wearing my best clothes and am on my best behavior. They're all wearing beach clothes and sunburns and look like they've known each other forever. I'm nervous as hell. Please let me have this room. I'm afraid that if I'm rejected, everyone in the mission will know and for the duration of my assignment here, I'll be an outcast. I'm sixteen again, trying to be a part of the popular crowd.

They never even offer me a seat. I just stand there at the head of the table, attempting to make eye contact with anyone who will look up from their meal. I feel like I am expected to perform. I imagine myself breaking into an aria, doing a little soft-shoe, telling jokes to amuse them. But my presence is not remotely interesting; they have no idea how important their decision is to me.

Chloe tells me a bit about the others and a lot about herself. They all seem to have significant positions here: everyone is "responsible for" or "in charge of" something for the election in May. Lawyers, doctors, Indian chiefs. She pointedly makes reference to each of their nationalities, obviously proud of the diversity. I look for solidarity in the one other American's face, but he's busy devouring a pile of rice and brown mush on his plate. Chloe asks me where I'm from, where I'm working in the mission, what my job is. I'm from New Jersey, I'm working here as a secretary. I say it as though I'm here to see about a job cleaning the house. Can it get worse? I want to plead my case, show them I can live up to their standards, but I'm intimidated by this woman and the silent diners before me, and I allow myself to be judged on the little information I've offered. I walk out feeling dejected and pathetic, unable to fit in once again. I'm right back at that modeling party wearing the wrong clothes.

Andrew
Phnom Penh

There's exhilaration in the air, and way too much carbon monoxide. Twenty thousand peacekeeping soldiers and two thousand civilians are on the loose in six thousand brand-new UN Land Cruisers, ruining the sleepy backwater I used to love. Phnom Penh is slowly sinking into the Mekong under the weight of these new arrivals.

And now I've joined them and made the problem worse.

Two days ago a one-page offer of appointment from UN Headquarters in New York rolled off the fax machine in the hospital office. It gave me carte blanche to save dying prisoners and was just too tempting to turn down. So I rinsed the dried blood off the floor of my Red Cross ambulance, turned it over to the new guy, and enlisted in the New World Order.

As I make my way through crowds of Cambodians toward UN Mission HQ, I pass through Oxford Street, which I used to know as Street #240. English is the coin of the new realm and Oxford Street is the center of the gold rush. Fluency means the chance of a UN job, and every Cambodian under thirty seems to be taking lessons. Hundreds of makeshift stalls have sprung up, sporting signs in English riddled with spelling mistakes and grammatical errors. They look like lotto booths. At four in the afternoon the street is impassable with avid young men and women jostling their way to class.

The French Embassy is trying to have Oxford Street shut down because it's sucking students away from language courses at the Alliance française. But young Cambodians want a language they can use to bootstrap themselves out of poverty, and it's not French. How quixotic, the former colonial power tilting at lotto booths.

UN Mission HQ is a sprawling art deco complex, splattered with shit from evil-looking bats that swing by their feet from overhanging trees. I show my fax to two UN soldiers with helmets, flak jackets, and automatic weapons. One is from Ghana, the other from Sweden. They make an attractive team as they smile and wave me through.

The personnel officer hands me a form with check boxes for the pass and ID unit, salary disbursement, bank account, next of kin notification, driving test, and communications for a radio handset. The last stop is the transport yard, where I strike it lucky and get assigned a brand-new Land Cruiser.

I drive back from HQ to my house in a village across the river, exasperated that it's going to take me an hour to get through the traffic on what used to be a ten-minute ride. All around me, white vehicles with *UN* stenciled in large black letters on the doors nose their way through a river of secondhand motor scooters. A UN truck has made a wrong turn up a one-way street and then stalled. An Indonesian soldier climbs out, shrugs, and ambles over to buy a cold drink from a roadside shack. A young policewoman wearing a pale blue UN baseball cap and an Irish flag shoulder patch stands in the boiling sun on an overturned bucket. She's trying to direct traffic, but no one is paying her the slightest attention—a lion tamer minus whip and chair. In the shade of a large mango tree, her partner, with a pale blue turban and Indian flag on his shoulder, has given up and is sitting on a parked motorcycle fanning himself. Cambodians were terrified of the ferocious-looking Sikhs when they first arrived here, but now barefoot kids are trying to pull his beard.

All this is disorienting because we once had this town to ourselves. We were a tight community of humanitarian aid workers, incestuous even, and could always figure out who was doing what with whom just from where each car was parked. I knew Communist Phnom Penh like the back of my hand and always felt good in my old truck with its red cross and bloodstained floor. Now I'm in a strange city in a UN peacekeeper's Land Cruiser with that new car smell and orders to clean up the prisons for an election that I'm not even sure I believe in.

But I'm always oriented in my house. It sits twelve feet up on stilts behind a large hedge, with a coconut palm on one corner and a mango tree on the other for shade. I'm the only foreigner living on the far bank of the Mekong and the villagers all know me. We watch out for each other and can recognize strangers, so it's safer than the city. I began building early on in my time here with the Red Cross, when I needed something creative to take my mind off amputations. I drew up the floor plans on a paper napkin one drunken night down by the river, and a gang of frenetic Vietnamese carpenters with hammers and chisels and not a word of English did all the work. I paid them in gold ingots whose weight tore holes in my pockets. An architect I invited over to help me design a roof deck told me that back home the hardwood floor alone would cost more than I paid for the entire house.

My house is all wood, with verandahs on three sides, wooden-louvered French doors, and shutters for windows: there's not a pane of glass in the whole place. A high tile roof throws an amber glow onto wide burnished floor planks. I'm proud of the five colors of bougainvillea I planted that now twist through the fence line. There is no phone and no address, so I can't be found out here unless I choose to be. With Phnom Penh becoming more of a zoo every day, that's priceless.

I share the house with my Cambodian friend Lumning, his wife, Sari, and their three children. Lumning works as a medic for one of the aid agencies. He and Sari were teenagers during the genocide and, like every other Cambodian, were forced by the Khmer Rouge to work as slaves in the rice fields. Neither Sari nor the children speak English, which has been great for my Khmer. The little one with curly hair is my favorite. She's just two years old and already a heartbreaker.

I fire up the generator to turn the ceiling fans and pull the cork on a good bottle of South African red that I've been saving. Tonight I think I'll drink the whole thing slowly, a toast to my new life. I don't miss the hangovers I used to get from drinking with Sasha and Alexi. They celebrated the Cold War thaw by pouring icy Sprite into warm Bulgarian red wine—called it Russian Champagne. I don't know how I drank that bubbling concoction and still managed to function the next day. Now the local Chinese merchant stocks Veuve Clicquot and Dom Perignon by the caseload.

We sip our drinks and sit on the verandah in sarongs and swat at mosquitoes while the sun goes down and the monks chant off in the distance. I thread a metal chain through my new ID card and loop it around my neck. This is a hard country, and I'm not convinced that the UN is able to do half of what it's supposed to here. But winter is bleak in Bosnia, and I want to tell Vary that I tried.

Heidi
Phnom Penh

I'm surprised when late one afternoon I get a phone call from Chloe offering me the room. She makes a point of telling me that only one person voted against me. I'm sure it was she who didn't want the lowly American secretary in her midst.

The day before moving into the house, I come down with something the UN doctors diagnose only as being "encephalitis-like." The slightest movement of my head sends my brain slamming, splattering into the wall. The tiniest shift of my eyes sends a bolt of lightning through my vertebrae. I'm deeply aware of my brain's connection to my spinal cord. The next day

I lurch slowly up the front stairs with my suitcase like the Bride of Franken-stein. I enter my new bedroom on the first floor, shut the door, and climb directly into bed.

For three days I don't see or hear from anyone in the house. Complete silence. Finally, I am forced to leave the room to search for drinking wa-ter. I hear voices and music coming from somewhere, maybe toward the back of the house, maybe upstairs. I wander, find a flight of wide concrete stairs, and ascend. In a sitting room upstairs, three or four guys whom I vaguely remember from my interview are sitting around wearing nothing but sarongs.

Ken, the other American, is telling a story about a classmate at Har-vard. I don't hear a word after *Harvard*. I'm ready to hate him. I've met guys like this. First thing they want to know is where you went to school. Say Vassar or Princeton and watch their face change. Now you rate, now you have their respect. I hate the way that makes me feel. I consider fab-ricating an entire Ivy League history for myself, but I probably can't pull it off. Those people can tell if you're in their club just by looking at your shoes or how straight your teeth are.

It's hot and I'm tired and just getting used to my brain feeling normal again, so I go out onto the balcony and slide down against the wall to the floor. The tiles are cool against the back of my legs and my neck. Ken comes out, hesitates a minute, and then slides down next to me. I decide just to be Heidi from Newark, New Jersey, without even a bachelor's degree from a crummy state school. Let him walk away. I feel like being alone anyhow.

But he doesn't walk away and I'm surprised that when night falls, we've been talking for hours. He does hilarious impersonations of guys from his childhood hockey team and of the big, doughy mothers in UAW jackets from the union towns surrounding Detroit, clanging cowbells, screaming to their eight-year-old sons to "Kill him!" Must have been con-fusing for an eight-year-old to hear that. There's something rough about him that makes me feel at home. Maybe he's the one who invented an Ivy League background.

March

Andrew
T3 National Security Prison, Phnom Penh

The UN Human Rights office was once the Soviet Cultural Center, but few Cambodians ever went in there. They were too afraid of the Soviets to want to learn about their culture. Now it's a bustling hub of activity. The boss has a corner office with a view of the Mekong. He has tension lines on his forehead and bags under his eyes, and I'm not sure yet whether to thank him or curse him for arranging the contract so quickly.

He tells me the UN lawyers have decided that inmates will be permitted to vote in the election, but an outbreak of a disease no one seems to be able to identify is wiping them out. The world is descending on Cambodia to observe the polling, and the prison just became a priority. Get inside quickly and see how many of those inmates need help, he says.

The National Security Prison occupies an entire block in central Phnom Penh, and Cambodians refer to it in hushed voices as T3. It was built by the French more than a century ago, and it looks as though it hasn't had a day of maintenance since. A twenty-foot-high, two-foot-thick concrete wall designed to withstand a siege surrounds it. I duck my head to pass through a rusting door set into one of the walls. Inside the gloom, it's a ruin. A large central courtyard is surrounded on three sides by cell blocks; the walls and roofs are dripping water from holes and cracks. It hasn't rained in months, so God knows where that's coming from. Multiple layers of chalky paint are peeling off the walls, marking the decades.

I introduce myself to the chief of police, who from his epaulettes looks to be a major. He doesn't introduce himself or shake my hand, but I know his name is Top Hong: he's infamous at our headquarters. He's solidly built for a Cambodian—thick neck, barrel chest, and a clever, alert face. His square glasses slide down his nose, about to fall off. I'd like to reach out and push them back up.

He's clearly nervous to have a UN doctor in his prison, but he has his orders and grabs a large iron ring jangling with keys and leads me to the nearest cell block. After seeing the first few cells, I want to smash Major Top across that clever face. The boss asked me to see how many inmates need help: everyone here needs help.

I've seen thousands of sick Cambodians in the past three years, but nothing like this. Oversized eyeballs stare unseeing out of shrunken faces from the darkness of dank cells. It's a pitiful sight, cell upon cell of emaciated human beings lying in puddles of feces and urine. They're dying of starvation, they're dying of disease, they've been abandoned and left to rot. It doesn't take much to finish off a malnourished prisoner with no hope; a common infection or a routine beating will do. One day they're there, and the next morning gone, carried out in a sack in the night.

Many are unable to stand. Some have huge infected pressure sores where their buttocks once were, and they're all shackled at night to long horizontal iron bars. It's to prevent them escaping, Major Top tells me. That's a cruel joke. They can't even get up to urinate.

I realize with a jolt that they might have beriberi, a scourge from another era. I've only seen it in black-and-white photos from old textbooks, but it ravaged whole populations in French Indochina and wiped out Allied soldiers in Japanese prisoner of war camps. I grab my medical textbook from the Land Cruiser and find beriberi next to scurvy and rickets. It says that in Ceylon *beri, beri!* meant "I can't, I can't!" First you can't stand and then you can't even sit up and in the end you quietly succumb on your back. Progressive, inexorable weakness leading to death—it fits perfectly. We have an outbreak of beriberi.

The cause is malnutrition. The body needs vitamin B1 and without it the nerves that control the limbs gradually degenerate. But it's curable, so I race to the market and buy up every vial of vitamin B1 I can lay my hands on. By the time I'm finished, the price has skyrocketed.

We flood the place with food, medicine, and light, and slop detergent and chalky yellow paint everywhere. Half of it ends up on the prisoners, but at least it reduces the stench. We fix the sanitation and get the water running. Major Top watches us from the sidelines, armed folded. How naïve we must look to this hardheaded Communist police chief.

The vitamin injections work. Cripples get off their filthy mats, stand, and then walk, rising like Lazarus. Even the guards are impressed. I feel like I did when Sofany woke from her coma and started eating, only times a hundred.

Ken
In the Field

Kill all the lawyers. It's a joke from Shakespeare, *Henry VI, Part II, Act IV*. Dick the Butcher plots revolution and conjures utopia: "The first thing we do, let's kill all the lawyers." But they actually did it here. They had a revolution, they killed all the lawyers, and it's not funny.

Nixon bombed the hell out of Cambodia at the end of the Vietnam War. The Khmer Rouge seized the moment of chaos, took power, and killed anyone they thought represented corrupt Western culture: lawyers, teachers, artists, people who spoke French, anyone who wore glasses. More than a million civilians died. It was one of those Maoist purges, inspired by the Cultural Revolution in China. I never understood in college exactly what that meant, "Maoist," but I think it means kill everything that moves.

Which is why this mission is so inspiring. The UN is sponsoring the election in May to create a legitimate, democratic government. If we can do it in one of the worst places in the world, then we can do it anywhere. That makes us the center of the New World Order. At least until June.

I'm a hundred miles outside the capital at the regional headquarters of a Cambodian human rights group. It's good to be in the field. The capital is full of political intrigue; everyone has an ax to grind and a distorted story to sell. But out here it's stark and raw, people are more honest and direct. The horizon is everywhere, the hills of Vietnam in the distance. But mostly you're far from the boss and you feel free and everything is an adventure.

It took six hours to go one hundred miles, lumbering around huge potholes, ox carts, minefields. Mile after mile of dry scrub brush and then pockets of sparkling green rice fields. Peasants in blue pajamas and straw hats make their way slowly along the road carrying rice and hoes and babies. We passed a dozen checkpoints on the road, bored soldiers with bored AK-47s slung over their shoulders looking for a bribe. You give them a few cigarettes and they wave you through.

At one desolate intersection in the true middle of nowhere, a scraggly old man—white hair, beard, and tank top over brown leather skin, you could still see the strength in his seventy-year-old arms from sixty years of hard work—ran out into the street smiling at us. When we got close he made the sign of a gun with his index finger and thumb and said *pa-pa-pa-pa-pa*, and grinned some more. Fighting up the road, no good, turn around.

My seminar is at a Buddhist pagoda. It sits on stilts, with a long creaky wooden staircase leading to the office upstairs. Above our heads we hear the gentle padding of barefoot monks. We sit below them on a groomed dirt floor. Every now and then a monk in an orange robe and shiny bald brown head descends the stairs and tosses out leftover rice to a waiting gaggle of chickens.

My classroom is overflowing with eager students. Dusty, grizzled peasants in flip-flops sit on their haunches next to the chickens, in rapt attention as I teach an introduction to democracy, struggling to explain concepts like "liberty," "dignity of the individual," and "the consent of the governed."

It's a remarkable sight and makes you realize the power of these ideas: we are literally exporting democracy. Maybe you have to be overseas to see the catastrophe of the absence of democracy in order to appreciate it. All that crap I learned in law school starts to make sense. This is my first real job and it's as exhilarating for me as it is for the Cambodians.

My translator's name is Pan Ya. He must be eighteen or nineteen. He's a good kid. He has a gentle face and always smiles. He doesn't say much except when he's translating. He generally seems to have a sprinkle of dust on his face that he never wipes off, a little powdery layer, like he just finished baking bread. He has shaggy jet-black hair, black eyes, and several moles on his face sprouting dark hairs that catch the dust.

Depending on how I phrase the question and what he thinks I want to hear, he says yes to everything I ask him, which is confusing.

"Pan Ya, do you think the class believes it when I say the UN guarantees the ballot will be secret, the government won't know how you vote?"

He faces me, shoulders drooping, eyes down but still somehow looking up at me intently. "Yes, Mr. Ken."

"But they told me there is a rumor in the village that the government has a satellite that can spy on them as they vote. They think the secret ballot is a UN lie, don't they?"

"Yes, Mr. Ken."

Heidi
UN Electoral Office

I'm finally assigned a job. They give me two choices: work here in Phnom Penh or out in a remote provincial office in the jungle, where elephants are the popular mode of transport. I spend a few moments savoring these options, unlike any I have ever had presented to me before. I'm tempted to choose the jungle office, but I'm not quite ready for that. Yet. Anyway, I'm enjoying living at the house with Ken, so I lie and say yes when they ask if I've ever worked with the software program they're using in the Phnom Penh office.

They hand me a slip of paper with an address on the other side of town and tell me to report there for work immediately. It was so easy to bamboozle them, I regret not having lied more. I arrive at the address, which turns out to be an old hotel converted to office space. The unit I am assigned to has a sign on the door, NO SPITTING ALLOWED. The woman I share the office with explains that the function of the Electoral Unit is to manage the logistics for the upcoming election, including keeping track of all the polling stations and Cambodian polling staff, which sounds interesting. I am responsible, however, for keeping track of three hundred vehicles allocated to Electoral Unit staff, which doesn't sound interesting at all.

She gives me the rundown. A ton of data entry, then filing, all cross-referenced in files located in cabinets in the bathroom. She demonstrates how easy it would be to take a leak, take a shower, and get your filing done at the same time. Get the work done quickly and you can spend the rest of the day writing letters home, she tells me. And we have two hours for lunch. Which, after an hour of puttering, we take.

We eat lavishly at a French restaurant—sign on the door, NO MARI-JUANA SMOKING ALLOWED—buy fabric at the market and take it to the tailor for dress fittings, and get measured for custom-made shoes at the Vietnamese shoemaker. Then we get caught in a downpour, during which the locals run out into the street and fire guns skyward, apparently in some traditional riposte to thunder and lightning.

In the afternoon I'm introduced to the boss. She's fat and stupid and evil. Well, there's one thing that's the same as in New York. My boss at HQ snapped her fingers at me whenever she thought I was on a personal call and was happy to criticize my wardrobe in front of the entire office. She won every battle of the war between us. In the end I usually found myself hiding in a toilet stall in tears.

But this time I don't care. I'm here for six months to make my money and then she can fuck off. No way am I going to take any more abuse or give any extra effort to my work. As a matter of fact, I'm going to be a bad employee. I'm going to relish being one of those workers who lingers at the watercooler and disappears just when you need them. Bad idea for her to start out on the wrong foot with me.

She very slowly explains her system of filing in detail. I watch her fat lips caked in pink lipstick roll out the carefully enunciated words for the retarded secretary. It's fascinating, like watching a sphincter muscle speak. "I will highlight certain words in every document and these highlighted words will indicate in exactly which files you should cross-reference the document."

My first document to file has eight words highlighted in blue. I make seven copies and start filing. One copy in the file headed "vehicle," one copy in the file headed "minor accident," one in "scratches," and so on. Twenty minutes I spend punching holes and filing a one-page report on a car accident that resulted in a scratch on the fender. I go back into the boss's office and tell her I'm ready for more. She hands me a six-inch stack of papers. I return to my office, dump the whole pile in an old cardboard box, kick it under my desk, and sit down to write my mother a long letter.

Andrew
T3 National Security Prison

As the prisoners regain strength, the guards begin to worry about escapes. Now whenever they see me approaching a patient with needle and syringe, they rush to tighten the shackles and leave them on permanently. The more I cure, the more they shackle.

For them, these men are criminals to be restrained no matter what, but for me, they're patients. I discuss the shackling repeatedly with Major Top, but he just says "yes yes" while continuing to ignore me. I even obtain signed documents from his boss, the minister of the interior, explaining that it's illegal. But no one cares. So I try to buy his cooperation, diverting UN food and medicine his way, but to no avail. The shackling continues.

I'm briefing a new UN lawyer in the prison courtyard. It's his first visit. The UN electoral officers are planning to photograph and register the inmates for polling day and have asked us for an updated prisoner list. As we check off each inmate's name against our database, I explain to him that we use quiet persuasion with the guards rather than confrontation. From near the bottom of the list, I call out a name and there's no answer. When I ask where he is, the guards just scuff their feet and stare at the ground. I shout out the missing name, but they shrug and turn their backs, so I scream it at them. Everyone in the prison turns to watch. The courtyard is suddenly very still.

Then there's a faint clink. We all hear it. It's the sound of metal on metal.

I run over and kick at the cell door, but it doesn't budge. There's a thick iron rod protruding from a hole in the wall. I peer into the gloom and am just able to make out a solitary figure, shackled to the far end of the rod by his ankles and wrists. I yell at the guards to open the door, but they just shake their heads. I'm bellowing it straight in their faces. The new lawyer looks scared: so much for quiet persuasion.

When we get into the cell, the guards remove the shackles from the slumped form. His head hits the concrete floor as he collapses sideways, catatonic in the fetal position.

He's dying in front of me. I grab my radio handset and call for the UN ambulance.

And then I snap.

I wrench the twenty-foot iron shackling rod out of the wall and drag it toward the front gate. It's heavier than I expected, but I can't let them see that. The guards start shouting and some cock their guns, but no one moves. The prisoners begin to cheer, adding to the tension. If I stop now, they'll go on torturing these people forever. But if I keep going, do they really have the guts to shoot me? In the emergency of the moment, it somehow seems worth the risk.

Major Top runs forward and cuts me off at the gate. I tower over him, but he weighs more than me.

"Are you going to shoot me?" I shout at him. "How are you going to explain that to the minister, that you shot me right in the face?"

He just stares at me silently, hand on the holster of his pistol. It's impossible to know what he's thinking: he's never had to deal with an out-of-control peacekeeper before. There's a serious loss of face looming for one of us.

It's too dangerous to turn back now, so I just walk past him, pinching my shoulder blades to make the space between them small. I wait for the shot, but the only sound is the iron bar scraping on concrete. I reach the safety of my Land Cruiser, tie the bar to the rear bumper, and speed to the office. It clangs and sparks like mad twenty feet behind me. When I go in to see the boss to make my report, my hands are shaking so badly I have to sit on them to hide the tremors.

Ken
In the Field

My translator, Pan Ya, is huddled with a small group of serious-looking students. He's writing like mad on a notepad. They are gesticulating and angry. That gentle look is gone from Pan Ya's face; he looks startled. He makes a beeline for me, shoulders up and eyes forward. I've never seen him so confrontational.

We're in a remote district near the Khmer Rouge zone conducting another human rights seminar. Pan Ya was scared to come here.

"Mr. Ken, Cambodian human rights worker killed by government maybe. No good. He was making investigation, maybe. I don't know."

Shit. I was afraid of this. I've been training this particular group of human rights volunteers for several weeks now and they seem a little overzealous. Part of the training is to encourage the members to investigate and report government intimidation of opposition parties. We even distributed incident report forms and cameras so they can learn how to document preelection abuses.

The problem is that no one knows what the rules are or where the line is. The government is still in total, autocratic control and their operatives are hardheaded assassins when they feel threatened. There is no legacy here of a loyal opposition; you rule and kill or lose and be killed. And then we parachute in, waving a human rights flag. The more we support the volunteers, the more active they are, and the more active they are, the closer they come to a line no one can see. In the back of my mind I've been worried that I'm training these guys in precisely how to get themselves killed.

I try to get the details straight, but it's difficult. Each iteration of the story is different. I can't tell if it's a translation problem, the story itself is unclear, I just don't understand, or some combination.

After half an hour of confusion, Pan Ya's ready to give me the abridged version. The police in a nearby village told the members of an opposition party that government spies will know if people vote against the government, and if they do, they'll be drafted and sent to the front lines to fight the Khmer Rouge. The local leader of the opposition party, Mr. So Ot, complained to the police, who proceeded to beat the shit out of him. Then he complained to the governor. The next day soldiers came to Mr. So Ot's house and asked him to come for a drink. While they were drinking late into the night, men in Khmer Rouge uniforms appeared at the bar and shot it up, but the only person they hit and killed was Mr. So Ot.

So Ot's wife heard about the human rights group and its UN sponsorship. She went to the pagoda and asked for help. A young volunteer decided on his own to conduct an investigation. He asked questions at the governor's office, the government soldiers' barracks, and police headquarters. Two days later his headless body was found in a well.

Oh Lord. I have to try to handle this. We tear back to Phnom Penh. I should probably shower and change into long pants and a real shirt for a meeting at the UN human rights office, but I don't want to wait, this is important.

The building is buzzing. Offices overflow with staff from every corner of the earth. Soldiers in colorful military uniforms move with martial discipline but stop smartly in the hall to let secretaries wrapped in Cambodian silk pass. Police in blue berets brief earnest young lawyers in khakis. Everyone has a military-issue radio glued to their ear. It looks like it could be a colonial administration in India or Kenya, except instead of British rule, it's the whole world, and instead of imperial occupation, we've invaded in the service of peace.

I've never dealt with anything even resembling the gravity of a murder case and I need good advice. The guy I want to talk to is Dr. Thomson. He's been working in Cambodia since before the UN came. He'll know how to handle this. Dr. Thomson is the real deal. Everyone seems to know him; he gets assaulted with questions and requests as soon as he arrives at our house parties.

Last week, without orders or authorization from anyone, he stole a huge iron rod the police used to shackle prisoners. By the time he arrived back at the office, the entire city had heard the story. I'm trying to translate "secret ballot" while Dr. Thomson is saving people's lives with his bare hands. It's embarrassing.

Andrew
UN Human Rights Office, Phnom Penh

There's a knock at my office door. It's a tourist, in shorts and a T-shirt. Then I recognize him from a party at Chloe's house. He was with that pretty secretary, Heidi. I've seen him running around town, another clueless American in a country that America carpet-bombed.

I'm busy. I'm sweating over the prison database, trying to separate inmates who have died from those still alive. The program seems to have a bug in it; the dead won't delete from the list of the living. I don't have time for a meeting, particularly not with someone in shorts. He hasn't been around long or he wouldn't be dressed like that. In this country only cyclo drivers and fishermen wear shorts.

He says he wants to talk to me about a political killing. He's oblivious and he's wasting my time. I'm overwhelmed with reports of hundreds of election-related deaths that would take a competent police force years to investigate. But then again, I think he's Heidi's boyfriend, and she intrigues me, so I invite him in.

I shake his hand and pull out a chair. He's younger than I am, maybe mid-twenties. Not that tall but not small either. He holds himself confidently and there's something about him that makes you think you wouldn't want to cross him. The absurdly casual dress belies a manner both articulate and direct, so I soon find myself paying more attention to what he's saying.

He tells me that he's just back from the field, where a young Cambodian has been murdered. I know the district. It's been a combat zone for years and is heavily mined. He doesn't seem to be aware of how risky it is up there, and it occurs to me that I should take him to the UN Mine Action Center for some decent mine maps. Otherwise he'll wind up on a hospital gurney with that tanned leg unrecognizable below the knee.

If he's in over his head with the death of just a single Cambodian, he can't have grasped yet that sooner or later here, but usually sooner, you have to deal with fatalities. He won't forget this, his first case, even if he ends up handling twenty or fifty or five hundred.

He listens, asks more questions, seems to get it. He's dressed for surfing, but he's got the mind of a prosecutor. I tell him I need much more information before even thinking about deploying our stretched investigative resources on this one.

"Okay," he says. "Thanks for the advice. I'll get you that information."

What he doesn't say is, *That will be difficult, I don't speak the language, I'm new here, someone ought to do it, but it will take time and could be dangerous*—all of which is true. None of the usual excuses, just that he'll get me the information. That vigorous confidence is unusual around here.

Sasha and Alexi moped around this town like beaten dogs and slunk back to Moscow sorry losers. A lot of the UN staff call themselves human rights experts but need a shoulder to cry on each time there's a killing. They belong in an office in Switzerland. Many of my French friends feign weary resignation whenever violence erupts, but that attitude was picked up on the cheap in some smoke-filled café. They haven't ever struggled and failed, haven't earned their cynicism.

Ken's problem isn't cynicism, it's optimism out of control. I watch as he bounds down the wide, curved staircase of our crumbling colonial mansion, strides into the street, and hails a cyclo, an American in motion. I have the impression he's going straight from my office to the helipad to fly back out there again tonight. He doesn't even know to slow down and pay the hot season a little respect.

Ken
UN Human Rights Office, Phnom Penh

I sat in the guest chair, he leaned against the side of his desk, arms folded, looking down at me, quiet and unresponsive, while I recounted everything I know. When he finally started to speak, it was in almost a bedside manner. He's thin, gentle, speaks the Queen's English softly. You'd never know if you didn't know.

Then I got hit with an onslaught of expertise. The doctor is a star all right, but the patronizing, half-British version. He looked at me like I'm the delivery boy who wants to marry his sister. He then proceeded to make it very clear he knows what he's doing and I don't. It was relentless.

"Where is the body? Did you see it? Do you know when he died? What political party did he belong to? Did you interview any witnesses? Alone or in the presence of others? How do you plan to protect the witnesses? How much do you trust your translator? Often these cases arise from property disputes, did he own property? Often these cases revolve around disputes over women. Did he have lovers? Did he drink? Owe money? How do you know the soldiers were Khmer Rouge? Often government soldiers act as agents provocateurs. They perpetrate acts of violence in Khmer Rouge uniforms, it's a classic trick. There's a lot of investigating you have to do before you come to any conclusions."

Yeah. There's a lot of investigating I have to do before I come to any conclusions. Classic trick? Classic to whom? We don't get many agents provocateurs in Ann Arbor.

I walk out of the good doctor's office dejected, ready to quit almost. Maybe I do belong in an office with a lawyer-man in a yellow polka-dotted tie telling me what to do all day. I think I'll go sit in the kiddie pool on the roof. It's so fucking hot, how can you work?

Encouraging peasants to confront the government is treacherous business under the circumstances, and here I am blithely marching around Cambodia waving a democracy and human rights flag like it's a maize and blue Michigan football pennant. I have a lot to learn. The doctor must think I'm a fool. I wish I had long pants and a dress shirt on.

It doesn't come cheap, does it? I rejected the hail-fellow-well-met club at Harvard and now I got what I wanted. I seek work of moral significance. A human dies. Then Dr. Thomson explains to me in detail how ill-equipped I am to understand political violence here, never mind constructively intervene.

But this time it's worth it. I'll earn my way into the doctor's club if it kills me.

April

Andrew
T3 National Security Prison

The boss suggested I give Major Top a wide berth for a few weeks, so I've been lying low at headquarters, working with UN lawyers to draw up a list of who is in prison for what. The B1 injections are holding the line, but what we really need to do is empty this prison before the election.

Only a handful of inmates have ever gone to trial. Many were arrested years ago on minor charges such as stealing chickens or bicycles. The police refuse to take them before a judge, so they languish indefinitely, with no sentence to serve. If you're a rich murderer or rapist, you can easily just bribe your way out of trouble. But if you're a poor chicken thief and you get caught, you're lost.

It's time to confront the major again. I take the list to Top's dilapidated office, where we haggle for hours over who should be released.

"No, not that one. He stole a policeman's motorcycle."

"That was in 1983. He's served ten years already."

"But he refuses to confess."

"Maybe he didn't do it."

He looks at me as though I'm stupid.

"We wouldn't have arrested him if he didn't do it." He's police, judge, and jury, and no one's questioned his decisions for a decade.

I tell him that after the election a new minister of the interior may want a new chief of police, that the new regime may not tolerate his treating human beings worse than animals in this dungeon. Apprehension momentarily clouds his face. I'm watching the power of a Stalinist state begin to dissolve before my eyes.

He goes back to the list, frowning.

"This one, I think we can let him go. He killed his wife, but she was unfaithful and now he's really sorry."

"That was just last month."

"But his family paid her family a lot of gold." I wonder what percent he took brokering that deal.

61

I negotiate hard. It's not the medical work I trained for, but it certainly saves lives. We finally agree on forty cases.

The release ceremony is inspiring and comical. Forty scared and confused-looking prisoners squat in the courtyard, with no idea of what's going on. They look like they're expecting a beating. I give them each a new set of clothes, a little cash, and some soap. You need to clean up, guys, that's a hint. UN diplomats make speeches about the importance of justice and rehabilitation, while Major Top looks on angrily. When his turn comes, he tells them they're all guilty and it's only because the UN insists that he's agreed to release them. Like the politician he is, he's covering his bets in case something goes wrong. They stand up slowly when they're told to go, look at each other in bewilderment, and begin to walk the thirty meters to the open iron gates.

The gates stay open, the guards don't shoot, and it begins to dawn on the prisoners that they're free. They take half steps forward, and then, all at once, break into a run. The frailer ones lag behind, limping toward freedom and sunlight, spilling out of the dark courtyard into the blinding day. Phnom Penh traffic screeches and honks to a halt. Drivers stop and stare and then slowly traffic resumes; the prisoners break up into twos and threes, weak leaning on the strong, and are swallowed up, gone.

The lawyers and I go down to the Floating Bar on the Mekong River to celebrate. It's a wooden barge tethered to the riverbank by steel ropes and a gangway. Through cracks in the floorboards you can see the water flowing by underneath. On hot days I want to dive straight from my chair into the river. We order beer from an ice chest. It comes half frozen and we watch without speaking while the melting ice expands into bubbly crystals that overflow and slide down the neck of the bottle. The wait is worth it and we drink until the sun is low over the water. A good day's work. As night falls and a breeze comes up off the river, we order fresh seafood and more beer and get so smashed we can't drive. So we flag down cyclos and get peddled home. None of us makes it into work the next day.

A week later a crime wave breaks out in the city. People are getting shot off their motorbikes in broad daylight. I don't know whether or not it's the guys we released who are doing it, but the police respond with hundreds of new arrests.

"I told you so," says Major Top, triumphant.

I think we've been set up: we just traded old innocent prisoners for new ones. It's a PR disaster for the UN, and our prison unit falls out of favor at headquarters.

Ken
Our House, Phnom Penh

Boutros Boutros-Ghali, the UN secretary-general, is in Phnom Penh to rally his troops. I leave work early to rally my housemates to go see him.

When I get home, Suliman is in the living room on the couch with Chloe. Suliman is a nice, thoughtful Egyptian guy who stays at the house a lot when he's in town. They look like they're in a tight clinch. That's an interesting development. I'm home early, I guess I surprised them. I can't help but investigate a little, so I stick my head in the door.

They're not kissing, he's hunched over on her shoulder, crying.

He isn't sad, he's angry. Atsu, a Japanese election worker, was ambushed and killed this morning in the north, he says, as he chokes down half-controlled man sobs.

Everyone assumes it was the Khmer Rouge. This is the first UN civilian they have targeted. They've killed a dozen UN soldiers, mostly Bulgarians, but no civilians. They shot him in the head. He was twenty-five. He was engaged. She's waiting for him back in Japan.

Suliman says the UN is risking our lives just to say they had an election, they don't care about our safety, and now a young man is dead. When they attacked Atsu's Land Cruiser, he knew he was going to die, he begged for help on the radio. It took the nearest UN forces hours to muster, decide what weapons to carry and who was in charge, find a map. Atsu was dead in half an hour. Suliman wails and punches the wooden table hard. He wants to write a letter, demand a meeting with the UN head of mission, organize staff to leave their posts and go on strike, anything, everything.

This is the first time I've been close to a colleague's death. I get the chills looking at Suliman, watching a man cry. It's like that Scud just landed again off in the distance. I'm in awe. He's had some derivative status bestowed on him that I can't name or describe but that everyone at the house feels. He's somehow earned respect and distance. I can see it in the way Chloe defers to him. I've never seen her defer to anyone before.

I pay respect too, but secretly challenge myself never to complain and cry like that if I lose a friend. I understand and accept the risks.

Everyone is agitated as we assemble for the secretary-general's speech. Will he mention Atsu? Does he know or care? How does a man like that assess the risks on our behalf?

He's surrounded by a phalanx of UN security officers in crisp blues.

They're not in the uniforms of their home countries, as the UN military forces always are, but instead represent UN Headquarters itself. They're lined up in a tight formation around the secretary-general—Asian faces, African faces, Nordic faces, all equally clean, sharp, disciplined. It's scary and thrilling. It looks like a cinematic image of the future, the living embodiment of a New World Order.

You are to carry out your commitment to hold this election even in the face of violence, the secretary-general says. We will not cancel this election. Cambodians deserve a chance at peace and it is your job to give them that chance. You are making history, you are creating a new world. *Bon courage.*

He doesn't mention Atsu.

Heidi
Our Roof, Upper Level

I drag Mr. Karim to the car to look for ice. We drive up one long, dark street after another. We slow down next to pedestrians and ask them, "Ice? Ice?" They look at us blankly. We get out of the car and approach men laying fish out on the sidewalk to dry. "Ice?" Wrapping our arms around our bodies, we mime shivering to get the ice idea across. How do you explain ice? How do you explain shivering to people who can't even imagine what a cold day feels like? Others come around and watch the spectacle.

A few blocks later, we stumble across the ice merchants when we almost hit one pulling a sawdust-covered block across the road with big iron tongs. I'm standing there worrying how Karim and I will load the ice into our pickup truck when the guy just snaps up a block weighing about the same as he does and hurls it into the back.

At the house, it takes five of us to drag the ice block in, leaving a long trail of slime and sawdust behind. Torches burn on the rooftop above. The sounds of Raï music float down to the street, where the cyclo drivers sit waiting for a fare. I stand outside and savor the moment. My house, my party. Everyone wants to be invited.

This is our last house party before the election. In a few weeks everyone will disperse, and we've earned a celebration. The rooftop is crowded with bodies swaying to the music. I move out among the dancers, casually checking out who's here. My eyes pass over each face; I smile, say hello, hold eye contact with a handsome man new to town. I take my time. The night's young and I can't commit yet.

I move up the staircase to the darker upper level where I can get a better view. Below, Ken moves from group to group offering fresh drinks. He stops to charm an attractive woman. It's fascinating to observe and I pay close attention. She's either seeing his Harvard side or his street fighter side, depending on which might appeal to her more. When she finally sees the side that appeals to her less, she'll be confused and think it's an act. But the truth is, it's all really him. She watches Ken long after he's passed on to the next conversation.

Ken
Our Roof

It's midnight and still ninety-five humid degrees. We are blasting Khaled again. Mr. Karim is in a sweaty trance, holding his gyrating arms up and out, hands twirling in a drunken Arabic salsa. His long curly black hair bounces around his face like a flamenco dancer's dress. Bloodshot eyes half shut, he swings his head back and forth with a half smile of secret pleasure, slowly saying no to an amusing question he asked himself. He's mesmerized and mesmerizing. Everyone knows the Raï rhythm, tune, and the *di di, di di wa* chorus, but Mr. Karim understands the words in Arabic, adding to the allure. He's surrounded by women trying and failing to match the contained Levantine ecstasy in his dance.

This is the best party I've ever been to, and it's my house. I never dreamed I'd attend a party like this, never mind host it. There must be three hundred people on our roof from fifty countries, and everyone is well-liquored. As the election approaches, as journalists and diplomats arrive, as the violence increases and everyone is tense and scared, these parties are getting even bigger and more drunken. Every time Atsu's name comes up, we pause, not exactly sure how to pay appropriate respect, not exactly sure how scared we should be.

A group of Africans takes over the dance floor. They replace the Algerian Raï music with dance music from Zaire. West African dance includes a graphic representation of the sex act, focusing on the rotating rear end of the lady. But it's done with dignity and joy. Exciting, not profane. The women are beautiful and have bright eyes and smiles that light up the night. They're having a riot. They draw a crowd of applauding admirers who all seem to know the words in French. I try and fail to get up the courage to introduce myself.

I went to school with African-American girls during my entire adolescence in Michigan and never noticed them as potential girlfriends, never even wanted to meet them. How did that happen? I'm nine thousand miles from home and a pernicious wall of segregation I never noticed in high school suddenly materializes before my eyes, ten years after the fact. A young man should travel.

Chloe joins Mr. Karim on the dance floor. The Spin Doctors come on.

Marry him, your father will condone you, how 'bout that now?
Marry me, your father will disown you, just go ahead now.
Marry him, or marry me, I'm the one who loves you baby can't
you see?
I ain't got no future or family tree, but I know what a prince and
lover ought to be.

This is the kind of scene that makes these parties famous. Mr. Karim wakes up out of his trance for Chloe. She's drop-dead beautiful and he's in unrequited love. It must be hard for him to sleep in the same house with her every night, all curled up in her bed just down the hall. The crowd forms a circle around them as she does the thing with her hips and ass, swaying under Mr. Karim's undulating arms.

Miss Heidi's surveying the party from a perch on the upper level that overlooks the official party and is a lot more fun. It's like a VIP room at a nightclub. You have to be invited up by someone from the house, so a select clique hangs out up there to dance in private and pair off discreetly. You can see a wide expanse of stars and dozens of ascending spiraled pagoda columns from up there, which makes for inspired jiggy-jiggy.

Miss Heidi avoids the official party and its official partygoers like the plague; she prefers the company of the sinners on the upper level. I go up the stairs to join her. We try to dance, we're both a little rigid, and she can't quite rotate her hips the way the girls downstairs do. I'm doing my hockey player dance, drink in one hand rocking back and forth, head bobbing, stiff as a board, like Billy Crystal's white boy dance. We're ridiculous and it gets funnier and funnier as we get drunker and drunker and we exaggerate how badly we dance for each other's amusement. I'm laughing so hard at her hips that jerk but don't roll, I'm crying.

I was wrong about Miss Heidi. I was the only one to vote against her when she interviewed for the room and I'm glad I lost. She's sharp as a whip and perceptive as hell. There's something of a 1940s femme fatale about her; she's a character actor playing herself. The lovely and talented Miss Heidi, playing a secretary from New Jersey.

She has big wet green eyes. She's tallish and has very short hair, reddish brown. It's not butchy short, still kind of feminine. She's got bones and shape, not big but not small. She's a woman, maybe, not a girl; she reminds me a little of Tali. She requires by her demeanor that you respect her, and you either learn how to do that or you can just fuck off. No hysteria, no politics, no finger-wagging lectures, just fuck off.

We call each other Mr. and Miss as terms of respect and endearment. Not everybody earns it. It comes from the maids and the cooks and the drivers. They called me Mr. Cain, which sounds too formal. So I said don't call me Mr. Cain, please call me Ken. They have their own sense of honor and duty, so they compromised and call me Mr. Ken. They did the same with Heidi and it caught on. Now when someone says "Heidi," I'm offended by the disrespect. It sounds naked. That's Miss Heidi to you.

I see Dr. Andrew standing ramrod straight on the lower level, far from the dancers, looking serious, locked in conversation with a bunch of senior UN graybeards. He sets the standard for this work and everyone knows it and admires him. I need more advice about the murdered human rights volunteer. I want to investigate, but I don't want to do any more damage. I trust Dr. Andrew's integrity, and so does everyone else. If I have his blessing, I'm protected; I'm officially doing the right thing.

The problem is that Heidi and I are in our own private drunken world up here. The good doctor will never take me seriously next to her. I'm going to have to leave Miss Heidi's embrace soon and get to his level.

Andrew
Heidi and Ken's Roof, Lower Level

The stifling air feels short on oxygen. Flames from the kerosene torches burn straight up without flickering in the torpid night, and the astringent odor of mosquito repellent steams off sweaty flesh.

I spot a large plastic bucket of chipped ice under a trestle table that serves as the bar, bend down, and grab a handful and press it against my forehead, hard. The sharp edges hurt for a few seconds until they start to melt, and I let the cool liquid run down my face and onto the front of my shirt until it's soaked. That should last me for the next half hour.

I mix a gin and tonic and lean back against a wall where I can observe, trying to spot Heidi. The crowd is packed shoulder to shoulder and I guess I should mingle, but I need to decide which knot of guests to aim for and who to avoid before I start making my way through. Much of it depends on language. I hate that feeling of insinuating myself into a conversation and having attractive women default to English as they stare at me.

The sages among us are debating the UN's role in the world, clustered around a VIP from the mission who's smoking a cigar on the sofa. I like him, he must be in his sixties, but he always turns up and chats until well after midnight with this crowd young enough to be his kids. So I sit on the couch and listen in.

From this angle I see Heidi right away, leaning over the railing of the upper level. She's surveying the scene, drink in one hand, cigarette in the other, and a wide grin in the middle. I try to catch her eye and when she finally looks in my direction, I wave. She points her chin toward the staircase up. Ken's up there too, at her side. I hope he doesn't come down here to try and talk to me about that case again. This is a party.

Heidi and Ken are inseparable; people say they're sleeping together. I can understand why Ken would pursue her, she's free and beautiful and I find her fascinating. She has an American accent that Ken says is from New Jersey. The sum total of my knowledge about New Jersey comes from a Simon & Garfunkel song—something about a turnpike. I've never been to America and am not even sure what a turnpike is. I have no frame of reference for this woman.

I wonder if she even knows three words in Khmer, or that to her cook and her cyclo driver, her presence represents the best chance of peace in a generation. But I do love those limpid green eyes. Tonight I want to be up there with her, and that little nod she just gave me is my invitation.

I try to edge away from the dance floor, but I get blocked by a bunch of humanitarian aid types. One of them grabs me by the arm and drags me into a conversation about the Khmer Rouge. Some wanker pulling on a pipe is holding forth about why they don't want the election to take place. He's boring. Either the Khmer Rouge will attack us and a lot of people including some here tonight will get killed, or they won't and the election will succeed and make history.

Someone else accosts me, wanting to talk about diarrhea. I dread these moments; it's bad medicine to be making diagnoses after gin at midnight. Sooner or later one of these de facto consultations is going to turn out badly, with me missing something really serious.

I'm still trying to get upstairs to Heidi. I love my job here and I work hard at it, but I'm not all work. Maybe up on her level, I'll be the boring one, but I'm going up regardless. I've been invited.

Heidi
Our Roof, Upper Level

Ken stands behind me in the darkness. He fumbles around, looking for a place to set his drink down. He washes his face in the ice bucket, mumbling to himself. He's combing his fingers through his hair, walking around in circles saying that he has to get down there and talk to Dr. Andrew, he's got serious shit to discuss with the doctor.

"I think he just said he's coming up here," I tell Ken.

"What? We can't let him come up here; this place is for sinners, not saints. Why'd you invite him up?"

"I didn't invite him. He waved and I nodded hello."

I don't want Dr. Andrew up here either. I don't want to stand there with him and Ken as they roll out sobering accounts of Khmer Rouge atrocities. Without Ken around, I doubt whether people like Andrew would even speak to me. I'll have to act all earnest and somber too and nod my head a lot. I'll have to ask relevant questions, and the whole time Ken will be nervously waiting for me to use foul language, and when I do, he'll smile and make that little coughing sound to show everyone he's disassociating himself from me.

But I don't want Ken to leave. I feel like he and I are the king and queen of the party, bestowing fierce judgment on the revelers below. I hate it when he gets weighty and serious, especially when he's in the middle of letting himself go. Interesting that Andrew is just the opposite. He's grave but wants to be allowed to play.

Ken hurries downstairs. He cuts Andrew off on his way up and leads him back to the main level. I can't help but feel betrayed.

Ken
With the Bulgarian Battalion in Western Cambodia

Mr. Karim controls the logistics for the UN helicopters in the provinces, a perspective from which he is able to offer stunningly accurate if untutored political analysis. After Atsu was killed, we had one of our endless house debates: "What is the UN going to do about all the political violence? Will we cancel the election?" After an hour of listening to our agitated chatter, which revealed only that we have no idea what the UN will do, Mr. Karim offered his definitive analysis: "I know what we're gonna do. We just shipped two hundred more body bags to the provinces for election week."

Dr. Andrew adopts that same hard-boiled attitude. He talks about his work as a doctor during the war almost with nostalgia, like it was a privilege to learn of war and he has some insight into the mystery you don't. The world according to the old Cambodia hands here divides distinctly in two: dilettante children who parachuted in just for the UN's show-election versus adults who by their mere presence prior to the UN's arrival know everything there is to know about death and war.

But I'm here and I'm mobile. It can't be so hard to cross that divide, they were newly arrived once themselves. So I arrange with Mr. Karim to get on the bird going west, where the Khmer Rouge are still fighting. I need to get out of Phnom Penh anyway. As the election approaches, it's getting claustrophobic in the capital with rumors, gossip, and diplomatic bullshit. I'll conduct a preelection human rights survey in the Khmer Rouge zone and make a report for the boss's eyes only. At least I can say I've been there.

But I'm alone when I get off the helicopter. Karim is airborne back to Phnom Penh, a dot on the horizon. I don't know anyone up here. The only soldiers I can find are Bulgarians.

Everyone hates the Bulgarians. The UN pays countries cash to send soldiers on peacekeeping missions. When the Soviet Union collapsed, Bulgaria lost its subsidies and was broke. The Bulgarian government wanted money but didn't want to send their best-trained troops. So, the story goes, they offered inmates in the prisons and psychiatric wards a deal: put on a uniform and go to Cambodia for six months, you're free on return. All you have to do is stand guard and give away food, they said, the UN is not a real military.

A battalion of criminal lunatics arrives in a lawless land. They get drunk as sailors, rape vulnerable Cambodian women, and crash their UN Land Cruisers with remarkable frequency. The Khmer Rouge is as genocidal and bloodthirsty a guerrilla group as any in the world, but they're not stupid. They know ordinary Cambodians hate the Bulgarians. So they attack wherever they can hit them. The Khmer Rouge get to stick a finger in the UN's eye, disrupt preparations for an election they reject, and kill foreigners that Cambodians loathe. You have to admire the strategy if not the tactic.

I have no other choices, so I flag down a Bulgarian soldier and ask for a ride into town. He laughs. There is no town. Oh shit. Where can I stay? He laughs harder and says you can stay with me in the Bulgarian house, have a drink with us.

No options, I go with him. His name is Alekko and he's not a bad guy. His friends are okay and they have good vodka. I ask him if it's true what they say about the Bulgarian Battalion. He says the guys in the first rotation weren't good soldiers, but they were replaced with a new battalion—his battalion—of professionals. I wonder if the Khmer Rouge know or care. The Bulgarians start to get drunk and I start to get tired, so I excuse myself. I have a big day tomorrow. I'm going to try to be a human rights lawyer in a war zone.

Deep sleep. Honking outside. Yelling in Bulgarian. Bright lights shine through the windows. Wide awake. Takes a second to remember where I am. More yelling, it sounds urgent. Front door bangs open. Loud footsteps inside the house. I'm blinking and worried now. Should I get out of bed? I look outside. A UN Land Cruiser tears away. Loud, fast footsteps up the stairs to my room. Insistent knocking on my door. Alekko bursts into the room in his underwear, yells in bad English, "Has been Khmer Rouge attack on Bulgarian compound close by. Get out of house, get out of house!" He runs back to his room. Are we under attack or is this a precaution? It would be silly to get shot because I insisted on putting my pants on, but it would be ridiculous if we're not under direct attack to run outside in my underwear. That possibility is more likely. So shame wins over fear. I dress and pack, thinking, Christ, what if I die because I decided to put my socks on? Should I brush my teeth? I run downstairs.

I'm alone with Alekko outside the house. He says we wait here for a Bulgarian patrol to pick us up. Great. Wait here for more Bulgarians. Why wait outside the house? For Bulgarians? Okay, friend, if there really is danger of attack, enough for us to evacuate, then maybe we should move out from under the fucking porch light?

So I go a hundred yards off to the side of the house and wait in the shadows of a clump of trees; at least we can see what approaches from here but can't be seen. Alekko comes but is agitated. Let's hide over there, he says, runs and crouches in a ditch beside the road. I follow him. The grass is wet and we are exposed. Fuck, why did I follow him? I go back to my clump of trees. He yells, Where are you going? and runs after me. This is defeating the purpose of hiding.

Now he wants to cross the street. I'm cursing him under my breath. "Just sit still and be quiet," I say. I'm giving the orders now, we must be in trouble. I'm back to the silly calculation: I don't actually know anything for a fact other than that a panicked Bulgarian drove up in a Land Cruiser in the middle of the night, told us to get out of the house, and drove away. There may be an imminent attack or this may be another Bulgarian circus. I'm a little scared but more angry at the idiocy of my host. Shit. I knew better than to stay with Bulgarians up here.

All of the lights in the neighborhood snap off. We look at each other. *Crack crack crack.* Shots fired. They sound close. This is the first evidence that this is real. I shrink further into the shadows. How much panic is appropriate now? Is my life in danger? Should I run? Should I stay with Alekko? Do I owe him anything? Heart pounding, no spit. I wish Dr. Andrew were here. My first exposure to the Khmer Rouge and I am alone with a Bulgarian.

I hear the rumble of a vehicle. I can see it's not a UN Land Cruiser, it's a pickup truck. The pickup turns onto our road and approaches. Khmer Rouge? Should I hit the deck? Climb the tree? Alekko hits the deck. I slink and crouch behind the trees, but I want to see the vehicle. Will it stop at the house? Do they see us? I should run now. Will that just attract attention? But if I stand here and they see me, am I dead? The pickup rolls calmly up the street toward the house. I can see half a dozen shadows in the flatbed with red checkered kaffiyeh-like scarves tied around their heads. They're holding Kalashnikovs. They look like the Palestinian guys from the Intifada. That's a bizarre thought in the middle of this shit. They drive past the house, past us, kicking up dust. They turn the next corner and disappear.

Alekko stands up and screams into his radio in Bulgarian. I can hear myself breathe and I'm blinking a lot. Alekko finishes on the radio. We walk up to the main street and wait for a UN vehicle to come by. After a few minutes, we flag down a Land Cruiser and jump in. I'm shaking. We look at each other and we both giggle. Suddenly I'm very fond of Alekko again.

The Land Cruiser drops us off at the nearest UN military compound. I walk up a hill and see lights, then a flickering TV. I get closer and I can hear David Bowie. It's Ziggy Stardust. It's MTV from Hong Kong via satellite. I walk in and it's a bar. There are a dozen soldiers dressed in civilian clothes, goofy tropical shirts, drinking beer, watching TV. There's an Australian soldier in uniform serving drinks. I say we heard there was an attack nearby and heard shots close to our house, do you guys know anything? He looks drunk. "Arw, there's shots fired here every night, mate, no worries." He moves off to serve drinks. WHAM! comes on MTV.

I find an officer and he says don't go back to your house, stay for the night. He gives me a comfortable air-conditioned room in the officers' quarters. He says people show up scared all the time asking for a room, no problem. Nothing is a problem here.

In the morning I find the Dutch marines who run the MoveCon, Movement Control, helipad. Mr. Karim works with these guys and said if I have any trouble up here, find the Dutch marines. They look hard and serious and disciplined. I ask the officer in charge if he heard of any activity last night. He says two hundred Khmer Rouge were on the move, and then he curses in Dutch and says something I can't understand about his orders from headquarters, then he says we have to hit the fuckers hard and he walks away.

As I walk to the helipad to jump on the bird, a pickup full of Cambodian government soldiers drives by, one of the guys waving a rocket-propelled grenade launcher. He yells something at me in Khmer. I have no idea what anyone is saying here and I still have no idea what happened last night and I'm getting out of here. I'm embarrassed all over again. How much of this should I tell Miss Heidi? I shouldn't tell anyone. Now that I'm safe, I don't want Dr. Andrew to know.

I get home grimy, sweaty, tired. I'm looking forward to a mango daiquiri and the usual revelry. Our huge house is dark and quiet, no music, no Miss Heidi, no Mr. Karim, no Chloe in any of the living or dining rooms. They say the Khmer Rouge used this house as a torture chamber in the seventies. I'm a little apprehensive as I walk around alone. Where is everybody?

Finally I stumble on Mr. Karim on the patio. He's brooding and drunk. He tells me MoveCon asked him to fly out to a remote field station to conduct the Muslim rituals for two dead civilians from Bangladesh before shipping them home. When he got there, the bodies had been lying out in the sun for days in a makeshift morgue, swollen, rotting with flies and maggots climbing in and out of every orifice. None of the Muslim rituals had been respected, no way their souls can go to heaven. He finishes describing the bodies and he grabs me by both shoulders and squeezes hard. He smells of cigarettes and rum. A lot of rum. His eyes are bloodshot and dark and crazy. "Mr. Ken, Mr. Ken, Mr. Ken, promise me, you gotta promise me, if I die here, you find me, you take my body home, Mr. Ken, don't leave my body, Mr. Ken, Mr. Ken, Mr. Ken, you gotta promise."

"Okay, man. I'll do it. I promise."

Andrew
A Reservoir Outside Phnom Penh

I'm becoming claustrophobic in the prison and need to break out, get some air. Windsurfing is one of the few things I miss from home. Cambodia, with its coastline and inland waterways, would be perfect for it, but I've never seen anyone with a board. Then last night I heard a guy at the Floating Bar talking about windsurfing in Thailand, just next door.

So I get up early, grab my passport and a wad of dollars, and make a ten-hour dash west straight to the Thai border. At sunset I cross a narrow track through a minefield, red skull-and-crossbones BEWARE MINES! signs everywhere, drink huge quantities of coffee, then drive through the night to Pattaya, the closest resort. I find a local guy running a windsurfing school on the beach and buy a board and sail for $700 U.S. Thais are good like that. If you're holding cash, you can generally get whatever you need.

I race home and set up the windsurfer at the first reservoir I hit outside Phnom Penh. The lake was part of one of those insane irrigation schemes leading nowhere, built by forced labor under the Khmer Rouge. Judging by the height of the dam, a lot of Cambodians must have died during the construction.

By the time I have the board and sail rigged, a crowd of villagers has gathered. They've never seen a windsurfer before. A cheeky soldier with a Kalashnikov rifle announces that I probably can't even swim. I ignore him and push the board out thigh deep into the muddy water. As the crowd goes quiet, a breeze comes up. I'm about to become the first person ever to windsurf in Cambodia. I sail out into the lake. They whistle and jump and clap and cheer. When I return to shore, the soldier taunts me again, saying anyone can do that, it's easy. So I swap the windsurfer for his weapon. Be my guest. He falls in right away. He falls on top of the sail, then the sail falls on top of him. He goes off the front end and he goes off the back. His trousers slip down, exposing bare arse, which sends the crowd into howls of laughter. But he's strong and persistent and by now has nothing to lose. Eventually he gets the hang of it and sails off on wobbly knees.

But like any novice in that initial moment of euphoria, he goes too far, doesn't know where to stop or how to turn around. So I have to swim out into the lake and drag him back. He's wide-eyed and addicted, ready to risk everything to windsurf. He begs me to swap the board for his automatic rifle, and I picture myself in the prison armed with his Kalashnikov and my vitamin B injections. Meanwhile he goes ripassing all over Cambodia on the board. It's hard to tell him no, so I promise that when the fighting's over, we'll trade in his weapon and go windsurfing together.

Heidi
On the Gulf of Thailand

I soon discover that I'm not the only woman in the office on the lam from a marriage gone wrong. One woman is running from a cocaine-addicted husband who spent all their savings, another from a marriage she entered on impulse after a romantic rendezvous in Indonesia. Together we form a sort of club. We do what generations of women before us have done in joyous celebration of newfound emancipation: we head south to the beach for the weekend.

The road is littered with potholes large enough to swallow a car and in some places is washed away entirely. At a small village we slow the vehicle to a crawl. The villagers have claimed the edge of the road here, making it just another piece of public furniture. Old men, mothers with babies tied to their backs, amputees: all sit resting along the edge of the road like a park bench. Women squat on the blacktop over iron pots, chopping vegetables or scrubbing laundry and chatting with their neighbors. They bring all the accoutrements of their daily life out to the edge of the road during daylight.

After a four-hour drive, the only thing that stands between us and the beach is a partially collapsed bridge. The left side of the road has come unhinged with one end submerged into the river below like a boat launch. We have to wait for the oxcarts and scooters to pass before it's our turn. The structure is rickety as hell and looks ready to give way beneath the weight of the Land Cruiser. We blast forward anyway, thrilled to be in motion.

At the motel we check in, throw on our swimsuits, and walk the short distance to the beach. Life is good. We spend the next few hours floating in inner tubes in the steamy waters of the Gulf of Thailand. We signal to the waiters, who wade out to us fully clothed, carrying trays of beer and cigarettes already lit. We talk incessantly about our good fortune, our winter lives at UN Headquarters a winter past. We decide this must be what it's like to be rich, to be entitled. At midday we wrap ourselves in sarongs and go over to the restaurant for lunch. We order literally everything on the menu. We don't even know what half of it is, but it's dirt cheap, what the hell. It feels good to say just bring us one of everything.

After showers, we're running around to each other's rooms in our bras, our wet hair up in towels. "Does this look okay?" "What do you think of this lipstick color?" "The black shoes or the tan?" We're four women getting ready for a night out. Only this night out is in Kompong Som, southern Cambodia. We can hear gunfire off in the hills; the night is black.

A checkpoint near the hotel spontaneously assembles. The soldiers need some cigarettes or a few dollars for beer. If they stop our car, maybe they'll shoot us, take the car, our money. Forensics will find our teeth in some pit in the countryside. The only protection we have comes in a small foil packet.

One of the women knows some French soldiers. We find the gate of the French Battalion and park across the dirt road. Around the perimeter of the base are hundreds of shacks hastily constructed to house young Cambodian and Vietnamese taxi girls. French soldiers exit the base and saunter openly to one or another of the whorehouses. The guys we are waiting for climb into the car and everybody's hugging and kissing.

After a long dinner, we speed defiantly through the dark and empty streets. We are eight people squeezed into the Land Cruiser on top of each other, but nobody minds. Salt n' Pepa's song "Let's Talk About Sex" blasts from the car radio. We're foreign and free and obnoxious and have dollars, so stay out of our way. We're immortal and nothing can touch us.

Except the checkpoint ahead. A face-off between a car packed full of drunk French troops with Western girls on their laps and Cambodian soldiers at a late-night checkpoint won't end well. The driver throws the car into a reverse U-turn and our laughter rings out through the otherwise silent night like a challenge.

We get the French soldiers back to base by their curfew. They check in at the front gate, all accounted for, and we drive off into the darkness. We circle the perimeter and park, lights out, by the back wall. Five minutes pass before we hear a thud on the ground, close by. Three more thuds as they each escape over the wall and climb back into our car. Back in their tents, their pillows lie propped under the blankets, masquerading as French warriors in deep sleep. We return to the motel as four couples.

The next day we abandon our warriors and drive recklessly fast to get back home before dark. We are only twenty minutes outside of Phnom Penh when the sun sets and the government soldiers establish their roadblocks. We don't even see the first one until our car slams through the narrow wooden drop gate, sending it splintering off to all sides. We hold our breath and wait to hear shots ring out behind us, but there are none. We don't slow down until we're back in the city.

Andrew
Two Weeks to the Election

I've been windsurfing anywhere there's water. I windsurf in flooded rice paddies and large fishponds and in the eddies on the edge of town next to the red-light district. The prostitutes love it; they glide out of their shacks half-naked to wave and invite me in.

My favorite spot, where the wind is strongest, is out on the Mekong River, which has the added advantage of being close to the Floating Bar. The breeze brings me back there in time for Space Shuttle hour. One of the UN guys from Jamaica has a secret marijuana drink recipe. The locals consider it just another herb and you can buy whole branches of the stuff in the market for a dollar. The Space Shuttle is made by distilling a pound of marijuana over a six-week period with increasingly good quality spirits. It's a work of love and the final product is an amber-colored liquid that tastes like cognac. We drink it on the rocks or with Coke. After a couple of glasses, I'm overcome by a complete sense of calm. As the sun sets over the Mekong, I down another one and watch mesmerized as pink tracer rounds curve in graceful slow motion over the shimmering water.

The Mekong is tricky though. It looks tranquil but the current can be swift, especially after it rains, when it's easy to get caught half a mile out by a sudden drop in the wind. Last week, I floated helplessly downriver toward Vietnam for two hours, and it was night before I managed to paddle back in. Try dragging a windsurfer up a riverbank knee-deep in thick mud after paddling for hours. The villagers were astonished at this cursing, bedraggled figure limping up out of the murk, hauling an alien contraption. They put me up for the night though, and fed me while their kids

77

pulled at the hairs on my legs. The children seemed to both worship and fear the board, creeping up on it, caressing its fiberglass, and then running away screaming, as though it might bite.

I was out on the Mekong again today when an entire village of refugees floated past. They had been attacked upriver by the Khmer Rouge. It was a pathetic sight, a flotilla of hundreds of ragged houseboats lashed together into giant rafts, drifting slowly. They were carrying their dead with them. I could see the bodies, wrapped in cloth. They stared at me blankly as I glided silently past, my multicolored sail bright in the sunlight. A small child waved but didn't smile. Then a gentle gust caught my sail and I was gone.

May

Heidi
Days Before the Election

The parties shut down, no more fun and games. All offices are working overtime, getting ready for the election. This is what we came here to do. For two weeks my team works nonstop, deep into the night, and all weekend long organizing the logistics for the three days of voting. Finally, I'm able to work on something related to the election like everyone else.

Outside our office UN soldiers are preparing as well. Steel reinforcements are constructed around all the fences with barbed concertina wire arrayed along the top. All military and security personnel wear their full gear with flak jackets, helmets, and extra ammunition. Radio messages report rampant rumors of Khmer Rouge attacks. There is a curfew imposed at dusk. Every corner along the main road is occupied by tanks and armored personnel carriers, soldiers everywhere. The road to Vietnam is crawling with military, and everyone is nervous. But rather than being afraid to go outside, I find it thrilling. I've stepped into a TV show and any misadventure can be undone with a flick of the remote.

Two nights before the elections begin, a group of us get together at our house. Andrew shows up. He's become a familiar presence around Ken. I'm glad he's here; he's calm and steady, almost fatalistic, as if the die is already cast. I don't know where he gets that from, but it has a reassuring effect on the rest of us.

We've never spent time in the formal downstairs sitting room, but on this night the mood is solemn and it seems appropriate to gather here. In the morning we'll each go our separate ways, off to prepare and observe different polling sites around the country. We've all heard the rumors about the Khmer Rouge, and it's obvious each of us is scared. It's as though we're here to say goodbye but not willing to say it. Dr. Andrew, the experienced one among us, half-jokingly gives tips on how to roll your body to the ground in the event of a grenade or mortar attack. For three days we'll have no contact with one another, won't know a thing until we all return to Phnom Penh and can do a head count.

I am assigned to monitor two polling stations near the sea. One is a schoolhouse in a three-room barn with a dirt floor. Narrow pieces of wood are nailed together and painted with a flat black paint for use as a blackboard. Drawings and records of exam results hang on the walls. I can feel the children's pride in having them displayed. I carefully remove and put them aside for safekeeping. There's no electricity and no windows, the only light comes through cracks in the barn siding. I imagine that one good kick would send the entire structure shuddering to the ground. This school makes the one-room schoolhouse my father attended as a child in Missouri look like a private academy.

The other polling site, across a dirt road from an abandoned railway station, consists of three large, open-ended military tents. As I enter one, my shoe is sucked off my foot by six inches of mud. There are no Cambodian polling staff in sight and I have no idea where to find them. Then it hits me that I'm in charge here. I've never done anything like this in my life and don't speak the language, but I have one day to get this mudhole ready for a national election. I walk through each of the empty tents and as I stand in the last, wondering where to begin, a huge, fat hog walks right past me and plops down on his belly. His friends and lovers soon join him. I spend the rest of the day alternately begging over the handheld radio for someone to bring some sand and cursing at the pigs, which makes me feel a little better.

I notice a small canteen close to the site. Soaking wet in the one-hundred-degree heat, I wander over in search of a Pepsi. I find the entire group of Cambodian polling staff catatonically engrossed in a soap opera direct from Hong Kong. I say nothing but am furious that they haven't started preparing the site. I've quickly gone from being the one who would have given anything to sneak off to watch bad TV at work to the one who is now self-righteous about work not being done. It feels good.

But the polling staff are in fact excited to start. This election is important to them and they are proud to be working for the UN. They are also happy to be getting paid $200 for one month's work. One of the women on the team is a radiologist at the local hospital. She tells me that she makes twenty thousand Cambodian riel a month, less than $5. She says this election is the opportunity of her lifetime. Mine too.

Andrew
Phnom Penh, First Day of Voting

A people and a country and the UN and the world hold their breath. Over four and a half million voters have been registered, and ten thousand Khmer Rouge soldiers have orders to stop them from voting. Hundreds of journalists are in-country to record the violence.

It's 7 A.M. but already way too hot. Lumning and Sari are dressed in their best clothes, usually reserved for weddings. He's combed his hair and she's put on makeup. They're even taking the kids with them to vote. I tell them not to hang around in the streets afterward, because today might be bloody. But Lumning, who is usually an overprotective father, seems unconcerned; maybe he knows something I don't. Before dawn he prayed beneath the pale bamboo cross driven by a rusty nail into the coarse grain of the bedroom wall, kneeling on the wide ebony planks of our hardwood floor. His little girl was holding his hand, still half asleep. Maybe I should have knelt beside them.

On my way into town, I'm surprised to see that Cambodians are already out in force; they look as though they're all on their way to that same wedding as Lumning. And instead of returning home after voting, they're milling about, making the most of the free national holiday. An eighty-year-old woman with no teeth buys a block of colored ice on a stick. It promptly melts all over her registration card. Whole families suck on mangoes, and the noodle soup street vendors are doing a roaring trade. Phnom Penh has turned into a family picnic with hundreds of thousands of guests.

At the prison the guards are bringing the inmates out of their cells in small groups. Even the hard men among them, the murderers and the rapists, are clutching their voter registration cards and dipping their fingers in invisible ink so they can't vote twice. The prisoners are standing on brand-new legs. Beriberi is a memory and that shackling bar is now mine.

Major Top looks relaxed and coiffed, and his glasses sit firmly atop his nose for once. Two months ago we both thought he would shoot me in the back, but now he shakes my hand and introduces me to his family as though I'm an old friend. He puts his wife and son in the same line as the prisoners and rests both hands on his son's shoulders while they wait. Today he's not an intelligence major from the Interior Ministry but a middle-aged Cambodian dad.

For the first time ever, all Cambodians are equal for a day. Prisoners with the same rights as their guards smile broadly at me as they stand in line. None of these ragged men in faded blue pajamas with invisible ink on their fingers has ever seen anything like this.

The scene in this prison courtyard is my own tiny triumph. I take a snapshot to show my grandchildren. Major Top watches as tears of joy smudge my lens.

Heidi
In the South, First Day of Voting

At daybreak on the first day, thousands of Cambodians are already calmly waiting outside my polling station. They squat on the ground, silent and patient. We didn't expect this at all. We thought they would fail to understand how democracy works. We thought they would be afraid of the Khmer Rouge. We thought they would passively accept their fate. We were wrong.

It is as inspiring a display of courage and faith as I've ever seen and I feel the need to go around and apologize to each person for the long lines and explain the delay. We are sorry but we had no idea that you would show up to your election. Even when the polls officially open, the wait is hours long, but the voters wait calmly. Six months ago Clinton was elected at home, and as I stood in line to vote in New York, we were ready to kill each other over a fifteen-minute wait.

Among the mass of dignified peasant voters, I spot a group of about forty taxi girls. Makeup in place, faces powdered white, sweating in their cheap, shiny dresses, voter registration cards in hand. Other than their inappropriate dress for daytime and obvious occupational status, the only thing that sets them apart is that they stand, rather than squat down on the ground. I wonder if squatting is something they were taught is unflattering or if their dresses simply don't permit it. I find their presence moving. I never thought they'd care about who holds power, but it's probably more important to them than to anyone. My own problems suddenly seem amazingly inconsequential.

The UN has supplied enough American military–issue Meals-Ready-to-Eat for all the polling staff. In the afternoon I sneak behind the tent for a smoke and find the ground completely littered with empty MRE packages. I confront the Cambodian staff. They confess that they've already devoured the entire three-day supply. A single MRE is meant to provide a full day's worth of calories and nutrients to a typical American soldier. I wonder what these tiny Cambodian bodies will do when ten thousand American military calories slam into them. Culture shock.

I on the other hand overdose on Pepsi and green mangos dipped in salt and continue to chase the pigs from the tents throughout the day. Everything else goes smoothly. The polls close on schedule and the UN French military convoy comes to collect the ballot boxes.

Ken
In the Field, First Day of Voting

There's a girl standing in front of me. She must be about seven, pageboy haircut, skin the color of dark wood, frilly yellow smock with white lace on the collar, dusty little brown feet in flimsy blue flip-flops. She has a wisp of white crust under her nose. She's holding her baby brother on her hip, two seven-year-old hands with dirty fingernails cradle him effortlessly underneath his naked bottom. He's weightless in her arms, he doesn't cry or squirm; they look like they were born in this symbiosis. It makes me want to have kids. Not just any kids, but a seven-year-old girl who holds her baby brother by the naked bottom effortlessly and without complaint.

Rumpled, unshaven Bulgarian soldiers in full battle dress lean up against a shade tree and smoke and smoke and try to look soldierly. I nod to one and he replies with a flaccid salute. Yeah, yeah, I know, this battalion is much more professional than the last one. But even they are caught up in the moment, shake their heads and grin as the line of voters grows. It was all too easy to forget in the revelry of Phnom Penh before the elections—our own brief Paris in the Twenties—but this is why we are here.

There's only been one report of violence so far today on the radio. The Khmer Rouge fired two 82-millimeter mortar rounds near a line of voters at a polling site in the west. But the voters held their ground, refused to evacuate, and just waited where they stood in line for their turn to vote.

My job is to compile poll monitoring reports from the fifteen hundred human rights workers who volunteered to serve as neutral civilian election observers. Pan Ya greets our team at the observation table and soberly collects their status reports, suddenly looking much older than his nineteen years. He looks me straight in the eye today. For the first time, I let him make the formal introductions to local officials.

Our human rights workers look somber and proud too, displaying their observer credentials like a passport to a new and peaceful future. Next to government officials, party representatives, and international delegates, they stand uneasily, apprehensive volunteers representing nothing more than hope. They forgot their gravity and broke into big smiles when I arrived. Now they glance up at me from the observation table every few minutes, as if seeking reassurance that this is real, Cambodia is voting. I get a lump in my throat each time we make eye contact. They're risking their lives and they know it and they fought hard for the chance to do it.

There are three possible results to this election. One, the government loses, refuses to relinquish power, declares martial law, and cracks down on all opposition, in which case the human rights groups are in deep shit—precisely what happened in Myanmar. Two, the government wins and then punishes anyone who stepped forward as a reformer during the election, in which case the human rights groups are in deep shit again— exactly what happened in China when Mao let a "hundred flowers bloom," then chopped off their buds. Three, the government either wins or loses but enters into a consensus coalition government and human rights are respected in a peaceful democratic transition.

The UN is betting $2 billion and a lot of human lives on option three, which seemed like a hell of an irresponsible risk to me after our human rights volunteer was killed last month. But if I believe my eyes today, Cambodians are eager to take that risk. It's patronizing for me to conclude anything else on their behalf. So I try to convince myself that I'm not responsible for that volunteer's death. I just gave him the reporting forms and the camera. Fifteen hundred more volunteers stepped forward today.

Heidi
Second Day of Voting

I spend most of the second day of voting sitting outside the tents talking to the two French soldiers stationed here. I realize by now that the polling staff are well trained and competent. I think I just get in their way, so I wait for them to hand me a paper to sign affirming that everything is in order for each batch of ballots, which is the only important part of my job here anyway. I go over and sit in the canteen for a while. The women who work there like to touch me, which at first was bizarre but now has become almost maternal. I feel lonely and the days are long and hot and tiring and it's nice to see their friendly, smiling faces.

Throughout the night I hear grenades exploding, gunfire and shelling, but all in the distance. I try to remember what Andrew said about rolling to the ground. Along with my head, which organ was it that's most important to protect? I close my eyes and pretend that I am actually in a really bad part of Brooklyn. Somehow, that scares me more, seems more real to me than the fact that I am alone in a field in Southeast Asia. The French military patrol comes by every two hours and stays for twenty minutes to flirt with me. It's a relief to see them coming down the road each time. As they approach, they yell things to me like "Honey, we're home" or berate me for not having coffee made. For once I don't mind hearing the sexist crap. In fact, by the end of the night, I'm wishing I was married to all of them and living in Paris, washing their underwear and making them big pots of couscous.

I spend the rest of the night sitting up in the dark tent, fighting the mosquitoes and listening to my shortwave radio. I find BBC and listen to a program about some Victorian poet. There is a brilliant electrical storm. Lightning bolts zigzag through the sky and light the ground every few seconds. Three full nights without sleep and I'm starting to hallucinate.

The sky lights up. I'm positive I see a silhouette of someone running low across the roof of the train station. My heart is racing and I rush to the back of the tent, not knowing what to do, sure that they will open fire at any moment. I pace around the back of the tent trying to determine the safest spot to avoid getting shot. It then occurs to me that I am all alone in a tent in a field in the middle of nowhere and if someone wants to shoot me, they can just walk up and do it. I go back to the BBC and the Victorian poet.

After three days of elections, we move down the road to a tent set up as a counting center to tally the votes. The counting of the ballots is exhausting and tedious work and takes all night, but I never complain. This may be the most important thing I have done in my life. Representatives from the twenty different political parties hang over our shoulders the entire time. A photographer from the *New York Times* sees my "I love Cambodia" T-shirt and shoots a roll of film of me counting ballots.

For all these months I've been writing my mother that I'll return home, buy a condo, go back to work at UN Headquarters, and see her on the weekends. I know she secretly hopes my husband and I will work things out. She just wants to know that I'm secure, provided for. It's natural and I don't blame her. But she also taught me that a woman should be prepared to walk away and take care of herself. I can do that now. I've discovered what had been missing in my life and can never go back. My role in the success of the election is small but I've been a part of something huge.

The election is over. Cambodians are on their own. But I'm not getting back on the Staten Island Ferry. There must be another election or land-slide or war somewhere where UN secretaries are needed.

Ken
Leaving Cambodia

I'm leaving tomorrow. Everything is folded, stacked, packed. Clothes, tickets, passport, pictures. Phone numbers of new, good friends from all over the world.

It worked. Ninety percent of registered Cambodians voted. The main opposition party won the most seats in Parliament. The government came a close second. The UN is helping to negotiate a power sharing agreement to create an internationally recognized, legitimate government. We actually made peace. That was fun, let's do it again.

There's been a coup in Haiti and Andrew is on the next plane. Fighting is raging in Bosnia, war in the heart of Europe. Our team at the Floating Bar can't just sit and watch, can they? Heidi is hand delivering my resumé and an impassioned cover letter in triplicate to the top of the in-box at person-nel in New York. The UN is urgently staffing a mission in Somalia and she's trying to get us both on the deployment list. We'll be there together soon, I'm sure of it. No one says no to Miss Heidi.

I said goodbye to Andrew, good luck on the Haiti mission. I'll see him again soon somewhere on earth, and on different terms, I'm sure of that too.

I never resolved the facts or my guilt, and I needed to hear Andrew's assessment of my human rights case again before I left. So we had a heart-to-heart at the Floating Bar. He said his office had investigated a list of 219 cases of election-related murders, none of them fully resolved, mine was just one. And four million Cambodians voted.

There's one last thing I need to do.

I find a cyclo driver and we peddle to Tuol Sleng.

It was once a grade school. Now it's a memorial to genocide. The playground and classrooms served as a Khmer Rouge torture chamber for twenty thousand enemies of the revolution. Almost everyone who entered died. First you were chained in a two-by-three-foot cell, deprived of food and water, forced to watch others being tortured, then tortured yourself and coerced to confess your counterrevolutionary tendencies, and finally transported to the killing fields and executed.

I wander the moldy museum alone. Picture after picture from Khmer Rouge files of inmates—who were not long for this world and must have known it—cover the walls in memoriam. Some of the terrified faces look just like Pan Ya.

They kept a few artists alive to create an endless series of busts celebrating the visage of Brother Number One, Pol Pot. They were among the handful of inmates who survived. After the Khmer Rouge were chased out of Phnom Penh, the artists painted eyewitness testimonials that hang on the walls now. I stare at a painting of soldiers laughing while one tosses a baby into the air and the other impales it with his bayonet.

The image of that laughing soldier will accompany me to Somalia and to the next ten Somalias. He'd turn over in his grave if he knew it, but he's my talisman. He is exactly what's at stake. We can save that baby. Dr. Andrew's done it a hundred times with his bare hands. That's my lesson in courage from Cambodia. The larger the threat, the more profound the doubts, the deeper you have to dig to find faith and conquer your fears.

This is the chance of a lifetime. I finally found my moment in history.

Andrew
Leaving Cambodia

We've each come a long way. Ken graduated from his apprenticeship, faster than anyone I've ever known. Look out, world. Four months ago Heidi couldn't find this country on a map or cross the street outside her hotel. Now she's run her small corner of a miraculous election. Ken and I are from dissimilar backgrounds, but he's still the kind of guy I'd have befriended anywhere, as my patient or my lawyer, or in a bar. Heidi's different. She intimidated me at first: nothing much about me seems to impress her. Those clear eyes see right through any pretense, so you just have to be yourself and hope that she likes you. Somehow Ken's figured that out and I haven't quite, yet. But I will. Because whenever the three of us are together, people stare and start listening in. Somehow we form an unlikely triangle I want to try to keep intact. I'm going to miss them, but Cambodia's just the beginning.

I'm a long way from that morning a decade ago when I walked into a physiology lab in New Zealand and sat down next to a Cambodian genocide survivor. I've been out of touch with the Medical Board for so long that they've probably removed my name from the official physicians register.

But I don't care. I'm stretching the usefulness of my training beyond any limit I'd ever imagined, happy to have exchanged my physician's calling for the bigger mission of serving as a peacekeeper. I'm a convert. There are jeeps and helicopters and jet aircraft lined up all over the world, waiting to take me everywhere there's war, anywhere but back home. Home is wherever the next mission is. It's a better high than the Space Shuttle and lasts longer.

I bid a sad good-bye to Lumning and the family and then get on a plane bound for the Caribbean, carrying everything I own in a single suitcase. As it banks over the tarmac, I look back at Phnom Penh shimmering in the heat. Down there are cerebral malaria patients whose lives I've saved, unshackled prisoners with vitamin supplements who've voted, and somewhere between the rice fields and the river, a banged-up windsurfer.

The jets thrust hard beneath me, we ascend, and it can't be stopped.

CONDITION CHARLIE
SOMALIA AND HAITI, 1993

Somalia. The Somali dictator, Siad Barre, had successfully played the U.S. and the USSR off each other for years, but his government collapsed at the end of the Cold War. Famine was rampant, warlords used food as a weapon and hijacked emergency aid for profit and political leverage. President George H. W. Bush ordered the marines in to deliver food and relief supplies. The initial phase of the mission was a success, and in 1993 newly elected President Clinton decided to expand it. It was a heady moment: the promise of democracy, human rights, and the peace dividend seemed to have no limits, as the mission in Cambodia demonstrated so triumphantly. In concert with the UN, Clinton ordered a full-scale "humanitarian intervention" in Somalia designed to impose peace and rebuild the nation. But one of the warlords, Mohammed Farah Aidid, decided he didn't like the "intervention" part and challenged America to a fight.

Haiti. In 1990 Jean-Bertrand Aristide, a former Roman Catholic priest, won the first democratic elections ever held in Haiti. But in 1991 the Haitian military and paramilitary forces that supported them carried out a successful coup. Exiled in Washington, D.C., President Aristide vowed to return to Haiti with U.S. and UN support. The leaders of the coup, led by General Raoul Cédras, took a bloody vice-grip on power and terrorized the civilian population of the poorest country in the Western Hemisphere, prompting Haitian refugees to flee for the U.S. in an endless flotilla of rickety boats. Together with the Organization of American States (OAS), the UN deployed an ambitious civilian human rights observer mission to document torture and execution of pro-Aristide civilians, hoping to pressure General Cédras from power and allow Aristide to return as president.

July

Heidi, Mombasa, Kenya
In Transit from Cambodia to Somalia
Bob Marley Is Dead

Inspired by my adventures in Cambodia, I decide to stop over in Kenya en route to Somalia. I saw a postcard once from Mombasa, a beach resort on the Swahili coast, and it stayed in my memory as this terribly exotic place I'd never get a chance to see. But I'm ready for anything now, so I just picked up the phone and made a reservation.

I spend my days dodging an Italian helicopter pilot on leave from Mogadishu. I made the mistake of having dinner with him a few nights ago. Now he unceremoniously installs himself in the lounge chair next to mine whenever he can, even as I sit silently reading my book. He has claimed me and no amount of rudeness on my part discourages him in his quest to win my heart or, at least, my bed.

I'm bored with the routine of a late breakfast of mangos and toast, a long day lying hot and sweaty under a palm tree, and an evening of "African cultural dance" staged for the tourists by disenchanted locals, followed by a nightly poolside barbecue of big hunks of dead zebra and antelope. This is the Hotel Intercontinental's idea of the African coastal experience. I have to get into town.

On my way out, I pass the hotel concierge. His starched white shirt and little black bow tie stand in contrast to the stretched earlobes that lie against his collar. He gives me a dirty look as I leave; he can't understand why I won't just stay where I belong, on the beach with the other tourists.

I walk out to the middle of the road and look both ways, trying to determine in which direction town might be. To the left, nothing but dry fields. To the right, the same. No shade, no life. Just the blazing Kenyan sun in front, and behind me, at the hotel, a cruel pantomime of Africa played out in blackface, replete with rich, tanned Euro-travelers demanding afternoon cocktails from illiterate Kenyan waiters in bow ties and white jackets.

I've walked about two miles when I start thinking this is a bad idea. I'm hot, I'm tired, I'm covered with road dust. Suddenly I miss the king-sized bed in my air-conditioned room. I pass a field and work comes to a standstill. Young boys lean on hoes or shovels and stare at me. They're laughing and yelling at me in Swahili.

Oh, fuck off, I yell back. Then I see myself in their eyes, this ridiculous white woman, her nose and shoulders burned red, shuffling down the middle of the road with a huge straw bag over her shoulder. I realize this is stupid. Stop whining, I tell myself. I'm made of steel. I'm tired and thirsty but I'm only two miles away from all the comforts of a five-star hotel.

I hear a car engine coming over the last rise, and although it turns out to be the Italian pilot and his friends, I'm happy to see them. I'm less happy when I realize that they have come looking for me after the concierge sought them out on the beach to report that I was last seen walking off alone, in the direction away from town. They turn the car around on the narrow dirt road with much loud commentary in Italian. As we pass by the workers, cheers go up in the field. Tools are raised in the air. The runaway woman has been captured.

The pilots aren't comfortable being outside the protection of their commanders or, at the very least, of the hotel's Pinkerton guards, but they insist on escorting me to town. My pilot keeps his hand tightly on my arm at all times, guiding me away from any undesirables who might approach and, God forbid, try to sell us a necklace or other local art object. I detest his protection and all it assumes and repeatedly pull away. He is not deterred, and finally the group gathers around me and gives me the girl talk. They patiently explain that I am being naïve and opening myself to known dangers by even speaking to the necklace sellers. I'm making it very difficult for them to keep an eye on me. Why, I'm even leaving them exposed if they have to constantly second-guess my every move. I'm just a girl.

Yeah, just a girl who in a week will be living in a free-fire zone in fucking Mogadishu, Somalia. Ken's been working there a month already. He said there are ambushes against UN personnel every day.

In the afternoon, back at the hotel, I search out a lounge chair as close to the hotel boundaries as I can get. Other guests prefer to be closer to the hotel and away from the Masai tribesmen who continually wait for the guards to turn their backs before approaching to show their trinkets for sale. Occasionally a Masai sneaks up with a discarded water bottle and asks me to fill it from one of the spigots scattered around for guests to rinse their feet.

There's a rustle in the bushes and suddenly this beautiful Masai head pokes through with a big smile. "Hi," he says. Hi, with these eyes that could look through you for a hundred centuries. It's always the eyes that get me. Before the guard can come to chase him away, he tells me to wait for him down by the water. I don't think twice. I throw my stuff into my bag, wrap a sarong around my bathing suit and within about thirty seconds am standing next to him at the water's edge. I keep giggling for some reason.

We walk along and talk. His name is James. He asks me a million questions, like where am I from and where is New Jersey in relation to places he knows. Is it near Jamaica? Well, sort of, in a roundabout kind of geography and taking into consideration how far both countries are from here. As we walk, I notice other solitary white women, all fairly young and attractive, with their own Masai tribesmen. Great, now I've turned into one of those rich white chicks who pick up poor, attractive men in third world countries for sex.

We climb aboard a dhow, which, after a short ride, deposits us directly onto the reef. Strewn around in puddles are the most magnificent sea creatures—anemones, urchins, starfish. Splashes of bright, living color everywhere—purple, red, blue, yellow—just lying in shallow pools of water, waiting for the tide to come in and rescue them. Not wanting to crush more than we have to, we sit in one place and smoke a joint. We're stoned and just sitting, staring at each other, smiling and smiling, the reef alive and pulsating around us.

Through the thick fog of my brain, I can hear this low roar. It's a noise I've never heard before but something that rings of danger. In between the looks of love I'm passing, I try to concentrate on this noise. I think to myself, *Focus, focus.* My brain says, *It's behind you,* so I turn. I watch as a wall of water smashes against the far side of the reef. *Hawaii Five-O* waves. The waves look far enough away to just give me enough time to review my entire life and anticipate my bloody death. Like those last four minutes or so when you know your plane's going down. That's how long I figure we have.

But I'm still not sure if the danger is real, so I compose myself and attempt to go back to our foreplay. All the while the wave-wall is getting closer and closer. I watch James's face for any sign of awareness that we are in trouble, but he seems oblivious to everything but me. I start looking at escape options. Behind is the life-crushing wall. Ahead lies more coral reef and in front of that, dead coral reef, which is a platform of razor blades. Okay, options considered, there are none. I picture myself standing, arms waving in the air, screaming for help from the shore. I imagine fat topless German women running to the Italian pilot for help. It would be too humiliating. I decide I would rather die. As they pull my skeleton, shaved of all flesh, from the surf, the pilot can shake his head and tell everyone how he warned me that I was just a girl. I was headed for trouble. Out of vanity, I add to the fantasy a few purple and red starfish entangled in my hair, which between the reef and the beach has miraculously grown halfway down my back and turned blond.

The only thing I haven't thought of yet is to ask James if the dhow will be arriving anytime soon for the trip back to shore. Silly me. Of course he must get himself into crazy situations like this all the time, but these guys know what to do. I'm sure he's arranged for the dhow to come back for us. I just missed it because I don't understand Swahili. "So," I say, "when is that guy coming back for us?" "You want to leave already?" he says. Casually, I sort of shrug and nod my head back toward the Big Wave. He turns and in one wild motion, flies into the air screaming, "Oh, shit, oh shit!" Maybe it wasn't just the joint we smoked. Suddenly his panic has made me calm. Accepting. I was right. We're fucked. Death is upon us. Lie down next to me. Rest your head on my bosom and let's enjoy our last good moment.

And then, sent directly from the spirit world, the guy with the dhow appears, three feet away from us. While the two of them scream and yell at each other, I nonchalantly lift my sarong and climb into the boat, primly adjusting my clothing and placing my bag squarely on my lap so the camera inside doesn't get wet. I've shifted rapidly from the death fantasy to really important matters: Are my panties showing? Is my camera safe from moisture?

Even as my guest, my new Masai friend is not allowed onto the hotel premises. He informs me of this after I invite him back to my room, and I am shocked. I'm also shocked that I'm so shocked. After spending five days here, I should have known this is the way it would be. We agree to meet the next morning to explore the caves along the coast.

At ten the next morning, he's waiting for me at the appointed spot. I light a cigarette and saunter across the beach, through the throngs of tourists baking in the sun, staring them down and daring them to make a comment. I feel like everybody knows where I am off to.

As we head down the beach toward the caves, no other hawker approaches us. I imagine there's some kind of code among them. Once in a while, he tries to kiss me, but I'm too aware of other foreigners nearby. The afternoon passes and we've done all the exploring of caves we can stand and I am not sure where to go with this. James saves the day by offering to show me his village, which, he says, is nearby.

After hours of trekking through the heat and brush of the Swahili Coast, we arrive exhausted at his village. The meaning of "nearby" is obviously elastic. We pass through the marketplace and unintentionally form the head of a small parade, as children and teenagers and barking dogs follow in our wake. The market is in full swing at this time with women choosing their fish and vegetables for the evening meal. Everyone stops to stare. I feel like a freak, which I suppose I am.

We enter a courtyard surrounded by a dozen or so identical huts. Each is made of compacted dung and sticks, with a tin roof and one door and one window on the opposite side. The floor is dirt and its only furnishings are a ragged mattress on the floor and several buckets that serve multiple purposes. And a cassette player.

Alone with me, James is suddenly shy. He flips over a pail for me to sit on and then sits facing me. There really isn't anything to look at, and what is there to say?

Soon enough though, James's friends come calling and the distraction is a relief for both of us. James immediately lights a couple of joints and starts passing them around. For a while we all sit on upturned pails, smoking our joints and smiling at each other, friendly, nice.

The men ask me almost the same questions that James had. Is New Jersey near Jamaica? Knowing now what "nearby" means in James's world, I figure I'm safe to say, yes, it's nearby. Then I think, what the hell, a flight from Newark to Jamaica takes as long as the walk to this village did, so yeah, I do live near Jamaica. Their eyes light up with excitement. One of them runs out and returns minutes later with a cassette tape. It turns out that James is the only one in the commune who owns a cassette player and his friend is the only one to own a tape, and it's Bob Marley's *Legend.*

We spend what's left of the afternoon smoking more joints and listening to *Legend,* over and over again. I'm hoping they don't share the hut with James, that they will go home soon. I'm also starting to get a little freaked out, maybe they think I'm just this big American whore who's here to fuck the whole village. Paranoia kicks in and I'm thinking, okay, after the village men have a big gang-bang, do I spend the rest of the night here in this room and then brokenly try to make my way back to the hotel, where the Italian pilot can say, ah-ha, told you so, girlie? Or do I leave as soon as I can and find a comfortable nest of grass to sleep in until daybreak? I never seem to be able to think ahead until the moment of impending catastrophe.

But then the friends are saying good night, shaking my hand, smiling. Off into the night they go and James and I are left alone again. I realize one of us has to make a move or we are never getting any sleep tonight. I move over to the mattress and lie down. I let my sarong slip off to the side. I let my bikini bottom show. He's busy, moving buckets from one side of the room to the other, shaking some dirt off the bottom of one, moving another just so. I'm wondering if this is some kind of Masai feng shui, or if he's avoiding joining me. I don't press him; I let him go on with whatever he is doing. A nervous man is a wonderful thing. It gives a woman all the power, but it only lasts so long, so I try to enjoy it, this moment of feigned control and confidence on my part.

Finally he lies next to me, still completely clothed. I lean over and kiss him. Kiss him some more and then I lose the control, feel it slipping from my grasp, and he takes over, sure of himself and of the moment. We make love for hours, and the last thing I think about before we fall asleep is bedbugs. Sleep tight, don't let the bedbugs bite.

In the morning I have to pee. I'm so dehydrated my body doesn't want to let it go. Ummmm, James, where can I find a bathroom here? I'm praying to God he'll tell me it's behind an as-yet-unnoticed door. But no, the toilets and showers are communal, just up the road. I want him to go with me: *All owners must walk their freaks on a leash.* But I brave the trip on my own. The courtyard is silent. Not a soul around. But then, as I pass through the alleyway to the street, I realize where everyone is. A large crowd of young women and girls has come to sit on the edge of the road opposite James's group of huts. A murmur runs through the crowd when I appear. Look! There she is! The freak lady! The girls smile and giggle at me. I wave and wonder if they stay there all day like sentinels. I picture them discussing me with their girlfriends later: "She finally came out of the room around three with her hair poking out all over, her eyes swollen shut by the daylight and stinking to high heaven, and she was still wearing that bikini/sarong combo." Better they think I'm the devil's spawn than some movie star. I don't feel like a freak anymore. Now I just feel nasty. Yes, girls, this is how American women behave. They fly around the world to spend their nights screwing men they don't even know. And they pay them too! God, let me just take a leak and then I'll go climb back into my dung hut and hide from the world, hanging my head in shame.

The shame part only lasts as long as it takes me to get naked and on the mattress again with James. Hours, which seem like minutes, pass by, and then James's friends are back at the door and we scramble to put our clothes on to greet them. There are used condoms everywhere and no place to dispose of them, so I lift an edge of the mattress and kick them all under. The afternoon is passed in typical fashion—having been here two days, I already know what is typical. We smoke, we listen to Bob Marley, we smoke some more, and occasionally we talk. Mostly we talk about Bob Marley. We are on our third or fourth joint of the afternoon when one of the guys asks, "Do you know Bob Marley?" "Bob Marley is dead," I tell him, although even as it comes out of my mouth, I'm thinking maybe he's not. I think to myself, he is dead, isn't he? Yeah, he's dead for sure.

Maybe an hour later, the other guy asks, "So do you know Bob Marley?" By now I'm really stoned and not at all sure anymore that Bob Marley is dead and I don't want to be the one to start spreading horrible rumors around the Kenyan countryside that a man so beloved here is dead. So this time I just don't reply. Another reason I don't reply is that I get so into pondering whether Bob Marley is dead or not that I forget the question. James takes my long silence as affirmation and says, "I like that you know Bob Marley." Several times my lips part. I want to say something but I can't speak. I'm thinking, okay, I'll go with Bob Marley still being alive, sitting down there in Jamaica, singing and smoking big Rasta doobies. Maybe it's true. Maybe it was somebody else who's dead, not Bob Marley. Yeah, Bob Marley is definitely alive. But I don't know him, that's going too far. Even here. Then I start thinking about how all my teeth feel like they're going to fall out of my mouth and I forget to deny knowing Bob Marley. My friend, Bob Marley.

Later, when we're alone in bed, James is lying quietly on top of me. Suddenly, he lifts his head and looks at me for a long time. There's something on his mind, a question he wants to ask me, but he hesitates.

"What is it?" I ask him. "Go ahead."

Shyly, he says, "Did you ever, you know, do this with Bob Marley?"

"Make love to Bob Marley?" I ask him.

"Yeah, make love to Bob Marley."

"No, never," I tell him. "I never made love to Bob Marley."

The look of disappointment on his face makes me wish I had said yes, yes of course, Bob Marley and I knock boots all the time when I'm back home in Jamaica.

By the next afternoon when we're all together again, I don't even bother to get off the mattress. I've barely slept in three days and have eaten nothing but bread. We're lighting up a joint every twenty minutes and James and I have even been smoking during sex. I'm alternating between being a zombie and laughing hysterically at nothing. I haven't bathed since I left the hotel, but I don't even notice. I'm no longer concerned with bedbugs. I can't remember when my hotel reservation runs out and wonder if the hotel will just set my bags at the curb or place them in storage. I have a brief moment of panic when I think that maybe someone has been looking for me or has reported me missing. Maybe the concierge has mentioned my absence to the Italian pilot, who then set off a panic. Maybe my parents are sitting next to the phone in New Jersey, waiting for the call that tells them my body has been found. Jesus Christ, I think, maybe they have already booked reservations on the next flight here to join the search for me! This thought actually gets me to sit up, ready to throw my shoes on and start tramping off through the fields and down the cliffside back to the hotel to call them and let them know I'm safe, that I've just been on a sex and drug binge for three days before entering the breach of Mogadishu, but I'm okay now, safely ensconced in my $200 a night hotel room with the nice pink German folk.

But then I think, naaahhhh, that's a lot of energy to spend on a big maybe, so I lie back down and start thinking about what I can eat for dinner.

Throughout the afternoon I field questions about Bob Marley's likes and dislikes. I actually know absolutely nothing about Bob Marley, but I'm not lying to them either. I no longer have any choice in the matter, for now I am channeling Bob Marley. They hang on my every word. It's astounding. I'm clairvoyant. It's been my lifelong dream that something like this would happen. And it all came to me so naturally. Just like that, I can see things. I sit on the edge of the mattress, my fingertips pressed against each temple. I've really got the Sylvia Browne thing down now.

But then I notice something move next to my bare foot. The tip of a used, slightly inflated condom pokes its little head up at me, trying to sneak out from under the mattress, where I have it pinned down. Bob Marley goes *bzzzztttt*—out like an old picture tube in my mind—and just as the little condom is about to heave itself out, James passes me another joint. I know that if I smoke it, the captured condom army will have me pinned to the dirt floor like Gulliver in a bikini.

I've reached my limit. I need a bath and some food. I need a tile floor and electricity. I need silence. I need detox.

* * *

James and I board a bus and, after a short journey, disembark in front of a small two-story concrete building. Painted crudely on the wall in the center of a big red heart, a sign welcomes us to "Sweetheart Hotel." At the reception desk, we awaken the clerk from his nap. James tells him we would like a room for the night. The clerk just stands there, his hands hanging limp at his side, not sure if we are real or just some figment of a bad dream. He looks desperately around the room, searching for confirmation that this Masai draped in red and blue beaded necklaces is actually standing there with a white woman who looks like Fay Wray after a really long trek through the jungle. Suddenly we all notice another man, who is in the same mute condition, on the stairway. The two lock eyes and only then does the clerk speak. Thirty shillings, he says, and hands us a key to a room upstairs. As we go up, his eyes never leave us and his mouth never closes. I feel three inches tall.

I'm better after a shower. My head is clearer and my insides aren't shaking as much now. The man from the stairs brings us some food—cheese sandwiches and Cokes. He leans across the bed and hands me a plate as I lie there. He's completely dumbfounded and I want to say, *Why? Why are you making me feel so bad about this?* But I know it's me, I'm making myself feel so bad about this.

James tells me he loves me. Then he tells me again. He tells me that in his village there is a white man who came and built a small concrete house and married a woman from the commune. They've lived there for several years now. They have children. They have a car. I picture myself living there in the village, raising children. I want to say, okay, I'll see you later, and run back and barricade myself in my room at the Intercontinental and watch CNN and order room service.

I tell James, "But I don't love you. I mean, I like you very much, but I don't love you."

"That's okay," he says. "I love you, you like me very much, no problem."

I tell him, "I don't really know Bob Marley."

"That's okay," he says.

"Bob Marley is dead," I say.

The next morning I'm dressed and ready to go before James even wakes up. I'm sitting on the edge of the bed, chain-smoking cigarettes and trying to keep from tapping my feet. He rolls over and smiles up at me. "Okay," I say, "throw those beads around your neck and let's get the hell out of here."

We hop another bus, twenty minutes and I'm standing in front of my hotel. I wrestled with my thoughts the entire morning. What does he really expect from me? Is it possible that this man with the body of a warrior and the smile of Cupid who spends his days walking half-naked with the tourists on the beach, who didn't hesitate to approach me, could not be a prostitute? At what point is one considered a prostitute? For men, it seems so clear: the woman is costumed; she stands in the shadows or under a street lamp; she approaches the car, gets in, takes care of business; a monetary transaction follows. It's over for him. The woman doesn't expect—doesn't want—anything more than the cash.

But what does a woman expect for her money? Why do we need to first be made to feel comfortable, flirted with, seduced? Why do we need to create the false sense of emotional ties? Why couldn't we just say, okay, that cave over there, we go in, we fuck, hand over some money, and go on with our lives? Why do I feel so guilty? The feeling that I have used and kicked to the curb another human being won't leave me.

He says, okay, I'll write you. Okay, I'll write you, too, I tell him. Then I hand him two hundred-dollar bills. He takes them, smiles, and walks away.

Two weeks later in Mogadishu, I get a letter from him.

"I love you," it says. "I miss you. Can you send me $700?"

I never reply.

August

Andrew
Port-au-Prince, Haiti

As the plane banks toward Port-au-Prince, I press my nose against the window, smudging the line half a mile out from the coast where the turquoise of the Caribbean turns murky brown. When the French were here, they began cutting down the trees. Haiti's dictators finished the job, leaving the topsoil to run into the ocean. All that splendid mahogany furniture in Paris salons and this is the result: a bald brown island with a muddy coast.

A blast of heat rushes up to greet me as I disembark. A derelict DC-3 rusting near the dilapidated arrivals lounge makes my shiny 737 look otherworldly. My sandals stick to the melting tarmac and my sunglasses aren't strong enough. It's a hundred degrees, the city looks burned out and run down, but I'm happy and confident. First burning breaths of Haitian air, screaming kids playing on the busted plane, smoldering garbage, bougainvillea vines twisting around the perimeter fence—all good omens. There's nowhere else in the world I want to be.

My thoughts swirl and I lose concentration on my bags and documents, almost forget where I am. I knew Cambodia well and felt competent there. But now I've landed in an unfamiliar drama, someone else's war. It might be more complicated here. No Ken or Heidi, no Floating Bar or Space Shuttle. And no windsurfer.

One foot inside the arrivals lounge and something is already different, not right. Phnom Penh's airport looked and smelled like this, with its Soviet fighter jets rusting in a heap and the overpowering reek of charcoal and burning hemp fiber. But the arrivals lounge there was so sleepy I often just smiled and walked straight through without showing any documents. Here, beneath the routine bustle, something is dangerous and disconcerting. Something I can't put my finger on.

Then it comes into focus, suddenly, like one of those dot paintings you stare at forever before an image materializes. The most routine movements—a girl reaching out suddenly to grab a suitcase, a mother chasing an errant toddler, an old man struggling with a luggage cart—everything in this place is being watched. I see a figure in jeans and T-shirt leaning in a doorway, expressionless behind reflective sunglasses. Then I make out another, looking down from a balcony, and yet another by the *bureau de change*, handgun bulging under his shirt. The place is crawling with them; it's clear there's no way out of here except through them. None of them is actually doing anything specific, but I can feel their menace thick in the air. These must be plainclothes paramilitaries, descended from the Tontons Macoute, former dictator Papa Doc Duvalier's despised secret police. The Haitian military carried out this coup, but it's these modern-day *macoutes* working in their shadow who are terrorizing Haiti.

My hands go clammy and my chest tightens and I think for a second I should just climb back on that shiny new plane before it returns to New York.

But I'm not here on a whim. I know how to save lives and it's my duty to do so. It's the Parable of the Talents, from Matthew's Gospel. Exercise your God-given ability and it will increase; squander your skills and they'll be taken from you. My father taught me that when I was a boy, when he would kneel beside the wooden bed, showing me how to pray to a good God. As I fell asleep, he'd trace out a cross with his thumb on my forehead before carefully tucking the edges of my mosquito net under the mattress. I had absolute trust in whatever this tall missionary with the kind eyes said.

It's been over twenty years since I prayed beside my bed with my father. But as I take my first steps on Haitian soil, I'm still answerable to those beliefs, not to the two-bit thugs terrorizing this place.

One of them is looking in my direction. He saunters over as I'm dragging my suitcase toward the exit. "Passport," he says with casual arrogance. I stop and try to look him in the eye, but all I see is my own reflection. Go to hell, I think. I just showed my passport to the soldier at Immigration. Who are you to demand anything of me? But I take it out of my pocket, drop it on his boots, pick it up again, and hand it to him upside down. I know it's brinkmanship, but I'm not ready to start the mission cowering.

He thumbs through my blue UN *laissez passer*, just to show me he can, then flips it back to me.

"Welcome to Haiti, Doctor. We need people like you here."

If you need people like me, it's because of people like you. I need to get hold of some reflective sunglasses to even things up a little. It's disconcerting how quickly he took my measure, looked into the back of my brain, saw who I am and why I'm here.

I push through the seething crowd to the UN car. The driver takes me past the slums by the harbor, up the hill to the lush suburbs where the rich, light-skinned Haitians live, far above poverty. He drops me off at a house that a friend from the Cambodia mission found for me, a Mediterranean-style villa high up where the road runs out. From my terrace by the pool, where it's tranquil and *macoute*-free, I gaze down through the heat and pollution into the city below, where the coup is playing itself out, violently.

Ken
Mogadishu, Somalia
Operation Restore Hope

I remember sitting with my father at the kitchen table years ago watching the news on TV. Mohammed Farah Aidid was surveying a refugee camp full of civilians he had starved, a tactic in his war of rebellion against the Somali government. Food as a weapon. He was walking slowly with a big wooden staff, smiling broadly amid the dying pile of humanity, like an African chief from one of the Joseph Conrad novels in our den. My dad scowled at the TV and said "swine," a level of opprobrium he generally reserves for Nazis.

It was the first and last time I had considered Somalia or Mohammed Farah Aidid. Until I landed here.

In June Aidid's militia ambushed a battalion of sleepy Pakistani UN soldiers who thought they were here on a safe, humanitarian mission to end starvation and keep the peace. Aidid preferred fighting on his terms to peace on ours, so he killed twenty-four Pakistanis, injured sixty, eleven of them crippled for life. The next day the UN issued a warrant for his arrest as a war criminal. It's been a full-on war here between the UN and Aidid since, and it's about to get worse because a task force of American Rangers and Delta Force is on its way to capture Aidid and his lieutenants. The best commandos in the world are about to show a Somali thug that the Cold War is over, the rules have changed. Our rules now.

An American Special Forces guy greets me at the airport. If you liked Beirut, he says, you're gonna love Mogadishu. I only half understand the reference and the implication. There's so much fighting in the city today, he says, that we have to shuttle incoming UN staff from the airport to the office compound via Black Hawk helicopter. Jump on, son, welcome to Somalia.

Helicopter rides are loud as hell. You can't really talk. Actually, you can scream and mostly be heard, but it's exhausting and eventually everybody shuts up and you're alone with yourself. In the heat, noise, and rush of the moment, my mind races. All my friends from law school are curious why I would abandon salary and prestige to sweat in these godforsaken places. Inspired by David Bruce, I told everyone I'd be a hypocrite to condemn tyrants and war criminals from the comfort and luxury of the most powerful nation on earth, but take no action myself. If I really believe and have any balls, I have to test the hypothesis.

So here I am. On a Black Hawk.

It's an extraordinary machine with the power and torque to fly straight up, backward, hold still, or bank at ninety degrees. The doors are left open to house a huge .50-caliber machine gun, manned by a boy in a motorcycle helmet and silver gloves. Takeoff is a combat operation to avoid incoming fire, so the pilot twists and turns the bird in evasive maneuvers like an unhinged roller coaster. I have a stiff new UN passport and an armed American escort. We have an enemy my father deemed a Nazi and a warrant for his arrest to complete the fantasy. The desert air and sand blast up into the bird from the downdraft of the blades, and I'm in a movie.

Heidi
Mogadishu, Somalia
Operation Restore Hope

After my adventure in Mombasa, I get a bus to Nairobi in high spirits. Next stop, Mogadishu. Bring it on. But then four American soldiers are killed when their Humvee hits a remote-controlled landmine, the airport in Mogadishu is closed down, and I get stuck in Nairobi for a week. I hate Nairobi. It's dreary and chilly and always rains, and the high crime rate doesn't help. They'll pull a gold chain right off your neck in broad daylight and there's nothing anyone can do. The cops are more corrupt than the thieves. We call it Nai-robbery. Just as I'm flirting with the idea of going back to Mombasa to wait it out with the Bob Marley Fan Club, I get a call to board a UN flight that afternoon. I hop an Antonov-32 into Mogadishu. I haven't seen Ken in months, since the Cambodian elections, and I imagine him waiting for me at the airport barefoot and sunburned.

We land and the tailgate jaws of the transport plane creak down to the tarmac melting in the desert sun. I grab my bags and walk down the ramp. Blinded by the sunlight, I make my way to the shade of a small lean-to, and when my eyes adjust, I take a good look around. Rolling hills of sand spread out to the edge of the Indian Ocean. Dozens of soldiers' tents dot the landscape. French and Italian and Indian flags flap in the hard wind above each. The snapping sound they make is somehow soothing and I'm sleepy standing here. I'd like to lie down in one of those tents with a nice cool drink and listen to the ocean and the *snap, snap* of the flags.

But my reverie is broken by the coughing, choking sounds of a diesel bus as it hurls itself around the corner of a nearby building aimed in my direction. The driver sees me, downshifts, and applies the brakes hard. A long trail of black diesel exhaust floats in the bus's wake. When he turns off the ignition, I hear Arabic music blaring inside.

The Somali driver gets down and smiles at me. He looks about fifteen. Three more Somalis get off. They also look fifteen and they're each carrying an AK-47. Fuck me, I'm not here twenty minutes and I'm in trouble already. There were a few other people with me on the incoming flight, but I've lost track of them. No Ken. I'm the only woman in sight. I'm alone in Mogadishu.

The driver reaches down, grabs my bags, and steps up onto the bus. He looks back at me, nods, keeps looking, and then climbs into his seat. I watch him as he looks straight ahead through the windscreen. I stand there thinking how to explain to the police, after the ransom is paid and I'm released, why I just got on the bus without any resistance, before anyone actually threatened me: *I felt stupid just standing there, Officer.*

The teenagers with the guns seem to be waiting for me to do something. I feel bad for them, standing in the sun, sweat rolling down their foreheads. Do I get on this bus? A long moment of indecision passes before an American-accented voice calls out from somewhere inside. "Well, are you getting on or not?"

So I get on. Toward the back a short, chubby white guy with glasses sits fanning himself. He looks pissed off. He won't make eye contact with me. "I'm with the UN?" I say, questioning it myself. "This is a UN bus?" I ask. One of the Somali guys with the guns comes up behind me. As I stand there in the aisle, ready to punch the silent fat guy in the head, the Somali gunman, nodding and smiling, says to me, "Yeah, UN, UN."

"Three kids armed with AK-47s, that's some way to greet people," I tell the fat guy.

"Yeah," he says, "welcome to Mogadishu."

Andrew
Port-au-Prince, Haiti

After a short briefing, my new boss sends me straight to the city hospital. The UN's mission here is to gather enough evidence of brutality to convince the world to reverse the coup and force the military from power. All over Haiti, 250 unarmed observers are investigating and documenting atrocities against the civilian population. Most of the victims are too terrorized to talk to foreigners or provide any meaningful evidence, but I have an advantage and the boss is happy to exploit it: victims need doctors and doctors get access.

My task at the hospital is to interview a beating victim, see whether there's anything we can do to help him, and take a statement. The sleepy receptionist thumbs through a grubby admissions book. He's in the surgical ward, she says in French, throwing her arm in a wide, unspecific arc, in the general direction right. So I head off down a series of endless corridors and soon get lost. Clouds of flies lift off the chipped floor tiles, resettling behind me as I pass. When I finally find the surgical ward, I give the victim's name to a nurse.

He was here but now he's not, she says.

I look at her, waiting for more, but she just stares off somewhere over my shoulder. She's uneasy. The ceiling fan turns slowly, cobwebs dangling from its blades. No air moves.

Well, where is he now? I need to talk to him.

She shrugs.

I start to lose patience.

I tell her I'm a doctor with the UN and I need to talk to the treating doctor now. She goes away and doesn't return.

There's no one around except patients and orderlies. I linger for half an hour until finally a slight man in his fifties appears. It's the surgeon. He invites me into his office and closes the door behind him.

Look, he says, I know why you want to talk to him, but he's gone. He was brought in several days ago after they'd beaten him terribly, for hours. He was barely alive when I first saw him, skull fracture, both arms broken, multiple rib fractures, smashed kneecaps, urinating blood. We did what we could for him, he says sighing, set the fractures, dressed the wounds. He did well, but he was weak and couldn't afford to buy any blood for a transfusion.

So where is he now? I ask.

When they heard he was still alive, they came in here last night and just dragged him away again, he tells me.

And no one did anything to stop them?

I was in the operating theater when I heard the screams, he says, and I ran down here in my greens and gloves to plead with them. But one of them just stuck his gun in my face and told me he'd turn me into a patient if I didn't back off. There was nothing I could do, they have all the guns. I have to go, he says wearily, there are patients waiting. A bitter look crosses his face as he opens the door to leave. They should have just finished him off the first time, he adds, it would have been much more humane.

I sit staring through the cracked pane of the office door at the post-op patients in their beds. I should write up a report, but I can't think straight, so I drive back up to the villa and gaze out past the bougainvillea at the pool. I can't quite believe what I've just heard.

In Cambodia I treated children who stepped on landmines, villagers stabbed in their sleep, shoppers shelled in the marketplace, drivers shot up at roadside checkpoints. The victims all made a beeline for our hospital and I was usually able to help. We didn't care who they were or how they got there; everyone knew that the killing stopped at the red cross on the front gate. Once you made it past there, you were safe, a custom of war so accepted that I never even heard it discussed. Check your weapons in at reception, get a receipt. Do whatever you must to your enemies out in the killing fields, but do not ever bring that shit inside my hospital.

Maybe there are no rules here.

Ken
Mogadishu, Somalia

For us, Cambodia was an election amid minor eruptions of political violence from a decrepit Khmer Rouge, just dangerous enough to add an edge to the otherwise bacchanalian proceedings. We thought Somalia would be similarly exultant, but instead we're inserted directly into combat. This is a hot war. It's hard to make peace in a society of nomadic warriors who like to fight, and twenty thousand UN and U.S. soldiers are failing.

My first work assignment as a UN Justice Division officer is to go see the force provost marshal, Major Foot. He's leaving, says the boss; you're taking over some of his duties. Go get a briefing from him before he goes. You need to get smart fast here.

Good then. But I don't have the faintest idea what a force provost marshal is. I find him at Force Command in an air-conditioned tent. He's a U.S. Army officer. Everyone calls him sir and defers to him. "You must be the new UN lawyer we requested," he says. "Finally. Now I can get the fuck out of here."

Uh oh.

I'm about to explain that I'm not a licensed lawyer in the U.S., but it's anarchy here, that distinction matters in Cambridge, not Mogadishu.

The UN's mission here is to restore order, Foot says. Our part of the job is to kick-start the judicial system, and the Mogadishu Central Prison is a good place for you to start. Aidid's militia is in control there. He holds prisoners because they attract resources, they're an economic and military asset. It's too dangerous for lawyers to get to the courthouse and there's no money to pay for judges. So there are no trials and the inmates languish, permanently untried and unconvicted. In the meantime, prisoners are dying of every imaginable tropical disease.

Then he changes his tone from a crisp military briefing to sharing a bad secret. The juveniles and the women are vulnerable to all manner of abuse, he whispers. Especially the girls. You should go there right away and make an assessment.

While he's briefing me, a sergeant interrupts, reminding him not to forget to eat.

By the way, he says as I leave, the Pentagon wants me out of here and the UN to take over my job because I've been ambushed twice coming out of that prison. Bring security when you go and watch your ass.

Why would they ask me to do this? I have no training or experience. I went to the most insulated, coddled law school on earth. I spent six months on mission in Cambodia, mostly drinking mango daiquiris on the roof with Miss Heidi and Mr. Karim. Those are my credentials.

Then I meet the one other guy in the Justice Division they could send and I understand.

Nicko is a Romanian Foreign Service officer the Romanian government decided they don't really need anywhere else and sent to Somalia. I ask him to show me how to get started at the prison. He pushes his face right up to mine and scrunches it up in a wince of consternation, confusion, anxiety, and very bad breath. He wiggles around and jumps and twists and swings one arm around his back all the way to his other elbow and says, "I can't go to the prison," his whole body is swaying, "I have too much work to do at the office."

I have to do it. This is my chance. Dr. Andrew did exactly this work in Cambodia. I was impressed and jealous. But this isn't Cambodia. No one was ambushed at the prison in Phnom Penh.

I go back to Force Command, find Major Foot, ask him how to arrange security, and an hour later I'm in an armored personnel carrier in a convoy with a platoon of twenty Pakistani soldiers, a tank in front and a tank in back.

I take a walk through the prison compound. It's a hundred degrees, the African sun is exploding overhead, but inside the cells are dark and moist and dank. The prisoners lie on straw mats and roll their eyes up at me and drop their jaws in amazement and hope. I'm not sure I can help you, friend.

There are pregnant women and young girls in a stinking, sweltering little pen. Boys mixed in holding cells with adult men.

Everyone is looking at me like I'm in charge. I've never been in an African prison before in wartime. I've never been in Africa before. Or in a war. Major Foot came here in a uniform with an American flag on it, with a weapon and a sergeant who reminded him to eat. I'm in khakis and a golf shirt and alone.

The militiamen that guard the prison tell me that if I bring food, water, and medicine for the prisoners, they'll institute release proceedings. I say what Major Foot told me to say: I want the young girls released. The girls get released, they say, as soon as you bring food, water, and medicine.

I bite and arrange for tons of supplies.

Heidi
Mogadishu, Somalia

The bus huffs and puffs at its full speed through the streets of Mogadishu. I watch through the windows, trying to get an idea of what I'm in for. We arrive at a checkpoint and pass through a gate manned by Pakistani soldiers in blue berets. The UN has set up its base within the walls of the former U.S. Embassy compound, abandoned by the Americans after the Somali government fell in 1991. It's about sixty-five acres in all, dotted with the remains of looted embassy buildings and white metal containers serving as the UN offices.

I leave my bags in front of one of the containers and go to explore a little. I've arrived at lunch hour and am hoping I can find the cafeteria. Maybe someone will know where Ken is.

A long line of Humvees passes me as I walk along the tarred road running through the center of the compound. Some of the American soldiers riding along smile, some don't, but they all look steadily at me. I'm the new girl in town.

Being married for ten years, I'd forgotten about the power of sexuality. The ring on my finger acted like a protective shield, giving me immunity from the heat, pain, elation, humiliation, joy, violence of that power. But it's all coming back to me now as I find myself surrounded by tens of thousands of men.

I follow the road up toward a circle of shipping containers, where I can see people passing through a gap. In the corner I find dozens of soldiers and civilians sitting at white plastic picnic tables, eating, drinking, laughing. Music blares from speakers. A camouflage net is draped over the area, giving some shade. Inside one of the containers, there's a little shop with beer, cigarettes, and toiletries and a hand painted sign that says ISRAELI PX.

I search the crowd for a familiar face and then I see him. Skin brown, nose peeling, barefoot in the hot sand, Ken breaks off the broken Arabic conversation he's having with a group of Middle Eastern women and turns toward me as if he senses my presence. He takes my face in his hands, kisses each cheek, my forehead, my nose, my cheeks again. We stand back and look at each other. I can feel the women's eyes on us, wondering. We go off in search of a quiet place to talk.

Later in the afternoon, I go over to the UN Accommodations Office, where, with a little scamming, I'm able to convince them to assign me to

116

the same residence as Ken. Then I go to the Personnel Office to get my work assignment. I'm holding all my documents in my hand and my passport falls to the floor. The personnel officer moves to help me pick it up. He stops, looks up at me, and quickly says, You're American. Oh, no, I'm thinking, they're stopping Americans from coming to the mission, he's going to make me go home. Shit. A dozen lies run through my mind, but none that doesn't sound ridiculous. I think of begging him to let me stay. Bribing him. I want desperately to be here. This is my proving ground, my chance to join the Dr. Andrew–Mr. Ken Mutual Admiration Society, to which of course I would refuse membership. I can't end up back at UNHQ in New York while those two overeducated, overzealous, undersexed adolescents get to play save-the-world for God and the American Way.

Reluctantly I admit to being an American. Good, he says, and gives me directions to the office I'll be working in. Wait a minute. He didn't ask me a thing about my background, my grade level, or my typing speed. What kind of job am I qualified for simply by virtue of being American?

My new office is set apart from the other offices in a guarded compound. I pass through two military checkpoints and see only soldiers until I enter the building. I ask directions to my post, the Intelligence Operations Center, India Base. I'm introduced to the boss—a retired U.S. Marine colonel—and my new colleagues. The boss describes to me the role of a watch officer. This mission is making history, he says, it's the first time the U.S. military has ever worked in joint operations with the UN in a peacekeeping mission. But the U.S. refuses to put its soldiers under UN command, so there are two parallel command structures, one U.S. and one UN. I'm not quite sure what that means, "parallel command structure," but I nod a lot. My job as a watch officer is to sit at the radio and compile all incoming information from U.S. military and UN staff into a duty log. At the end of each day, we prepare an intelligence report for UNHQ: who's fighting whom, for how long, where, with what weapons, how many casualties.

Watch officer. Intelligence report. My job. I'm hallucinating. This isn't a job they just give to a woman. Not when there's plenty of typing to be done.

But this time my job is determined by my nationality, not my lack of a penis. Funny how that works. Because the U.S. is agreeing to a joint operation, the UN has agreed to appoint an American, a retired four-star admiral as head of the UN mission. Most of his staff are American and they only seem to trust Americans. Fuck it, I'll take the job. It's the first advantage I've had since I started working for the UN, where I've practically had to wear a giant red *S*—for secretary—on my sweater every day.

The walls of India Base are covered with maps and charts. The maps are littered with colored pins stuck in at different coordinates. Matt, another American watch officer, tells me those are the sites of all hostile incidents within the last twenty-four hours. Places where there have been significant exchanges of small arms fire or mortars have impacted. Or an ambush. Another board relates to this map and describes the incident in detail. In the background I hear the scrambled noise of a half dozen walkie-talkies as soldiers and civilians around the city make contact with one another. Matt sits at a desk logging the calls. I'm standing there in awe, trying to memorize everything I'm seeing so I can describe it in my next letter home to my mom. She became a mother at twenty, spent all her time raising my brother and me, and now lives vicariously through me. I owe it to her to share the details of this other world.

My gaze wanders and falls on a piece of paper taped to the wall. A flyer with a picture of Mohammed Farah Aidid advertises a $25,000 reward for his capture—dead or alive. Is this a joke? No, they tell me. The admiral has put a reward out. Wait a second, the United Nations is putting a price, dead or alive, on someone's head?

I seem to be the only one in the room who has a problem with this, so I shut my mouth.

Andrew
Port-au-Prince

The boss asks me to go down to the morgue at the hospital. He tells me they've received a report of a headless body and wants me to check it out.

"Well, is there a head with the body?"

"We don't think so."

"What exactly do you want me to do if I find it?"

"We think it's important to try and determine the cause of death," he tells me. First I'm supposed to treat a victim who's already been hauled out of his hospital bed for execution and now I'm asked to ascertain the cause of death of a headless man.

But I go anyway; maybe I can learn something. I get lost again at the hospital, half expecting to run into more *macoutes*. I know I'm close to the morgue when I round a corner and can suddenly smell it, that sickly sweet odor of rotting flesh. The morgue assistant, a toothless old man, apologizes for the broken air-conditioning.

It didn't used to stink like this, he tells me.

Feeling slightly ridiculous, I tell him I'm looking for a headless body.

We've got a few of those, he says helpfully. Come inside and have a look for yourself.

When my eyes adjust to the dim light, I see that the room is strewn with bodies and body parts.

We get all sorts in here, he says. They're all mixed up.

There are surgical dressings still attached to some of the corpses and drainage tubes hanging out of others. But some bear unmistakable signs of the *macoutes'* handiwork: fingers bent at strange angles, thighs and buttocks pulped from beatings, fractured skulls.

Look, he says, here's a body without a head and there's another one over there.

I scribble notes and take photos. There's just him, me, and a hundred cadavers, interrupted only by the buzzing of flies.

This might be the one you're after, he says. It came in two days ago, found on the beach somewhere up the coast.

He rolls it over onto its back, revealing a young male. It's not exactly headless but ninety percent of the neck and most of the left side of the jaw and face are missing. From the deep gashes it looks as though they tried to hack his head off with an ax or machete and when they couldn't quite do it, just threw him in the surf. Microorganisms are still feeding on what's left of the neck. There's no tag on him. His identity is a mystery, but there is no mystery to the identity of his killers: they're running this country.

I thank the morgue assistant and promise to find him a new air-conditioner.

Anything you can do will help, he replies graciously. Come back any time you want. He looks around furtively. I can let you know whenever one of these comes in, he says, pointing to the one with no face.

No, don't try and contact me; that's too dangerous, I tell him. I'll find you.

He pauses, sad eyes.

"It's not right what the *macoutes* do to people," he says. "Haitians doing this to Haitians."

I'm a million miles from the Floating Bar, but I'm not getting back on that plane. By your acts you shall be judged.

Ken
Mogadishu

After a month of mucking around dangerously alone in the 'Dish, I'm joined by a new lawyer in the Justice Division—Danny, a criminal defense lawyer from Dublin. He used to do IRA cases. Hard guy, rugby player. Bald shiny head, thick neck and shoulders, scarred hands. Big smile. We go for a drink at the Israeli PX and after a few beers he starts to warm up. He's been working in Africa for years, Sudan, Uganda, up north in Somalia. Knows the country and knows how to do human rights work in a prison. Thank God. He calls me "ye wee cunt ye." I think it's meant as a term of endearment. He says "Oh Jeeeysuz" all the time, crumples up his face, the wrinkles climbing right up to his bald skull, and squeals when he laughs, which is often. "Oh Jeeeysuz, ye wee cunt ye, whadya dooowin' in the prison aloown?"

So we go together. It's a hell of a lot better that way and I almost start to enjoy it. The road to the prison takes us past the port, which is a hornet's nest of militia activity and technical vehicles—pickup trucks with crew-served, high-caliber weapons bolted onto the bed—as well as random, *khat*-addicted, lunatic Somali assassins. Occasionally someone takes a pop at our convoy as we pass.

We're asked to bring visiting officials from a Saudi Arabian charity to the prison to try to raise money to pay the judges. As we round the corner of the port, a barrage of automatic fire cracks over our heads. When we get to the prison, one of the Saudi officials rolls out of our armored personnel carrier clutching his genitals and a big wet spot around his groin. "Oh Jeeeysuz, ye wee cunt ye," Danny says after. "Didja see da looouk on dat cunt's face when he pissed himself? Oh Jeeeeeeeeyzus," he squeals, all wrinkles and dancing green eyes. He can't contain his glee. I love this guy.

We work hard and well together. We install a jerry-rigged sanitation and water supply system in the prison, so at least the stink gets slushed away in a stream along the gutter. We segregate the prisoners with TB and get them a doctor. We try to release the young boys, but when the doctor gathers them in the middle of the courtyard to examine them, reaches down and squeezes their balls to ascertain their age, he says he can't tell. They're so malnourished they stay prepubescent into their late teens. There are no birth certificates and we can't find the parents and we just don't know if they qualify for release as juveniles.

An American Intel officer pulls me aside one day at the morning senior staff briefing. A group of terrorists have infiltrated from southern Lebanon and are operating under Aidid's command near the port, he says. They're placing remote-controlled land mines. There's a list of UN officials Aidid wants to kill and you and Danny are on it. He hates what you're doing in the prison, trying to restore order where he thrives on chaos. That's his neighborhood, he's the law there, it's personal. That's how you get killed around here. That's why they ambushed Major Foot.

So now before each convoy we have to choose our preferred mode of transport: an armored personnel carrier, which is hot as an oven inside and can withstand gunfire but will set off an antitank mine and poses an attractive target; or, a naked jeep, which can withstand nothing, but is air-conditioned and usually doesn't draw fire or set off antitank mines. Tough choice—a hot, sweaty, rushed, and important choice—and there's no good way to know what's best.

The Pakistani drivers in the convoy don't speak English, can't find their assholes with a shovel, and often get lost. One day we took command of an APC that kept turning back into Bakara Market, the worst place in Mogadishu, which might well mean the world. There was Danny, his bald shiny head sticking out of the hatch of the APC turning blood red, as he waved his arm wildly in a direction the driver couldn't see, screaming, "Turn *away* from the market, *away* from the market ye stupid coont!"

But we return to the prison every day anyway to try to monitor the supplies, because it's our job and because neither one of us has the courage to say we're too scared to go.

The food, water, and medicine I arranged for the prisoners are gone, but the prisoners didn't eat, drink, or medicate. The militia stole it all and sold it. The Intel guys actually saw it for sale in the market. In the meantime inmates die every week.

We panic and bring more food, water, and medicine and attempt to control and monitor its disbursement, with smiling assurances from the militia of full cooperation this time. We're trapped. The moment we announced that we wanted to help, we'd already lost the game.

This isn't quite the kind of logic I learned in law school and there are no provisions in the Universal Declaration of Human Rights to negotiate with a murderous militia in control of a prison. I have trouble wrapping my mind around how cheap death is here. It's a commodity to negotiate and trade. Three dead prisoners for a ton of rice. The release of one girl who's been gang-raped for months in exchange for a shipment of penicillin. The joyous look on a child's face when she realizes she is free from a Somali prison seems, momentarily, to justify our work. But the next day they pick up three more girls. There is no way for us to win. The more effective we are, the more damage we do.

On the way to the prison one day we get caught in a crossfire outside the port. We scream at the driver to go forward. But there's a nasty checkpoint in front of the port. If we rush them and they don't see that we're UN staff, they'll shoot at us. Go back. Stop. Wait. Shit. We're in a crossfire, there's no way out.

Danny slinks down into his seat and says, "I'm fifty-five years old, I've drunk a lot of beers in my life, seen the world, lots of lasses, you know what, son, I'm ready to die."

Fuck you, I'm twenty-eight. I scream at the driver to floor it forward, screw the checkpoint.

We speed through, they just wave us in, and then we're safe inside the port. Like nothing ever happened. Another day at the office. Beat that, Dr. Andrew.

The Indian Ocean sparkles through the windshield. I radio Heidi at India Base.

"India 7, this is X-Ray 4, reporting small arms fire outside the port, you copy?"

"X-Ray 4, India Base, copy, we have that report already, there's small arms fire every day outside the port. India Base out."

Thanks for the love and warmth, India Base. So cool and professional in your new job and its air-conditioned safety.

Every few days someone from the UN does get killed—Pakistanis, Nepalese, Nigerians, a few Americans. You can always tell who their friends were as they shuffle broken-hearted around the base. You just put your head down and walk past. There but for the grace of God. But it's not real. It's *M*A*S*H*, it's *China Beach*, it's the 'Dish.

The disc jockeys from A-farts, Armed Forces Radio and Television Service, brought down from Desert Storm a tremendous collection of classic rock. We kicked ass in the Gulf War and of course we will here too. Heidi and I dance on our roof as the sun sets to Jimi Hendrix, Black Hawks buzz overhead, we can feel the heat from the exhaust. "You're listening to 99.9 FM Mogadishu, Rockin' the 'Dish. Keep your head down and the volume up."

Rockin' the 'Dish. Beats the shit out of practicing law in New York.

SEPTEMBER

Andrew,
The Morgue, Port-au-Prince

A crowd of demonstrators forms when the former mayor of Port-au-Prince, an Aristide ally, tries to reclaim City Hall from the *macoutes*. The crack of automatic weapons fire comes over my handset radio as a hysterical observer reports that the police are shooting into the crowd. I go back down the mountain to the hospital to find my friend the morgue assistant besieged by journalists and cameramen looking for fresh bodies.

No new civilian casualties today! he shouts in Creole. He looks like a shopkeeper who's just run out of stock. The media stampede off, but I stay.

Come in, come in. Of course there are bodies, he whispers to me, same as every other day—it's Haiti—but my job is hard enough without journalists in my morgue.

He tells me the police weren't just shooting at the protestors but also waded into the crowd and ripped people up with knives. One man ran from the scene trying to hold his intestines in with both hands. He pulls back a blood-soaked sheet off one of the protester's bodies to reveal a jagged tear from where the blade was plunged deep into the lower abdomen and then dragged all the way up to the sternum. It's a true evisceration. Someone tried to stuff the intestines back in, but they are beginning to bloat out in the heat.

How many more?

Three or four like this one, he says. They're trying to save them right now. Go check in surgery.

The operating block reminds me of the hospital in Cambodia after a Khmer Rouge attack: wailing, blood, and chaos, lives running out onto the floor. Never enough surgeons. I'm just a voyeur here; there's nothing useful I can do. So I go back up the hill to write another report no one will ever read. The following day the *Washington Post* reports that the police failed to control the crowd or arrest those with weapons. They apparently missed the fact that the police were too busy carving up civilians to worry about crowd control.

Heidi
UN Civilian Compound, Mogadishu

We're living in an enclave of ramshackle old villas near the sea, behind high walls covered in twisted bougainvillea. From the rooftops we can see small groups of armed Somalis lurking at the perimeter, waiting for the right moment to slip down an alley to make their fortune by stealing a UN vehicle or kidnapping a UN staff member stupid enough to roam the streets without an armed guard.

We're forbidden to go outside the gates of the house, but some nights we just can't take it anymore. Screw the rules, we go anyway. The guards at the residences sit bored all night with their weapons slung across their laps, chewing *khat* and talking, so they're happy for a little action. The guard cracks open the gate, looks out. Nothing. He steps out into the road and looks both ways, his weapon at the ready. All clear. He nods back to us, and Ken and I are off, trailing close behind the guard, running low like cats in the shadows, up one street and over another until we get to our friend's gate and our guard gives a coded knock and the gate opens. It's just as dull at the next house and I would just as soon have stayed home, but Ken would go without me and I can't let him go alone.

When there's nothing to do at the house at night, we amuse ourselves by writing erotic short stories. I sit in one armchair with a laptop writing, while Ken sits across from me in the other and throws out ideas. "She has long, curly black hair, she's barefoot, torn jeans and a white T-shirt . . ." Usually they're Israeli—some obsession he has—with names like Nili and Arieli.

Each day an elaborately staged armed convoy transports UN staff from the group of civilian residences near the sea to the Embassy Compound a few miles away. On days when the fighting is bad, we skirt around the city on a supply road built by American forces. It's beautiful out there; nothing but rolling sand dunes and herds of camel and then suddenly, around a bend and across a broad expanse of sand, the sea appears. It's an hour-long ride, but it's tranquil and safe and the only chance most of us have to see anything outside the walls of the compound.

But if things are quiet in Mogadishu, the convoy travels straight through the city to the compound, a ten-minute ride. The line of buses, interspersed with cars carrying Somali gunmen—"shooters" we call them—looks like a fast-moving Gypsy caravan, but with an armored car in front and an armored car in back. We're supposed to travel only the roads designated by India Base as all-clear and alter the route every day. The back of the convoy is always supposed to be in visual contact with the front. There are supposed to be two shooters in every vehicle, one to cover each 180-degree fire radius, forward to back on the left, back to forward on the right. None of this ever works out right, and we stop every few hundred meters for the drivers and security officers to scream at each other.

Heavy fabric edged with pompoms is draped across the windows of the buses, hiding us from view—as though the Somalis won't know the buses are transporting UN staff. It's like traveling to work blindfolded. I part the drapes and watch as the buses fly over the unpaved roads, through vegetable markets, past the camel market and dozens of houses destroyed by shelling. The convoy stops for nothing but our own mistakes, and I spend the day wondering if that flash of color I saw out the windscreen made it to the other side of the road. Once we traveled the entire distance with a bright orange head veil hanging from the antenna. When the shooters sense any kind of threat, they fire warning shots freely out the window. I spend half the ride on the floor. So I'm happy when I'm told that because the working hours at India Base are different from the rest of the civilian staff, I'll be taking a special India Base convoy with the other watch officers.

But my happiness is short-lived. I soon find I have even less control of my destiny in the India Base convoy. We climb into the backseat of a car driven by a security officer, who casually hands an AK-47 back to Matt. A Somali vehicle follows us with three shooters. With a pistol clutched between his hand and the steering wheel, the security officer flies through streets virgin to UN vehicles—uncharted territory. I know we are not supposed to be on these streets, because I log and announce the fucking no-go directives. The security officer knows them as well as I do. It would be easy for us to disappear in the maze of sandy back roads here. It's also insane for Matt, my young and vastly inexperienced colleague, to be sitting at the back window with an AK-47 in his hands. It's anarchy here; everyone's a cowboy, armed and dangerous.

At dinner Ken and the other housemates argue about Clinton's peacekeeping policies in Bosnia and Haiti, but I don't even hear the words; my nerves are shattered and the noise gets to me. I lash out angrily at them,

"You're all so full of shit, who cares what you think about U.S. policy?" and then run crying up the stairs, with Ken at my heels. Upstairs in my room, I tell him I'm leaving the residence tomorrow and moving to the Embassy Compound, I'm too scared to ride in the India Base convoy anymore. I'm afraid that idiot security officer is going to get me killed. I try to tell him about my ride home, how we were lost and we had no shooters. Ken stops me and tells me that I have to keep it together, the security guys know what they're doing, it's a war, we've all got to hold on, the last thing to do is panic.

I can't believe he's treating me like I'm a silly girl with premenstrual syndrome, like I don't know what I'm talking about. He wasn't on that convoy and he's not even hearing what I'm saying. Like he's the big man, the daddy, and I should just trust him and The Men because it's a war and what would I know about a war? Men know about war, not girls, like it's something they're born with. Tell that to the Somali women. They'll laugh in your face. The truth is that he doesn't want me to leave him alone in the house.

Everyone wants to control my security but no one cares how secure I am.

Ken
Embassy Compound, Mogadishu

I'm at the Israeli PX drinking with Danny. A lot. It's tense now. There's more fighting every day in the 'Dish. I'm pissed off at Heidi for moving out of the house, and Danny's the next best option for a drinking partner. It's like those summer nights in high school when you have so much nervous energy you need to drink yourself silly or you're going to burst. Danny doesn't even eat dinner. He just sits all night drinking beer after beer.

It's hot as hell and he's funny and there's a lot to talk about and no reason to stop. I'm well-liquored when Miss Heidi saunters by with a lanky Somali guy on her arm. The notion of Miss Heidi captures my Stolichnaya-enhanced attention for a long reverie while Danny launches into another soliloquy about how worthless an IRA ceasefire is.

No one believes Miss Heidi and I aren't sleeping together. We're not. I swear. I mean, sometimes we do sleep together, in the same bed. But like a brother and sister.

I had a girlfriend in Cambodia once, Elodie. Beautiful girl. She was a political affairs officer for the UN envoy. She spoke perfect French, Spanish, and half a dozen African languages, but not much English. So she spoke to me with body language. One day Elodie couldn't take it anymore and asked, raising her eyebrows quizzically but nodding her head vigorously in affirmative answer to her own question, "You?" Nod. "Miss Heidi?" Nod. She thrust her elbows up and down rhythmically and rocked her hips, like riding a horse. Her version of what jiggy-jiggy looks like. It was a very funny sight, but she was serious. Her mind was made up that I was sleeping with Miss Heidi and I couldn't convince her otherwise.

But I'm not. I wasn't. I guess I've thought about it. But she's the sister I never had. Anyway, someone else is usually sleeping with her. And she seems to prefer men who are taller and darker and, well, more exotic than I am. I can usually tell when they walk into a room. She has big green eyes—Dr. Andrew says they are limpid, and I think he's on to something important. She does this thing with her eyes and her neck and her chin, and if she can catch the man's eye, it's just a matter of time before he succumbs to his fate. It's like watching a good movie you've already seen. There's no drama in it, but it's still entertaining.

A woman appears out of nowhere and sits at my table. It's Gisella, the Brazilian finance officer the UN brought in to help raise more money for the good work we're doing. Well how are you, Gisella? Miss Heidi's eyes instantly catch mine from all the way across the PX. Good. I want her to see. Watch this. Danny's face is all squelched up and he's squealing a lot. We talk and drink and talk and drink. Gisella's excited to hear about our convoys to the port. What's there to lose? I reach under the table with my feet and cross my ankles over one of hers, taking her feet captive. Pause. She doesn't blink and chats with Danny. Can Heidi see this under the table? Gisella rotates her ankle in a caress, wraps the other one around mine and our ankles are the center of the universe. We stagger out of the PX. I feel Heidi's eyes burn on my back as we leave.

Gisella's hooch is a mess, there's paint and easels and paper and brushes everywhere. I'm so drunk I can barely see. There are paintings all over the bed and walls—weird red and pink figures flowers bushes faces fish—wait shit they're all vaginas. There are paintings of vaginas everywhere! I look at her cross-eyed, woozy. She giggles a little Brazilian giggle. She says painting vaginas relaxes her. She sits down cross-legged on the floor and starts to paint. Different shades of red begin to form a tortured triangle.

She says, "Tell me the most awful thing you've seen at the prison, tell me more about the fighting outside the port, tell me everything about your work while I paint." No, no, I'm not sharing that. It's mine and it's Danny's, not yours. Instead I sit cross-legged facing her. I dip my fingers in the red paint and rub a line across her neck slowly, hard. She stops painting and looks up, concentrating. I get more paint and run my fingers across her clavicle and down. It degenerates. Soon there's paint all over everything. It's humid and hot and doesn't smell fresh and my head is spinning. An alarm goes off. Where am I? It's morning. Ooowwaahhhh. Paint and clothes and sand and vaginas. I'm nauseated; 7:45, I'm gonna be late for the morning follies staff briefing.

I run to the bathroom, vomit hard, then dry heaves. Everything hurts. Shit, there's even paint on my shoes. I splash water on everything, the paint bleeds, I sprint to HQ. I'm the Justice Division briefer and I can't disrespect the admiral, he needs to know our status every day, I gotta be there.

I turn the doorknob as quietly as I can, hoping I can slip in unnoticed. Heidi's conducting the briefing today. There she is, up on stage with a pointer and a combat operations map—all sexy and in control. I love it when she dips her shoulder and drops her chin, revealing a lovely shot of cleavage each morning at the end of the briefing, and breathily asks the admiral, "Any questions, Admiral, *sir?*"

I slink to the back, try not to catch her eye. She'll want to know everything in detail and I don't want to relive it. I have shame. But it's okay, none of this is real. It didn't really happen. No one paints a room full of vaginas in real life.

Heidi
Embassy Compound, Mogadishu

It's nice to just walk across the compound to my office in the morning, relaxing even. It's quiet at this time of day, before the convoy arrives. I take the path that runs straight through a group of U.S. Army tents and all the boys are outside, bare-chested, shaving over washbasins filled with water. They smile at me through faces covered in foam. It's a good way to start the day.

After being trapped in the residence, I feel free here in the Embassy Compound. Acres and acres of wide-open space, broken up by a crumbling wall here and there and surrounded by a high perimeter wall. In the evenings I can be alone in my room, a quarter share of a shipping container tucked into a corner of the compound, or I can wander over to the Israeli PX and catch a movie and a beer.

But it's not just a sense of physical freedom. There are thousands of anonymous people here from all over the world. Few know me or where I come from. When the soldiers ask my name, I tell them Mary Anne Bell. It's easy to reinvent myself. The few I do know think that because I work for the admiral at India Base, I must be CIA. They give me a whole lot more power than I'm entitled to and I take every bit of it.

And I'm one of only a handful of women, surrounded by twenty thousand men in uniform. Coming from New York, it's an interesting role reversal. I take my time to explore options my mother never had. No commitments assumed on either side, you're free to be yourself, move forward at a comfortable pace. The flirting and seduction can go on forever. With so few women available, the men have to try harder, offer more of themselves. There's no rush to do anything, even if sometimes it can't be helped. It's always an adventure, or at the very least, a good story to tell after.

In the permanent emergency of the mission, I suddenly don't have to play by the boys' rules. Which only proves the boys' rules were bullshit to begin with.

Last night I had a drink at the Israeli PX with a handsome soldier I met there. He invited me down to his post, near these enormous bladders they brought in from Texas to store fresh water for the troops. The guys on duty there built a little platform in a tree where they keep a small blue monkey they bought from the Somalis outside the gates. If you sit in the chair under the tree, after a few minutes the monkey will drop down and pop you on the head. He does this a few times and then, when he feels safe, he falls onto your shoulder and lets you pet him.

We sat for hours, just me, the monkey, and the soldier. We were having a good time, and he suggested we move over to the water bladder, where we would be more comfortable. The bladder was only half full so it wasn't easy to scramble onto, but when we finally made it to the middle, it was incredible, like lying under the stars on a giant waterbed.

After, we lay back naked, sweat drying, smoking cigarettes. Nice. Then I spotted an observation tower not fifty feet away, where two soldiers with night-vision goggles were peeping down at us. The double green glow is a dead giveaway. I was cursing, trying to pull my clothes on with the water sloshing around under me. Finally, I just rolled off and did a furious walk of shame back to my room. I think they set me up.

As I hurry down the road to work, I can see the civilian staff getting off the convoy from the residences, just starting their day but already weary and frightened. I wonder how long it will take them to realize their lives are in the hands of incompetents. I'm an outcast now for speaking out too loudly against the lack of security, but fuck them, it's every woman for herself. I'm staying alive.

At my office the night shift gives me the morning briefing: a quiet night in the compound, but a wild night in the city. Normally we get two or three mortar rounds fired into the compound. The routine is that when you hear the explosion, you run for one of the sandbagged pits scattered around outside and bang on every door you pass along the way. I don't know why we do that. If you didn't hear the explosion yourself, it's because you're already in a thousand pieces. I sleep with a helmet and flak jacket on, and another flak jacket draped over my hips and thighs. You lie in bed almost wishing the damn things would drop just to get it over with so you can sleep.

I gather my charts and maps and head over to the briefing room. I line the boards up behind the podium, next to the UN flag, and wait while the senior staff shuffle in and take their seats. An admiral, a general, an ambassador, and a handful of colonels sit at the long table directly in front of me. The door is shut and all eyes are on the podium. "Good morning, ladies and gentlemen," I begin. "The security designation remains at Condition Charlie today."

The little rubber tip of my pointer dances across the map grids as I point out locations of hostile activity last night, detail the militias involved, weapons used, estimated casualties. Five minutes into the briefing, the door at the back of the room cracks open. All heads turn to see who is about to violate the sanctity of the briefing room. It's the Brazilian finance officer, Gisella. I expect her to slip quietly into the last row, whispering apologies. Instead, she strides forward, her head held high, big smile on her face and looking dead at me. She takes a seat front and center. Something clicks and I realize there's a message here for me. Somehow, this is between me and her. And then my vision zooms forward three feet at a time until it zeros in on her neck. Hickeys. Big, purple bites all over her neck.

She's modeling them for me, turning her head at angles so I can get the best view.

The door opens again and, with his head buried deep between his shoulders, Ken slides into a seat in the back row and commences an intensive inspection of his shoes. He won't make eye contact with me. Gisella, in contrast, is triumphant. Okay, I get it. I'm disgusted by her pride and furious with him. "A convoy of fully armed technical vehicles was spotted last night on the Kismayo road, moving in the direction of Mogadishu," I hear myself say, slamming Kismayo on the map with my pointer.

Andrew
Port-au-Prince

After just a month in-country I'm already enraged, not by the work, but by being unable to work. My patients are all either headless and rotting or alive and rotting, out of reach behind prison walls. I became so enamored with peacekeeping that I never even stopped to consider what might happen if there were no peace to keep, if a country, and a mission, were at the mercy of malevolent men. The war years in Cambodia should have made me hard, but here in Haiti I'm feeling strangely brittle.

I want to go back to Heidi and Ken's roof in Phnom Penh, drink their mango daiquiris again, and soak up their friendship. I've never met anyone quite like them, still can't figure out whether they're lover close or brother-sister close.

They're more intimate than any lovers I know. Without words, they toss three separate ideas across a noisy bar in a split-second glance. They get a kick out of screening lovers for each other, then get jealous. They bicker like an old married couple. It's a wonder to watch. If one of them does go down in Somalia, it will be a catastrophe for the one who survives.

I miss my old life in Cambodia, so I drive the winding road to the northern coastal town of Cap Haitien. Three hundred years ago, when the French made Le Cap their colonial capital, it was a flourishing seaport. Now pastel-colored paint is peeling off crumbling buildings, mongrel dogs scavenge in piles of uncollected garbage, and teams of kids roam the streets under the ever-watchful eyes of armed *macoutes* in arrogant control. When I ask where the best beaches are, I get another of those profoundly unhelpful roundhouse waves to nowhere, so I just drive west, in the general direction of the gesture. The path, more of a goat track than a road, runs along lonely cliffs. Even the Land Cruiser, made for this, struggles.

Suddenly, towering over the bay, I see a giant white cruise ship. On a gorgeous white sand beach are hundreds of tourists. They're lounging on plastic deck chairs, playing volleyball, and frolicking in the turquoise water. There has to be a windsurfer down there somewhere.

I scramble down the rocky cliff, strip off my shirt, and merge with the vacationers. A long yellow inflatable rubber boat in the shape of a giant banana speeds up and down the beach. Tanned young men serve frozen cocktails from behind a palm-fringed bar as hunks of red meat sizzle on huge gas grills. It's Miami Beach. I join the line for steaks and salad, grab a rum punch, and sit down at one of the tables.

People are friendly. I find myself next to an older American couple.

"Ha d'ya like it so far?" the man asks in a heavy Southern accent. "Isn't it great having these beaches all to ourselves?" I look around at the crowd. There's hardly a square foot of free sand anywhere. "Where are you from then?" he inquires.

"I work here."

"Really, how did you get on this cruise?"

"Well, I'm not on your cruise," I tell him. He looks puzzled. "I'm here with the UN because of the military coup." That catches his ear.

"I used to be in the military," he says, "went everywhere. But I didn't hear about any military coup; where did you say it was?"

"In Haiti."

"Where's that?"

"You're in Haiti now."

"No, this is Labadie Beach, on the island of Hispaniola, look it says it right here on our map. It's the last stop before Miami."

He shows me a map of the Caribbean, with Labadie Beach, but not Haiti, indicated. "Okay, but didn't they tell you what country Labadie Beach is in?"

"Well they didn't really say much about that. We've hit a series of beautiful beaches like this one. It's been great. Sure got our money's worth."

"But didn't you need a visa to enter Haiti, show a passport?"

"Nope, we just got off the boat each time it stopped. So you didn't come here with us from Miami then?"

"No, I drove here."

"From where?"

"From Port-au-Prince, the capital. Of Haiti, the country." I wish I had an atlas. "Look, there's my car way up there on the cliff." He's still not convinced. But his wife begins to look worried and others at the table are starting to listen in. Let's not start a panic.

"What's all this military coup stuff anyway?"

I try to explain the politics and the work of observing and reporting on the illegal actions of the coup authorities. I tell him the government uses many different armed groups to maintain power: army, police, paramilitary attaches, and the FRAPH, their political wing. But for us, they're all *macoutes* and it's our job to monitor them all.

He grasps at it. "So you're kind of fighting the *macoutes* on behalf of the people?"

"Well, not exactly. We're two hundred and fifty unarmed civilian observers, here to help apply pressure on the coup leaders as part of a UN deal to bring President Aristide back to power."

"Must be dangerous," he says, glancing over his shoulder at the fence.

"Well, yes, certainly for Haitians."

"What's the point if you just observe and can't really do anything?"

That's a good question. I tell him that I'm a doctor, that at least I can help the victims. It doesn't sound convincing.

"Something should be done," he says. "It sounds terrible. Maybe this Labadie place, I mean this Haiti place, needs an old-fashioned American invasion, you know, marines, to get the bad guys out."

He's a little confused, but I'm beginning to get confused myself. I gaze out at the shrieking young women in bikinis riding the big yellow penis of a banana boat. Which of these worlds is real, Labadie Beach or the morgue?

I try a Cuba Libre—they have great rum in this part of the world—but what I could really use is a Space Shuttle from the Floating Bar. And my windsurfer. I want my old life back.

Four shrill blasts on a whistle. It's 5 P.M. and the party's abruptly over. Everybody begins to pack up and head back to the boat. It looks like a reverse invasion. Someone pulls a plug and the banana slowly deflates, hissing out hot air in the shallows.

"Well, nice to have met you," says my new friend, sticking out his hand to say good-bye. "Keep up the good work."

A few minutes later the boat gives a solitary honk and steams slowly off into the sunset. As it shrinks over the horizon, I first feel relieved, and then lonely. The beach, frivolous just an hour earlier, is now deserted and vaguely menacing. I feel sorry for them, so innocent and clueless. But maybe they're sailing off to Miami feeling sorry for me.

Heidi
Mogadishu

For weeks I've found myself drawn to the group of Somali interpreters who live in the compound with us. The men are handsome, tall, statuesque; they have beautiful smiles and never stop talking. One night I was alone at the Israeli PX having a drink and a whole platoon of them arrived and sat at the table next to me. After a while, I noticed one guy who stood out. He kept looking over at me, but maybe because I was staring at him. I heard someone call him Yusuf. Over the course of the night, each time Yusuf or I got up to buy a beer, we returned to a seat closer to each other until, many beers later, we were side by side.

"Do you think you know me from somewhere?" he asked.

"No."

"I'm wondering then, why you were looking at me. You were looking at me, no?"

"Yes, I was. I find you very attractive."

And, voilà, the deal was done as he turned bright red. We stayed for hours, drinking, smoking, talking, tension building, and then I decided it was time to break his heart a little by leaving suddenly. Let him find me.

It only took him a few days. We started meeting for coffee every afternoon at the Israeli PX. At one point I focused in on the wedding band on his finger and now I can't take my eyes off of it. Every time I try to forget about it, a ray of gold pierces my eye. But I can't help myself, I want him badly.

Last night I thought it would happen. He stopped by my room and we sat on the bed and talked, but he couldn't stop looking at his watch. Ready to leave, he stood stiffly at the door, telling me about his wife and how he had never cheated on her and now he is confused. Then I kissed him. Shocked, he stood with his mouth hanging open, not knowing what to say. Then he opened the door and ran out. I could hear him tripping and cursing as he ran down the sandbagged alley.

I usually eat dinner alone at the mess hall each night, later than the other civilian staff whose workdays end earlier than my own. I often look up from my plate to find that every soldier in the mess has taken a seat facing me. You start to feel like you're nothing but an enormous animated vagina perched atop two legs. I'm trying to ignore the stares, keeping my eyes focused on my plate, when I hear someone ask, "May I sit with you, Miss Heidi?" I jerk my head up, on guard. But it's Yusuf. I smile a surprised smile and he sits down, thankfully blocking me from view.

After dinner we take a slow walk back to my room. As we pass through a hole in the wall into an open and lighted area, a burst of tracer rounds sails over our heads. We snap our heads around to follow the pink neon line from a rooftop across the road. Fuck, it's a sniper. We panic and start running nowhere and everywhere in circles. A passing UN soldier grabs me, and rolls me to the ground up against a building. Yusuf dives under a jeep stuck in the sand nearby. A round pings off the driver's door.

After a minute, or five—time loses all meaning—Yusuf and I get up and run around to the safe side of the building. And then the strangest thing happens. I want to rip my clothes off, rip Yusuf's clothes off, and just fuck him right there. I can feel this pounding inside me and I can't wait. It has to be right now, not in ten minutes, not five. Now. An emergency. Emergency sex. I grab his hand and we start back toward my room. As we pass the Somali tea shacks lined up empty along the road, I pull him into one and grab him and kiss him as I hard as I've ever kissed anyone, unzip his pants, and pull him into me. My head is pounding and I feel a need to howl.

It's over and we pull ourselves together and leave the tea shack, still clinging to each other. As we pass a dark lumpy form in a doorway, Yusuf says matter-of-factly that it's a dead body. I make this whimpering noise and then I just start sobbing, tears and hiccups and big gulps and I can't stop.

Andrew
Port-au-Prince

The *macoutes* torture and we write reports and nothing changes. We're very busy and very useless. So I decide that I'm going to get myself inside the National Penitentiary, where I can do some good. It's full of political prisoners and torture victims and offers my best chance to be useful here.

But the authorities won't give us permission to enter: they don't trust our intentions once we get inside. The boss has been negotiating hard but getting nowhere, so I propose we bribe our way in. We have nothing to lose by offering them something in exchange for access, maybe food and medical assistance. That helped us get inside the Phnom Penh prisons. It's worth a try: take the politics out of it and just make a deal. The boss is nervous because he's never seen it done like this before—just pragmatism and a truck full of medicine.

I've done it before and know it can work. I'm envious of Ken and Heidi, working with the might of the U.S. military behind them in Somalia, while I sit here begging for access to a prison that's guarded by three sleepy soldiers wearing uniforms that don't fit. I got on the wrong mission.

I want one of those U.S. Marine colonels that Heidi's got for a boss in Mogadishu to parachute in here and fix this. I'm having trouble imagining her in that environment—this is the party girl secretary from Phnom Penh, mango daiquiri in one hand, cigarette in the other, French soldier's hand on her ass, as she grins over her shoulder at Ken. Now the party's over and she's in flak jacket and helmet, way out of her depth. She's too headstrong to follow orders and she'll have no idea how to function under fire. I'm sure she'll snap.

Meanwhile that marine officer's barrel-chested blind confidence is exactly what I need here, along with three soldiers to carry out his orders: *At 0800 hours you will escort Dr. Thomson by Humvee convoy to the National Penitentiary and introduce him to the Haitian Armed Forces officer in command at that institution. Thereafter provide close protection while he negotiates for access and furnish him with the required quantities of food and medical supplies. And you will incapacitate and arrest the aforementioned officer should he attempt to obstruct this operation.*

Instead I go alone. The police colonel keeps me waiting ninety minutes outside his office, while armed guards in dark glasses lounge in the hallways. When I walk in, he leans back in his chair and puts his feet on the desk to welcome me. There's a handgun, a pair of handcuffs, and an open box of condoms arrayed in front of him, along with reams of dog-eared papers with what look like lists of names. I'm sure those are the names of his prisoners, the names I've been after since I stepped off the plane. People are disappearing in here and if I can just get a copy of that list, I can prove it. I feel I'm getting close. There are bulging file cabinets behind him containing hundreds of dossiers. It's the mother lode.

I tell him the UN brought me here because I'm a medical doctor who has worked in prisons, that I know he doesn't have much of a budget, so we want to bring a team of doctors, nurses, and sanitation experts down here to help.

What makes you so sure we need any help? he asks.

I tell him I've interviewed patients who have been in here and conditions don't seem so good.

Who told you that? he snaps.

I ignore him, and persist. What have you got to lose? I ask. We're offering free medical care and food for the prisoners, and while we're here, we'll treat your men as well. That's it. I'm a doctor, I'm not here for the politics.

You're all here in Haiti to bring down this government, he says dismissively.

This is getting tricky. A bead of sweat rolls off my forehead and into my eyebrows and he's close enough to see I'm struggling. He wants to know why it's so important for me to get inside his prison. A long silence follows. I'm getting nowhere, so I decide to go for broke.

Look, Colonel, I say, people are dying here in your prison and that's your fault. I'm here to make sure you have fewer deaths; that can only be a good thing, right?

I think of the headless corpses and figure that maybe his orders are to keep mortality high and rising. Maybe that's his goal and this is a complete waste of time. I never imagined bargaining with a prison chief who wants all his inmates to die.

He hands me a mint from a rusting tin on the desk. As I unwrap it, the thought occurs to me that it might be poisoned. *UN doctor dies mysteriously after visit to Haitian police colonel.* But when he takes one himself, I realize he's thinking the offer over, weighing the inconvenience of having to beat prisoners somewhere else versus all the free supplies.

He tells me to just give him the money and that they'll do it themselves, jutting out his chin to indicate that's his last offer.

We have no cash, I tell him.

The terms of the deal are simple: UN food and medicine in exchange for access. He stares at me, playing with his handgun. I can't help noticing he has a small globule of pus draining from a painful-looking infected tear duct. I begin to feel a little sorry for him; it would be easy to treat.

He swivels his feet off the desk.

You can come once a week, he says, but only you. I don't want any of the other UN people.

Thank you, Colonel, I say and start to leave. That's all the foot in the door I need. There'll be time later to discuss broadening the access once they get dependent on our supplies.

Arrange it all with my deputy, he says.

I move to shake his hand, but he's already distracted, fiddling with his condoms, counting how many are left in the packet.

"We'll bring a bunch of those too," I tell him, "blue ones, with a UN logo on them."

Whatever it takes to get inside is fine with me. Condoms for the colonel, antibiotics for his men—we all have our price. At least it's healthier than the cigarettes we used to toss out the window to get through checkpoints in Cambodia. I begin to wonder how many condoms he goes through per week, and with whom, but the thought is sickening.

"See you next week, Colonel." I slip out of his office, my mission achieved. As I walk out the gate, I start laughing. The guards look at me, then at each other. I'm so giddy it makes me wonder who really needs whom in all of this. Do I need sick prisoners as much as they need a doctor?

Ken, September 26
Mogadishu

Danny and I decided to concentrate on the prison because we thought we could do the most good there, the most quickly. We're supposed to be lawyers, and lawyers need clients, and we found five hundred desperate ones at the prison.

The boss, in contrast, is very excited to set up a court, empanel judges, find salaries for all the Somali judicial staff. It's an impossible task in the middle of a war and we're not exactly sure why he's so committed. But he spends all day every day cajoling, insisting, threatening, begging the Somali Judicial Reconciliation Committee to agree to a bench of judges and negotiating the salary the UN will pay if they agree to sit. It's tedious and silly, a bunch of lawyers in flip-flops squabbling about salaries.

The boss is a big French man with a big head; he looks a little like Gerard Depardieu. Built like a heavyweight boxer and just as focused and relentless. And he finally did it. He has an agreement for the judges to reconvene the regional court. The UN agreed to pay if they actually agree to sit. The U.S. is all for it; we need to show progress in building a nation. Christiane Amanpour has descended upon us and is watching us destroy, not build. The boss has planned a big ceremony at the Supreme Court building in Southern Mogadishu. There's even an announcement in the local paper with the times and the names of the judges.

Which seems a little overambitious because it's getting ugly in that neighborhood. Last week Delta Force and Ranger commandos raided a house in South Mogadishu and captured Aidid's deputy, Osman Ali Atto. It was a lightning raid, in and out in twenty minutes. They brought him in flexicuffs to an isolated island off the coast, guarded by American warships. We had no idea they were planning it, none of the civilians knew. I don't think even the regular army guys knew. There was nothing on the radio. But suddenly we were holding Atto on this island no one had ever heard of.

Aidid threatened massive retaliation and killed three Pakistani soldiers the same day. Fired a rocket-propelled grenade at their APC, frying them inside. And yesterday they shot down a Black Hawk with an RPG. Killed three Americans and wounded three more in the rescue attempt. They dragged one of the bodies out of the bird and paraded it around town. Brought it into a house and charged money for people to see the charred, burned-up body of an American soldier up close.

So maybe it's not the most opportune moment for the boss to open up his court in the middle of Aidid's neighborhood. With a ceremony announced in the paper. And I'm not so sure I should participate.

The UN chief of staff is a retired three-star U.S. Marine general. Scary motherfucker, built like a tank. For some reason he seems to like me and if he can't help, no one can, so I go see him.

There's a huge, hard, shiny marine posted outside his door with a huge, hard, shiny gun. It's not slung casually across his shoulder like usual when they're inside, but he has it gripped, finger poised just outside the trigger guard, pointed down at his feet, which are spread shoulder width, knees a little bent. He looks like a defenseman lined up for the drop of the puck before a play-off game. Is the general in? Nod. Is he available? Dunno. Why am I so nervous? This is my job. I knock because I can't stand there softening in front of the hard marine.

"What?"

I crack the door. "Sir?"

"What?"

"Sir, we have an opening ceremony at the court tomorrow and Intel told me at the briefing this morning that, um, there is information that Ai-

143

EMERGENCY SEX AND OTHER DESPERATE MEASURES

did will attack the court tomorrow, and, ahh, they suggested I ask you for, I guess, additional support." Shit. Just say it, you fool.

Big sigh from the general. He looks at me, eyes narrowed, teeth clenched, corners of his mouth shooting straight down. He's about to spit. Crosses his arms hard. I've never seen anybody cross their arms like that. Each hand is in a fist, bumping into the opposite bicep, not hugging himself, more like getting ready to launch his shoulder into someone. I want to remember how to cross my arms like that.

"Okay. Go to Ops right now and see the commander, tell him I said you need support."

Good. That's what I wanted. "Thank you, sir." I start to back out. When I move my arm to close the door, I can feel a pool of sweat. He stops me.

"Son." His face softens.

"Sir?"

"Watch your ass."

I should be worried if a three-star marine general is worried, but instead I'm happy and almost proud he noticed and cares.

At night there's a party hosted by the Jamaican security guys. Ja love and a lot of duty-free liquor. Danny and I sit in the corner and drink and drink. We don't say anything, but tomorrow hovers, so what's the harm in one more drink? Then someone fails to respect someone at the bar, two security guys square off and strike that dominance pose, chin up and forward, circling each other. It's like a radio wave that instantaneously reaches all the other security guys, they strike that same dominance pose before they even know what's happening, and they all surge toward the bar. Someone thinks they see a gun muzzle and panics and calls the Quick Reaction Force. Three minutes later a squad of Nepalese soldiers arrives at the party, guns drawn. Fun's over, I'm going to bed, see you at work tomorrow, Danny. "Say your prayers ye wee cunt ye, oh Jeeeysuz."

Ken, September 27
Mogadishu

Splitting headache in the morning. I put a handful of aspirin in my shirt pocket. I'm conscious of everything I do. Boxers, khakis, fake Polo shirt I got for a dollar in Phnom Penh. Shoelaces, wristwatch. What would I look like on a white slab?

Our convoy of Pakistani armored personnel carriers pulls up to the courthouse. It's a hundred degrees and my flak jacket is heavy. I can't get the strap fitted right on my helmet and it's choking me, feels claustrophobic, echoes when I speak. I can't wait to get inside to take all this shit off. We dismount from the APCs, and they start to turn around like they are headed out. I run after them, "Where are you going?" "Orders are to drop you off and return to base," they yell back as they leave.

I see two skinny Egyptian peacekeepers posted at the outside gate with vintage World War II rifles. "Where is the rest of the security detail?" I ask the brightest-looking of the two.

"We are your guards, sir," he breathes.

Wait. This is our security? We're dead. I look at Danny, he's wrestling his helmet off. "I taught ya arranged security, son, ya coont, what da fook iz whicha?" The tenser he gets, the broader the brogue.

My headache is pounding and the sun is screaming. I'm soaked with sweat and the day's barely begun. We walk into the courthouse. The Judicial Reconciliation Committee is assembled, proud and erect. We're going to convene a functioning court here, you gotta give the boss that. He's been bickering with these guys for months, but here we are.

There's a rumble outside and a lot of dust kicks up. Two Malaysian APCs arrive; they're the new kind, sleek and low to the ground, with a huge .50-caliber machine gun mounted on top of each. The officer jumps out and introduces himself, Captain Halim. He's younger than me. He speaks perfect English, is clipped and confident. He says his Special Forces platoon was sent directly on orders from command to support us. This is more like it. He will act as a liaison to us, both APCs will wait outside the gate, his men will deploy in a secure perimeter on the ground during the ceremony and cover our exit, then reassemble at the APCs and escort us home. Good. I go back inside happy and relaxed. Let's open this court, this is what we came to this country to do.

The ceremony is fun. I'm used to seeing the Judicial Reconciliation Committee squabbling, yelling, storming out. But today they look noble and dignified and ready to claim authority back from Aidid's militia. It's the most inspiring thing I've seen since the election in Cambodia. We can start releasing the juveniles tomorrow.

There's one little guy on the Reconciliation Committee I especially like, Abdi. He's from a minority tribe that's treated brutally here by everyone, but he's always smiling and joking. Dusty yellow afro and big ears, he looks like an African leprechaun. He sits with me for hours sometimes after meetings, telling stories about Somalia before the war and even before that, when the Italians were here. He studied law in Rome. Imagine what he's seen in his life. He keeps smiling at me during the ceremony and motioning that he wants to talk.

Captain Halim checks in through the front door smiling too. I give him a thumbs up. The ceremony starts to wind down, we're all shifting in our seats, it's too hot to sit still this long. Everyone is relieved there's been no attack and is anxious to scram. Let's declare victory and go home. The boss gives a ridiculously long speech mostly about himself and then it's over.

We walk back out into the yard, sun slicing down. I swing the flak jacket over one arm—it's too hot to put it on—and look for Captain Halim. I want to give him that index finger circling in the air sign. Let's mount the APCs and go home. *Crack crack crack whomp.* Shit, AK-47 fire. That last one was a rocket-propelled grenade? Fuck. I run, but where? I turn and run, turn and run, *crack crack.* Danny flashes past, he's running and turning too. The judges are kind of walk-shuffle-skipping and turning but it's just a courtyard, there's nowhere to go. Each time a new shot is fired, we change directions, turn again, we're all just running and turning at ninety degrees going nowhere. I can't tell where the fire is coming from and I don't see the Malaysian soldiers. *Crack crack crack crack crack.* Wait, that's heavy incoming fire now, it's close, we gotta get out of here. I run back to the court entrance and see a little anteroom off to the side. Some of the judges are in there. I stick my head out and yell for Danny. I can't see him. I run back out. He's still outside looking for the APCs. I motion for him to come to me. He pauses and looks at me quizzically. Come back, I yell, get out of the line of fire, there's a safe room here. He runs back, everybody follows him and piles in.

Then there's a different, steady, low, thud sound. *Kug-kug-kug-kug.* It must be the .50-calibers on the APCs. The Malaysians are returning fire. Good. Those slugs are huge. Then there's a wave of incoming AK-47 fire, *crack crack crack crack crack crack crack crack crack.* It's relentless.

We put our flak jackets and helmets on, fuck it's hot. The boss gets on the radio and calls India Base and starts screaming, "We're under attack we're under attack," but he's not making any sense, he hasn't identified himself, his location, he hasn't even established contact with the base yet. He's not following any of the radio protocols. They won't know what's happening. Then he runs out into the yard waving. He must be looking for the APCs, but he's right in the line of fire. We scream at him, get out of there, you idiot! He's standing out in the middle of the courtyard shouting into the radio.

He runs back in the anteroom, his hands are shaking and his whole huge head is trembling and he's yelling into the radio about opening the courts but he's not making any sense. Wow. I grab the radio out of his hand. I don't even think about it. He's supposed to be my boss and it's his responsibility to coordinate with India Base, but fuck it, he's a mess.

"India Base, this is X-Ray 4, copy?"

"X-Ray 4, what's your location?" It's Heidi on the radio.

Something about hearing Heidi's voice puts me deeper into a panic than I already was. I asked for the radio, now I have it. My heart is pounding harder than when I was outside under fire. When I depress the talk button, India Base will hear the fire outside. Everyone at India Base will stop working and listen. Then the news will spread and the entire mission will go to the channel I'm on and listen.

I don't want to speak but I have to, I already identified myself.

"India Base, this is X-Ray 4, our location is an anteroom at the court house, over."

"X-Ray 4, what's your status?" Heidi's voice has changed entirely, it's dropped three octaves. She's heard the firing in the background. She's scared, which makes me more scared.

They are going to judge everything I say from my tone of voice, each word I choose. I gotta get this right.

I don't want them to know I'm on the edge of panic, but I want them to know what's happening. We might need to get pulled out of here. I take three deep breaths before I speak, to calm myself down.

"India Base, we have heavy incoming small arms fire and heavy outgoing fire, over." Good enough, I got that out.

There's a pause on the other end, no answer. Then a different American voice comes on, a man's voice. "X-Ray 4, keep us apprised of any change in your status, over."

It's Matt, the other watch officer. Heidi must have heard the fear in my voice and can't function at the radio. The more I understand that they are concerned, the more I panic. I have to control myself.

Whomp whomp. The air reverberates. I feel it deep in my ears, not a sound but a vibration. RPGs. Close. My right ear is ringing profoundly.

Do I call this in? Should I ask them for more support? Maybe a helicopter could pull us out?

My hand is shaking. I take three deep breaths again. I have to call this in and ask for help.

I'm about to press the talk button when a Somali guy appears out of nowhere at the other side of the room, screaming at the Somali judges. He must have jumped in over the wall; one side of the roof is open to let in air. He's sweating and his eyes are huge and the judges are screaming back in Somali.

I ask Abdi to translate for me. He says the guy is a representative from Aidid's militia. He says we have five minutes to stop the Malaysian big guns or they will come in over this wall and kill us.

Abdi looks at me and says, "Just tell the Malaysians to stop firing."

How the fuck do I do that? The Malaysians are not on our radio frequency, they have their own internal net. Anyway, what am I gonna do? Tell the officer not to return fire? It's suicide. I can't tell him what to do.

Okay, maybe I can find Captain Halim. I have five minutes. I look at Danny. He shakes his head, no, don't do it. I walk outside. The firing is loud and I can't see anything. No good. I go back in. Now what?

I'm stuck, I have to call in to India Base, but what do I tell them? I can't explain the situation in detail over the radio, the Somalis monitor everything we say.

Maybe I can ask India Base to radio Malaysian Battalion HQ and relay the message for the captain to come talk to me in the anteroom. Right. Do that.

"India Base, this is X-Ray 4, are you in contact with Malaysia Batt?"

"X-Ray 4, India Base, affirmative, via Joint Operations Command, over."

"Roger. Request you pass a message for the captain to come find me. I say again, I need the captain to come find me for discussion, over."

A new voice comes on.

"X-Ray 4, this is Bravo 2. What's your status?"

Oh, fuck. Bravo 2 is on, the U.S.-UN military liaison officer. That means someone went to get him, they've stopped everything, the top of the machine is involved. Shitfuckpisswhore. If I screw this up, it will be headlines tomorrow. If I get anyone killed, I'll kill myself. If my voice is shaking on the radio, I can't look Heidi in the face. My father can hear the whole thing. I hate this shirt, I'm never wearing it again. Three deep breaths. They're waiting.

"Bravo 2, our status is heavy incoming and heavy outgoing, over."

"Roger, X-Ray 4. What is X-Ray 1's location?"

I smile at Danny. They must have heard the boss lose it on the radio earlier and wonder where he is and why I'm coordinating the communications.

"Bravo 2, he's with me, here, over." I got that one out without hyperventilating first, I'm okay, I got it.

A message goes out over the entire net from Matt. "All stations, all stations, this is India Base. Be advised we have a security emergency, all stations clear the net, clear the net until further notice. India Base out."

They only do that when it's bad. It's official. This is real. I'm fully in this. This is exactly what it sounds like over the radio right before people get killed. I've heard India Base do that half a dozen times; each time it was a disaster.

Suddenly I'm thinking clearly and quickly and see a pattern to everything.

I have to get to Captain Halim.

No spit in my mouth. "India Base, X-Ray 4." I have the radio net to myself now, I don't even have to wait for them to acknowledge, they're listening.

"Confirm you have passed the message to Malaysia Batt, over."

"Roger, X-Ray 4, confirmed, over."

Right. Nothing to do but wait. They could jump over the wall any moment. For the first time in my life I wish I had a gun. Get small in the corner, watch them come over the wall, and whack them one by one. Too bad I have no idea how to load it, aim it, or shoot it. They didn't teach us that in torts class.

We settle in a bit. Danny slouches down against the wall and smokes a cigarette. He has that placid resigned look again like that time at the port when he said he felt old and was ready to die.

The boss is pacing and talking to himself. "Don't they want judges here? Don't they want a court?"

Danny looks at him and squeals out a laugh. "Jeeeysuz."

Abdi, the little Somali judge I like, slides over to me and smiles and starts to whisper conspiratorially. He's not scared at all, he's been living with this for years.

"You're doing the right thing," he says. "We wait here for a while."

"Good. Thanks, Abdi. Stay with me, okay?"

He has a funny look on his face; he wants to tell me something. "Hey, Ken, you know why your boss was so insistent to open the courts and have judges paid salaries, right?" His eyes are twinkling like the sun off the Indian Ocean on the other side of this hardscrabble court.

I'm trying to think. The boss pushed and cajoled and even put an ad in the fucking paper in the middle of the most violent days of the mission, but I can't guess the answer. "No, Abdi, why?" I can't help but smile at the leprechaun Somali judge.

He's enjoying himself somehow. "Because we must to give him fifteen percent of our salaries." He shows me his pocket and pulls out the lining, big grin, eyebrows and eyes shooting sparks.

He thinks it's funny. I want to kiss him.

And I want to kill the boss. I want to drag him out into the line of fire headfirst and watch his body buckle and jerk as the bullets hit him. I want to watch him bleed to death.

The incoming AK-47 fire is louder and closer, and the outgoing .50-caliber fire is constant now. I have the chills but a bad version. Each one of those little hair follicles burns.

I slouch down next to Danny. He's quiet. Then he says, "You never told me about your family, son. Brothers and sisters?"

"Older brother in San Diego," I tell him. I wonder what he's doing right now. What time is it there?

"What about you? Kids?" *Whomp whomp.* Fuck, the RPGs are getting closer.

Captain Halim comes flying in from outside, fully helmeted, M-16 in fire position, drenched, wan, and breathless. He looks like a soldier from one of those Vietnam War movies. He comes right up into my face, "Sir, I have a message to find you, it's not easy, sir, we are under heavy fire, my men are separated. I have to coordinate, what do you want?" He's calling me *sir*?

I tell him about the sweating Somali and the threat from the militia. He looks at me like the general did when I asked him for support. I'm making these guys' days hard. We should all just go home.

Captain Halim says he can't order his men to stop defending themselves. Anyway, he's not in contact with all of his men, they're separated, he can't just order a ceasefire. "Especially the .50-calibers, no way," he says, "that's the only thing I've got the Somalis are afraid of."

Which is probably why they're threatening us now.

A couple of the Somali judges spring outside and run, keep going, disappear. Maybe we should make a break, run, but where to? *Whomp.*

Fuuuuuck. RPG close. The whole room reverberates; my right ear is ringing like hell.

Captain Halim pivots and sprints out, gone.

The Somali militia guy jumps back in over the wall. This time I actually see his skinny fingers on top of the wall first, then the flecks of gray hair on top of his head, then his shoulder, then one foot, then he jumps in. We have no gun in here, we're defenseless.

Most of the Somali judges have gone, there are only a couple left, including my friend Abdi. I wonder if he stayed as a favor to me. He talks in staccato bursts to the militia guy. Christ, I wish I understood that. He turns to me and shakes his head. He says two minutes, the .50-calibers are killing a lot of militia, cease fire now and you can leave; no ceasefire and they come in over the wall.

They think I can give the Malaysians orders.

I can't even get them on the radio.

I tell Abdi to tell him to give me more time, tell him we are sending a message to the soldiers outside now.

But wait, maybe this is a bluff. Maybe those .50-calibers are indeed hitting their targets and this is just an empty threat to get us to stop firing and leave. Maybe they are establishing an ambush or laying mines for us when we exit, because they can't get close enough through the .50-caliber fire. Maybe this is a full-on setup. Maybe I shouldn't pass any of this on to Captain Halim and get in the way of his operation.

That's a hell of a gamble though. At least I have to talk to him about it.

"India Base, this is X-Ray 4. I need to communicate with the Malaysia Batt Captain again, over."

"Roger, X-Ray 4, will pass your message on Joint Operations Command net now, over." It's Matt again, where's Bravo 2, where's Heidi?

Captain Halim appears at the door forty-five seconds later. He's dripping with sweat and out of breath. How bad is it out there? This is our fault, stupid, stupid idea, to open a court in the middle of a war.

He's in my face again. We can withdraw if you want, he says, but I'm missing one man, I can't leave without him.

I tell him about the last message from the militia. He says, "Okay, but I can't leave without my man. When I find him, I'll pull the APCs up into the courtyard and you run for it, okay?"

"Wait, can you send one of your guys in here with an M-16 to guard the wall? What if they attack here? I'll be more comfortable waiting for you to finish up outside if I've got a shooter in here with us."

Everyone is pinned down, he says. I can't spare a man. He runs out.

Wait. I want to discuss my theory that this is a bluff and a setup, but he's gone. I guess a theoretical discussion isn't the best use of Captain Halim's time and talents right now.

We wait. Alone. I hear a loudspeaker. It's not English, it's not Somali. It sounds like Thai or Chinese. It's Malaysian, it must be Captain Halim on a speaker from one of the APCs. He's shouting and repeating something over and over. Just a few words. Maybe it's a name. He must be telling the missing guy to try to make his way to the APC. What if his guy is injured? Or dead?

It's time to call India Base and ask for help. But if I'm right and this is a bluff, they send soldiers in who get killed, then more to rescue them, and it goes from bad to worse, it's my fault for panicking. Yesterday they passed an American soldier's body around in the street celebrating the kill and people paid money to see it. These are some of the most bloodthirsty humans on earth. They took a Nigerian hostage last month and still have him. Fuck. Hostages.

Captain Halim flies back in. He looks different, better. I found my guy, he says. We're pulling one APC back into the courtyard, we'll open the side door wide and when you see it open, run to us and jump in.

The APC pulls into sight and stops on the sand, they throw the door open. I hear the incoming fire but don't see any impact. We look at each other and sprint for the door. I run through the sand in slow motion. The last time we were out here we were turning at ninety degrees toward nowhere each time we heard the crack of a shot. This time we beeline for the door of the APC. When we get there, we have to wait a moment for the guy ahead to bend and climb in—that's a long moment. Finally we all plop down, close the hatch, and roll out. We should be safe. That's what the armored part of the armored personnel carrier is for. Unless they laid antitank mines. Then we're dead.

My eyes adjust and find the Malaysian soldiers inside. One guy is hanging on his buddy, shirt open, heaving, body soaked. Oh shit, he's hit, I did this, my fault, fuck he's gonna die. He looks over at me and nods. Wait, he seems okay. "Are you all right?" "Tired. Bad day. No good." He's just tired. They're all exhausted. I wonder what it was like outside. They must have been running back and forth in the heat returning fire and covering one another and the guys on the mounted .50-calibers. Jesus. I try to call India Base to tell them we made it out, but the radio can't emit from inside the armor. They have no idea where we are now; they must be worried.

We roll and rattle and bump. There are no windows in back, we can't see outside. I have no idea where we are. The APC smells of hard-work sweat, like a locker room after a hockey game, except for the burning smell from the weapons. Not like after a hockey game. We stop and the hatch opens. We're home. That was fast. It's only a mile between the court and the safety of the Embassy Compound. It's over.

I shake hands with Captain Halim. We smile and pump each other's hands. What do you say? Thank you, Captain. Thank you very much.

I go straight to India Base to find Heidi. Everyone looks at me funny on the way to the office. She's sitting next to Matt at the radio and looks stricken. She sees me and brightens. She stands up and we circle each other warily, like the Jamaican security guards posturing before the fight. But this is no pose, it's something at the core. I don't smell so good. We don't talk. I sit. She brings me a big glass of cold water. Exactly what I want. I dig into my shirt pocket for the aspirin. The shirt is soaked through, the aspirin is sludge. I'm throwing this shirt out, I never want to look at it again. We just stare at each other.

Finally I ask her what they were saying here. She somehow knows exactly what I mean. She says she was too upset to stay on the radio and so she ran messages back and forth to Joint Operations Command. The orders were to listen to X-Ray 4 and follow his lead.

I knew it. The whole world was listening to every word. I've never been more exposed.

She says, "You did good. I followed the whole operation, everyone says you did the right thing."

Thank God. I finally feel like crying. I couldn't take it if the conclusion were anything else. I could never look at her again. I'd leave the mission.

At night I take a shower, crank up the air-conditioner, lie on my bed naked. I watch my fist clench and unclench, flex my thigh muscle, look at my dick. I sleep in a cycle of two or three minutes, then I dream and my body jumps and I wake up and remember. My brother and all his friends from home are watching me play hockey and a big defenseman comes to hit me hard and I fall in front of him, weights on my stomach, and I can't get up and everyone is laughing at me, the other team is laughing, surrounding me, and I'm on a white slab of ice and can't move. And I wake up and remember then sleep again and dream an RPG explodes near my ear and I'm deaf and all my friends are yelling at me, they're angry and I can't hear and I fucked something up badly but I don't know what and I float above myself and I watch my eyes roll up and my jaw drop down, like the prisoners when they're dying, and I'm dead and I wake up and find my dick and I'm alive.

I've been seeing a Swiss girl who works for the Red Cross. It's their job to collect the bodies those big Malaysian guns cut down when we returned fire. The next day she comes stomping into the mess hall looking for me, wild-eyed, dripping with sweat, seething, "You killed twenty Somalis just to open your stupid American court!"

I hadn't thought of that yet. How many we killed.

October

Heidi, October 1
Mogadishu

The fighting is so bad now that they've stopped sending new personnel into the 'Dish, leaving us understaffed. I haven't had a day off in weeks and my nerves are fraying. The boss senses it and finally gives me a day of R&R.

Nothing much to do in the compound besides sleep and eat, but today I'm invited with a handful of other American civilians to the U.S. Liaison Office compound, where Yusuf works as an interpreter, for an American-style barbecue. Yusuf comes over to my room early and we sit outside chatting and drinking beers before we go. After two beers he starts to hint at dark secrets that somehow implicate me.

I find some of the things he says so strange and paranoid, but maybe he knows what he's talking about. When he comes into the room, he usually hides his walkie-talkie in the back of my closet under a pile of clothes. He's convinced that the Americans at USLO only half trust him because he's Somali, so they've put a bug into his radio. He'll whisper in my ear, "CIA," and then put his finger to my lips . . . *ssssshhhhhhh*. Sometimes, he'll only write on a piece of notepaper what he wants to tell me and I'm expected to reply in the same way.

One night I made the mistake of asking him aloud if he didn't think the USLO people had anything better to do than to listen to our pillow talk and he was furious and walked out on me. Now I just humor him and go along with the note writing.

But I think his paranoia is starting to get to me. I went to my room in the middle of the afternoon yesterday on a break from work and found the door unlocked. Inside, a white guy with an American accent and three Somalis were standing around the circuit breaker box. They just looked at me when I came in and the white guy told me they were repairing something, but none of them seemed to have any tools. I stared silently back at them, all of us bunched in my tiny room. Then they just put the cover back on the breaker box, turned around, and filed out the door without saying another word.

I tossed this incident around in my mind for a few hours and finally decided to tell Yusuf. I was afraid that if he got too paranoid, he might refuse to spend nights in my room, but my need to share this amazing information was stronger than my fear of his reaction. I motioned for him to step outside, and then I told him what happened. Hands on his hips and nodding his head wildly, yep, he said, they were planting a bug. I think I believe him. I think it's true. Those fucks planted a bug in my room.

Later, back in the room, we wrote notes to each other and then, once in a while, Yusuf would start some strange, fake conversation. He wouldn't let me go near the breaker box to take a look. I have no idea what's really going on. But one thing's for sure, there's nothing like the CIA listening in while you're getting laid. It's like your mother being in the next room; you're trying not to make a sound or let the bed squeak. Adds an extra thrill.

It's a ten-minute walk across the compound to the USLO gate, where the marine guard checks Yusuf's ID and thoroughly looks my passport over before issuing me a guest pass. People I've never seen in the compound before are standing around a barbecue, drinking beers and talking. It's like some strange parallel world I never knew existed.

All the earnest Mormon-looking guys Yusuf works with seem to know me. I'm pleased at first, thinking he must talk about me a lot. Then I introduce myself to one who says to me, "Yeah, I know who you are. I recognize your voice." I'm stunned as he leans toward me and quietly repeats word for word a telephone conversation I had recently from my office. He smiles and wags his finger in my face and says, "Remember that. Be careful."

At one point during the party, I can't find Yusuf and I start to feel uncomfortable, alone with sixty drunk men. I'm angry with him for not watching out for me and decide to go back to my room. When I get there, the combination lock is off the door and I'm assuming I'll find him inside.

But instead there's another strange white man perched in a chair facing two Somali guys sitting on my bed. I must look scared because the white guy says, "Heidi, it's okay, I'm with the U.S. Liaison Office." The creepiest thing is that the guy knows my name. I slam the door so hard the container shudders. As I flee my own room, I can hear the white guy inside calling someone on his radio.

So this is why they bugged my room: to record conversations with Somali informers. Yusuf had to be in on it. I feel exposed, used, and stupid, like with those assholes with the night-vision goggles but a hundred times worse. It starts to rain. I run up to the women's showers and hide in a stall with all the lights out and cry. Fully dressed in the shower crying.

My life here is coming undone quickly. I'm in the middle of someone else's nightmare and even my boyfriend is a spy and there are tapes and bugs and radios everywhere and every clean-shaven white man in Mogadishu knows my name and my room is a fucking secure Intelligence hangout and I can't trust anyone.

Andrew, October 1
Port-au-Prince

Haiti is unraveling fast. There are fresh bodies in the streets every morning now. Today I almost drove over one as I was pulling in to get gas. He was lying facedown, shot in the head, ignored. The *macoutes* are running riot and there's nothing 250 unarmed observers can do to stop them. Our database of victims is growing and these are the survivors, the ones that we were able to treat. Hundreds more are dead, filling up morgues all over Haiti.

- Number 57, 46-year-old male, arrested 3 September, smashed across the face with a brass knuckle, forced to lie facedown while soldiers jumped on his back, then beaten into unconsciousness with batons in the kidneys and buttocks. Left for dead in the corner of a filthy cell with no food or water, comatose for two days. Finally dragged out and taken to hospital, where he required hemodialysis to save his shattered kidneys.

- Number 72, 24-year-old male, arrested 7 September, attacked in the Cité Soleil shantytown and then dragged to the local police station. Trussed and suspended from horizontal bar and beaten repeatedly on lower back and testicles with baseball bat. Repeatedly punched in both ears. Injuries are bilateral ruptured eardrums, extensive skin and soft tissue loss from both buttocks and left testicle swollen with blood to 2.5 inch diameter.

I'm called to treat a twenty-three-year-old man just released from the central police station. His injuries are massive tissue damage to buttocks, thighs, arms, and face from hundreds of blows from rubber truncheons, fractured right arm and wrist, ruptured eardrums from blows to the head and strange burns on his skin.

How did you get these? I ask.

I don't know, he says. They tied me down and the next thing I knew there were wires on my abdomen connected to some kind of current.

Then I treat another young victim with deep, strange gashes in both thighs, all the way down to white bone. I've never seen an injury like it.

"They beat me with a car," he says.

My Creole isn't great, but that can't be right. I grab a translator. He says there was an old car in the yard of the police station and the police got drunk, ripped off the front metal fender, and beat him with it. Tears well up out of nowhere as I look at his mutilated limbs and realize that he'll never walk straight again. I'm only days from my twenty-ninth birthday, and I understand nothing.

The guy from the cruise ship was right. This country needs a good old-fashioned American invasion. U.S. Marines to land here hard and well and kill *macoutes*. Kill Haitians so Haitians can live.

My parents get a telephone call through for my birthday. I tell them I'm doing fine, then I have to cut the conversation short before they realize I'm not.

Ken, October 3
Mogadishu

Sundays at our house are almost normal. I crank up the AC, sleep late, and pretend it's an autumn football weekend in Ann Arbor. We taught the cook how to make pancakes, someone brought a case of syrup in from Nairobi, and we call it brunch. Sunday afternoons we eat lasagna. It's the one thing the cook makes well.

Everyone trickles away from the table for siesta. I miss Heidi now. These were the best moments with her, when the house got quiet and we would gossip about our housemates and write crazy short stories together. She went into a frenzy about the driver of the India Base convoy though and left the house to avoid traveling with him. I tried to convince her to stay, but she was hysterical, wouldn't listen.

I go up on the roof and read under a weakening sun. I put on A-farts. They have a sexy-sounding female DJ on Sundays: "99.9 FM Mogadishu, Rockin' the 'Dish. And you thought the desert was hot." I plop down and try to do a few push-ups. It's too hot and I'm too lazy on this Sunday. This is the first day I've been able to relax since the ambush, and I'm happy to be alive and to have eaten lasagna and to feel the setting sun on my face.

But I'm horrified I was ambushed and horrified we killed in response. It's different from getting caught in crossfire or a mortar landing nearby. It's personal: you are the target, they want to kill *you*. Bad, bad chills.

So we killed them. We came hoping to save Somalis and then we killed them.

There's a lot of helicopter traffic visible from the roof. Four or five Black Hawks are in fixed positions about a mile away near the Bakara Market. They usually don't do that. Another one keeps flying right over our roof like he's patrolling in an indecipherable pattern that takes him right over my head. I go over to the edge and squint into the low sun. The roof is bright with whitewash reflecting off the Indian Ocean. It would look like one of those pretty villas on the Greek Islands if on the other side of this wall it wasn't an African version of the Apocalypse.

There are three or four pockets of black smoke billowing near the port. It looks like the black smoke from burning tires, which isn't unusual, but there's too much smoke for it to be just tires. There's gunfire crackling in the distance, but there's always gunfire crackling in the distance.

It can't be that bad because there's nothing on the radio. We would have been warned to go into lockdown if there was anything to worry about. It's getting dark and the mosquitoes are coming out, so Joseph Conrad and I retreat to my room.

Heidi, October 3
Mogadishu

India Base never sleeps, so watch officers work in two twelve-hour shifts. Day and night we log the details of battles that shift around the country in patterns and rhythms I start to recognize, like water flowing around a rock.

Matt and I usually work the day shift together. We've been learning the intelligence business on the job, fast. Matt arrived in-country a few months before me and is territorial about his position in the office. He's secretive and tries to keep the most interesting jobs for himself, including those that require contact with any of the U.S. military commands. But when Luke, the intel officer from the U.S. Liaison Office, comes looking to share information, Matt knows I'm all he has to barter with. Women are the only things the Americans at USLO don't have.

So when Luke stops by every afternoon, I make him coffee and Matt slips discreetly out the door. Even the boss, when he walks into the room and sees us talking, abruptly leaves. Is obtaining intelligence a cover for flirting, or is flirting a cover for obtaining intelligence? In either case, I'm crazy about Luke and look forward to his visits.

He brings me chewing gum and jars of peanut butter and Ziploc bags, the wartime equivalent of flowers and candy. Even if I'm not on duty that day, I always make sure to show up at the afternoon Joint Operations Command briefing, where he and I stand on the dark side of the room, side by side, just barely touching. I can smell his scent and it gives me an enormously pleasurable sensation right at the front of my brain, a few inches above my eyes. I'm afraid that if I let myself turn toward him just a bit, our bodies will slam together like two magnets and I may not live.

It's a wonder to me how this blue-eyed farmboy from Montana wound up in the intelligence business. "Major," I asked him once, as I fondled the U.S. Marines patch sewn on the chest pocket of his uniform, "can you get me one of these patches?" It was a good excuse to run my fingers over his chest. Without hesitating he pulled an assault knife out of his belt, cleanly severed the threads anchoring the patch, and slapped it down on the table in front of me. In unison the baby marines gathered around us at the PX sucked in their breath, wide-eyed at the sacrilege, waiting for the earth to crack open and swallow Luke up.

I feel oddly ashamed in these moments and I blame it on Andrew. Everything with Andrew is work and saving lives and God forbid you should enjoy yourself while you're at it. I think I can make love with a few sexy young soldiers, and a Somali or two, and not forget that children can't go to school in this country. Does he think the Haitians or the Somalis aren't making love? Somehow I can't imagine him throwing his clothes off and lying underneath a naked woman. Funny, I torment Ken about his hero worship of Andrew, but here I am worrying about what Andrew, who's on the other side of the world, thinks of me. And I haven't even touched Luke yet.

It's a sleepy Sunday, and I'm the only one on duty. I'm thinking about Luke, and then he walks in, calm but deadly serious. He stands very close to me and, quietly, he tells me, "The shit has hit the fan. Start asking questions." He keeps his eyes locked on mine as he backs out the door. That's all he says, so I call JOC and ask if there has been any activity in the 'Dish. No, the sleepy Italian watch officer tells me, nothing all day. So I sit at the radios for a while, tuning in to six different channels and trying to sort through the information being passed. After you do this for a while, you don't even need to listen to the words being said; you become so sensitive to tone of voice that you immediately hear it if it's bad. I knew after three words that Ken was in deep trouble last week.

I call the boss on the radio. He knows if I'm calling him, it's for a good reason, and he's at the office within minutes. I tell him what I heard. He doesn't ask who told me or how I know. He sits and thinks and then says he's going to take a walk around, see what he sees.

When the boss gets back an hour later, he's red-faced and sweating. When he's angry, he starts yelling and spit flies from his mouth. His face gets really tight and his teeth show. He's exhibiting all these symptoms now and I'm a little scared. "We don't know much more than that we've got a bunch of Rangers and Delta Force trapped downtown, surrounded by Aidid's militia. There are a couple of Black Hawks down and a lot of casualties on both sides," he says. I get out of his way as he starts rocking filing cabinets side to side until he gets each one across the room. He starts piling office furniture in a corner. He's building a fucking fortress. "Get your helmet and flak jacket on now," he commands.

As daylight turns to dusk, U.S. troops in their chocolate-chip uniforms race past our office and up onto the roof, preparing to secure the perimeter of the compound as a precaution. They're carrying weapons so heavy they have to be lugged up by two and three soldiers at a time.

The night shift never arrives from the residences, so I stay on duty. Another watch officer who lives in the compound comes in and we spend the night on the floor against the desks, helmeted and clad in flak jackets. Spent shell casings rain down sporadically outside our window from warning shots fired indiscriminately into the night. The perimeter wall stands twenty feet away, bougainvillea grows lazily up its interior. We see and know nothing about what's on the other side.

We take turns every hour going over to JOC to check for new reports. I try not to run, and to stay in the light, so the snipers on our roof can clearly see me coming and going and won't shoot me. But I'm also conscious that there may be Somali snipers on other roofs, and I'm presenting an easy target. I remember to switch to the heavy flak jacket with the armored plates when I leave the building.

In JOC the Italian officers, who usually have their feet up on the desks while they play solitaire on their computer screens, are milling around the room anxiously. Nobody knows what's going on or what to do. The Americans are sharing little information. In a back room, through a window, I can see uniformed Americans in intense conversation with some of the JOC officers. Everybody's sweating.

I think about making a dash over to USLO to see if I can find Luke, but I know there's no hope of the marine guards letting me get anywhere near the gate.

At daybreak I'm exhausted but still on an adrenaline rush. Things seem quiet for the moment. I decide to go down the corridor to brush my teeth in the women's room. As I stand at the sink swishing some Crest around my mouth, I have a fleeting moment of normalcy. But then the bathroom door slams open. The boss is coming at me fast. Red-faced, teeth bared, spittle flying from his lips, he's so angry he can't form words. "You are never, ever to leave your post," he screams inches from my face.

"I just wanted to brush my teeth."

"Men are dying out there," he screams.

As my mind tries to process the implications of what he has just said, I try for one last defense. "I'm just a secretary." I start to cry.

He looks in my eyes for a long moment and then says something that changes my life. "No, not anymore you're not. I need you to be more. You're a marine now, and you are never to leave your post again."

I'm left standing alone at the mirror, watching tears run down my cheeks. I have so many thoughts at once, my emotions are crashing together. I'm embarrassed to look myself in the eye, but I force myself to. I'm ashamed to have failed this man whom I respect more than any other person here. He gave me a chance to prove myself as a watch officer, when no one else has ever given me that much credit. I replay the scene over and over in my head, and after maybe the twentieth time, I finally hear it. "You're a marine now," and suddenly, I realize I am. Because he said so and he never would have if he didn't believe it himself, and that's good enough for me.

Ken, October 4
Mogadishu

Early morning. The radio crackles. Wide awake. It's Heidi. "All UN staff, all UN staff, this is India Base. Be advised, all activities are canceled for today, all convoys are scrubbed. All staff are instructed to go into lock-down. Stay inside your residences and await further instructions from India Base. Stay off the net. I say again, stay off the net. We are in a security emergency. India Base out."

A few minutes later India Base announces a general request to staff for blood donations of all types: If you are willing to give blood, contact your security coordinator immediately. That means it's bad.

I go up to the roof. The sun is already hot. UN staff look like scarecrows on their roofs all over the neighborhood, peering into the city. Everyone has a radio pressed to their ear. Our Somali guards stand watch in the alley below. A chopper flies over the roof, the pilot waves me down violently. He's not screwing around. Okay, I'm off this roof.

Downstairs everyone is already up and watching CNN. There's break-ing news about Yeltsin and Russia and then they say there has been fight-ing in Mogadishu with American casualties, as many as five dead.

The roof is off limits. We are in lockdown, all I can do is listen to the radio and watch CNN. But it's the same thirty-second clip every fifteen minutes with nothing new. Yesterday was so nice and domestic: I'm sun-ning myself on the roof, thinking it's the fucking Greek Islands. Mean-while Americans are fighting and dying a mile away. And I didn't even know until CNN told me. I'm useless and frustrated and there's that surge in my chest and tightening in the stomach but nothing to do and nowhere to go.

And then there is somewhere to go. At noon the security coordinator arrives at the house and asks for me. They want me to come to the com-pound for a meeting. Okay. Wait. Maybe I should shave. I'm not sure I'm ready for this.

First I felt useless, now I'm not so sure I want to be useful.

They've called a special briefing. It's not the morning and it's not the follies, but it's all the same people. The faces are grim. They all look like they want to spit. The look on the general's face etches into my mind. The corners of his mouth are shooting straight down again, his head and neck are forward, his crossed hands are balled into fists, rammed into his armpits, he's staring down and out and a thousand yards away.

We get a brief, staccato review. Delta Force and Rangers attempted to capture two of Aidid's top lieutenants yesterday. They succeeded but two Black Hawks were hit with RPGs and went down. The Rangers ran to the crash sites to protect the pilots' bodies from the mob. There was a firefight that lasted all night. We don't know the exact number of casualties, but so far the estimate is twelve Americans dead and a few still missing, over fifty injured. Hundreds of Somali casualties. The Rangers didn't inform anyone about the raid until after it started, and the UN didn't get involved until last night when the Pakistanis and Malaysians were asked to join in the evacuation. We are asking for blood donations. If we need you, we will notify you. Otherwise everyone is in security lockdown.

I look over at Heidi. No cleavage today, no hickies, no smiles. She says she's been at the radio for eighteen hours passing messages between UN and U.S. JOC and it's as bad as it could possibly be.

On my way out, the chief of staff calls me into his office. He says, The commander of American Forces in-theater is convening a Hostage Task Force meeting and I want you to attend, representing the UN civilian side. Be careful, he says, the official U.S. position will be that the U.S. refuses to negotiate for hostages, but they may try to enlist the UN to do it. Don't let them railroad you into making a commitment at that meeting, son. Listen to what they say, bounce it back to them, and report back to me.

How am I going to bring myself to bounce anything back to the commander of U.S. Forces, for Christ's sake? I'm not even in command of my secretary.

The meeting is two buildings over at U.S. Joint Operations Command, a three-minute walk but a world away. This is the top of the American military machine here. A two-star general chairs the meeting with senior U.S. Command staff flanking him and a team of civilians from the U.S. Liaison Office. They must be CIA. The general looks tired and the Agency guys look mean.

The general gives a brief, gruesome review. Aidid's militia has desecrated the bodies of several American soldiers. They were dragged through the streets by rabid crowds, mutilated and worse. CNN is going to be running clips of the soldiers' bodies in the streets soon and the shit is going to hit the fan in Washington. A number of soldiers are still missing. It's not clear if they are dead or alive. They may be hostages. We are sure they have at least one hostage, a Black Hawk pilot. We are going to send helicopters out tonight calling the names of the missing men, telling them to hold on. We have to try to make contact, intervene, and request humane treatment ASAP. We all know what they did to the bodies of the guys from the Black Hawk that went down last week.

They go over the military options, none of them attractive; too much

166

blood has already spilled and the White House is not interested in a robust use of force today. So what are the other options? The U.S. will not
negotiate for hostages. But maybe the UN can. That's why we've asked the
UN side to join us.

It's sweaty and hot inside and there's constant gunfire outside.

They all turn to look at me. I'm the youngest person in this room by ten
years. I'm afraid my voice is going to shake. It reminds me of the first time
I was called on at law school, but then it doesn't remind me of that. I say
I'm here to listen to the options and report back to the civilian command,
that's all. This is probably enough for them to know I'm worthless to them,
which I think is the role I'm supposed to play.

What if, hypothetically, they ask, the UN negotiates a deal and pays?
Can you get the UN to authorize a payment? We're just running the scenarios, we're not saying we're gonna do it, we're saying could it be done?

This is precisely the trap I'm supposed to avoid.

Don't commit to anything, you were told to bounce it back. Okay, here
goes. "I can't answer a hypothetical question, sir. The UN is very bureaucratic. If there was an actual request, we could then see if New York HQ
would authorize it, but I don't think we could authorize it here." I made
that last part up, I have no idea how this would actually work.

The head CIA guy sweating bullets doesn't say anything for most of the
meeting, then he looks at me, disgusted. There's a hostage crisis and I'm a
bureaucrat.

"Why don't you go talk to some fucking imam?" he says.

Yeah, I can check that. An imam. I'll check that.

I've seen a hundred movies where American commanders hold a
meeting to assess the various scenarios and someone always has a brilliant but risky solution and the balls to attempt it. I've imagined this
scene a thousand times at the White House: mature, steady, rational
men—leaders addressing the issue head on, choosing a response, fixing
the problem. That's what Americans do, that's why we dominate. They
study this shit at Harvard, case study after case study of decision makers
making the right decisions. We can do anything if we put the best people on it. The Hostage Task Force meeting is full of courageous, responsible men. I am honored to attend. But American bodies are being
desecrated, and men are unaccounted for. And the task force doesn't
know what to do.

Because there's a frenzied mob outside these compound walls, not afraid to die, thrilled to kill. And to desecrate. Maybe there is no rational response. Maybe that was our first mistake.

Andrew, October 5
Port-au-Prince

The U.S. has finally decided to send troops to Haiti to restore democracy. There's so much shooting in the city that the boss put my prison operation on hold until the Americans arrive. All I can do now is wait, so I stop pretending to work and start drinking gin and tonics each morning. This seems the only sane option.

The gin says, *Whatever your hand finds to do, do it with all your might.* It isn't really the gin, it's Ecclesiastes. But the sum total of my doing my work with all my might is a stack of UN memos about cadavers. The *macoutes* are terrorizing Haiti, with all their might, and they're mightier.

I've never been shot but I think I fear a bullet entering my flesh much less than the prospect of everything I believe melting down into this malignancy. The gin says, *They can only kill your body, they cannot touch your soul. Fear only God, who can destroy both body and soul in hell.*

Suddenly a crowd of observers gathers around the TV at the bar, craning their necks. It's CNN breaking news. The announcer is wearing a weighty look and speaking in one of those grave tones they put on for tragic stories. It's Mogadishu. There's been a major firefight between the Somalis and U.S. Rangers. I'm glued to CNN, adrenaline pumping, drinking coffee now, not gin. Wanting to be there but glad that I'm not. They're dragging a battered body naked through the streets. "Victory!" they shout to reporters. "Come and look at the American!" They're destroying body and soul on earth.

I want to turn it off before I hear that an American civilian has been killed. Ken wanted so badly to get into the action in Cambodia to prove himself, and now he's got his wish and that's exactly how you get yourself hurt. If an AK-47 burst kills him, the real cause of death won't be bullets but something that burned right through his fear and turned him into a target.

Heidi mocks him mercilessly for looking up to me, and she'd no doubt hold me responsible. But who looks up to whom is irrelevant now. We're all in way over our heads.

Ken, October 8
Mogadishu

I'm down at the airfield. It's quiet. No Black Hawks swarming. No air traffic at all. There's a Hercules C-130 supply plane though, with its jaws hanging open, waiting for cargo. Soldiers are gathered in a room by the hangar, next to a broken green board on a trolley, no it's a bag. A big green bag. And that's a stretcher. Wait. There's a coffin in the room. Oh shit. That's a body bag. I stop dead in my tracks. On the tarmac there's a pair of boots, with a helmet nestled in the middle and an M-16 resting across. That must be some kind of traditional tribute. I bet it's a Ranger tribute. Oh. My. Christ. That's the body of one of the Rangers from the firefight Sunday.

I don't know what to do. What's my tribute? It would be silly for me to salute, I'm not a soldier. Maybe say a prayer? But I'm not religious, I wouldn't even know what prayer to say. So what do I do? There's no music in the background, no parade. But that's an American soldier going home in a body bag, his boots, helmet, and gun providing the tribute. Okay, my tribute is to try to think about it.

How many times have I read about body bags in poli-sci class, in my literature from the Vietnam War class, in *New York Times* editorials? Well there's one, in all its glory. I don't know what to think. I'm impressed and sad.

And angry. Clinton was on CNN last night announcing that U.S. forces will exit Somalia in March. But in the meantime he's sending double the number of forces and is adding more armor to cover the exit. He said it would be "open season" on Americans all over the world if we pull out now. But then he announced we are pulling out soon. Which is it, Mr. President?

Then they showed a speech by Senator Robert Byrd from the Senate well. He was saying Somalia is a quagmire, no more body bags. He's all puffy, blow-dried gray hair, hands shaking. You could see the piece of paper in his hand—it must have been his speech—trembling like a kitten's ear. He looked like he was on his sixth vodka tonic, an old Senate blowhard. Quagmire, Senator? Wrong war. I wonder what the soldier in the body bag thinks. Thought.

Abdi, the Somali judge I like, came running into my office yesterday all excited. He said, Why did the Americans stop the attack, *why did you stop*? He was pounding my arm. He said that was the biggest firefight they've ever had here, Aidid's militia ran out of ammunition at the end. "You had them weak, why did you stop?" I have absolutely no clue why we stopped. I didn't even know that we had started until it was over. He said he tried to contact me and every other American he knows to tell us Aidid was vulnerable, no more ammunition, you can walk right into his compound, why are you stopping now? He was smiling and laughing like always, but he was in agony. "I couldn't pass any messages," he said, "usually we have a CIA contact in my neighborhood, but we couldn't move. We could have told you where Aidid was, you had him, you had him!"

Then he stopped smiling. "You know, Ken, if you were out of ammunition, he would never stop fighting, you know that, right? Right?" He was pounding my arm again. "You know that, right?"

If Abdi's right, then those eighteen soldiers didn't need to die in vain. If it would be "open season" on Americans everywhere if we leave now, Mr. President, then what would it be if we stayed and killed the cocksucker?

I'd like to know Dr. Andrew's view from Haiti and the Space Shuttle crew's from Bosnia. I bet a lot of folks whose hands shake a lot less than Senator Byrd's do want us to stay and fight.

It was only six weeks ago I was flying around in a Black Hawk for the first time, lost in a post-Holocaust, post–Cold War, preadolescent fantasy powered by the might of the American military. Ready to kill Nazis, make peace, introduce the New World Order to starving Africans. Now the Black Hawks are grounded. All that American military might is in a useless, ceasefire funeral procession under the airport hangar.

Andrew, October 11–12
Port-au-Prince

The U.S. chargé d'affaires goes to the docks to greet the American soldiers and their landing ship, the USS *Harlan County*. The chargé's car is kicked and rocked by a gang of drunken *macoutes* with crude weapons. "Haiti, Somalia! Haiti, Somalia!" they shout. "Aidid, Aidid!" Their eyes are wide and bloodshot and gleeful. Goliath is wounded and confused. Democracy in Haiti is no longer worth American blood.

So President Clinton orders the American soldiers and their ship to withdraw from the docks and from Haiti. It's too dangerous.

But it isn't. The American military could crush the *macoutes* in an afternoon's training exercise. They know it, and the *macoutes* know it.

The problem is not military; it's psychological. Fear ripples from Somalia through Washington to Haiti. A few punks with small guns and big mouths and the world's only superpower is in retreat.

Far up the hill at the Hotel Montana, the UN's special representative for Haiti is on TV assuring the world that the USS *Harlan County* will soon dock and American soldiers will disembark before dark. Someone forgot to tell him that they've withdrawn and that the whole city is watching as the ship grows smaller and smaller and disappears over the horizon, past Cuba, toward Miami.

It's a lonely and demoralizing sight. The chargé d'affaires is almost in tears on TV as it dawns on her how badly she's been betrayed by her superiors. She denounces the *macoutes* as gangsters who don't want the future of Haiti to arrive. But it's her ship that didn't arrive. Last week it required eighteen fallen Rangers in Somalia to get Clinton running scared. This week a group of loudmouthed thugs did it.

How in hell is he ever going to face down the Bosnian Serbs, who, unlike their Somali and Haitian brothers, have a real army?

Ken, October 12
Mogadishu

I check in with Heidi at India Base. She's watching CNN with the American Intel officer who's been hovering around her lately. Wonder what's up there. They're watching breaking news from Haiti. The Intel guy says the USS *Harlan County* arrived yesterday to deploy American and Canadian peacekeeping troops and a crowd of Haitians came to the dock to greet the ship, shot in the air, shouting "Aidid, Aidid," and the *Harlan County* was ordered to retreat. Turned tail. Withdrew.

From *Haiti*?

I look at the Intel guy. Are you shitting me? *We* retreated from *Haiti*? They barely have an army for fucksake. The *macoutes* will run riot now. Open season. They win. He looks back at me with a cold stare. I try to hold his gaze. There's an entire doctoral dissertation communicated in the three-second silence of that stare-down. It's the most coherent articulation of an American foreign policy critique I've ever heard in my life, and he didn't have to say a thing.

I'm ashamed in front of the officer. For being a civilian. Like I personally represent everything that's wrong with the policies we're all watching fall apart. Only civilians would imagine that you can keep the peace in a hot war without fighting.

This will never work now. It's over.

I gave this idea everything I had, literally.

Why am I taking this all so personally? It's not about me, I tell myself, even as I talk to myself. This is exactly why Heidi thinks Andrew and I are full of shit: it's always about us and our ideas, not about individual humans. But an idea died this week, just like a human dies. How many successful peacekeeping missions will never be sent now? How many lives we could have saved will be lost now? The question is palpable as India Base Somalia watches CNN Haiti.

Andrew, October 14
Port-au-Prince

The cook runs into the kitchen in a panic.

"They killed him, they killed him," she screams, shaking and weeping.

I turn on the radio to find they've gunned down Guy Malary, Aristide's justice minister, in the middle of town in broad daylight. I drive down there right away but it's all over. His overturned car is riddled with bullets; his body, his driver's, and his bodyguard's are all lying inert among broken glass in the street in front of the church. I return home, nothing I can do. The cook says she wants to run into the hills. You can take to the hills, but there are no trees left to hide you. You can kneel in a church, or lie in a hospital bed, but there's no sanctuary if the *macoutes* have orders to kill you. You might as well just put your affairs in order and wait for them at home.

The mission is imploding because of a tragedy in Mogadishu that has nothing to do with us. I receive a radio message to muster at the Hotel Christopher downtown. The parking lot is an ocean of white UN-marked Land Cruisers: it could be a Toyota convention. CNN is filming from the back of the meeting hall as the UN chief of mission announces that it is no longer safe for us to work and we are to evacuate immediately across the border to the Dominican Republic. Silence. Then as the news sinks in, an angry, confused buzz spreads across the room. Dozens of hands shoot up with a torrent of questions.

"What about our Haitian staff?"

"They're staying."

"What do we do with the computer files and the database of witness statements?"

"Destroy them quickly."

"How do we protect the witnesses? The *macoutes* will kill them if we leave." More silence. The staff are angry now and a young observer, shaking, voice cracking, leaps up and shouts, "Who made the evacuation decision, did you?" There's a long, uncomfortable pause.

"UN Headquarters in New York together with UN Security here on the ground in coordination with the American Embassy." He's already being vague, trying to dilute the blame that will surely follow.

"Sorry, no more questions. The first plane leaves in three hours. We're calling in all staff from around the country, and the second plane will leave tomorrow morning. And there's a ten-pound baggage limit, so pack only essentials."

The meeting breaks up and suddenly, from one minute to the next, life is totally changed. Observers are crying and you can feel the beginning of a roiling panic in the parking lot. Hysteria is contagious, so I get out of there quickly.

It's dark by the time I get through the traffic back up to the house. I drain the pool, open a beer, and sit on the terrace, staring at the twinkling lights of the tortured city far below. I never did find an air-conditioner for my friend the morgue assistant. The prisoners won't get their truckload of food and medicine, nor will the colonel get his condoms or percentage of the supplies.

I told you it wasn't a serious offer, I can see him telling his men. *Look, a little confusion in the streets and they all just get on a plane and leave.*

My dreams of being useful here are vanishing, like the water in my pool. I still have to decide what to do with my database of interviews with torture victims, eighty detailed descriptions of acts of brutality and sadism that I could never have even imagined before I came here. I want to carry a copy of these witness statements out of the country with me to preserve the records, so I can't just destroy them. But if the *macoutes* find those files, they'll hunt down the witnesses. It's past midnight but I drive to the office, grab the hard drive from my computer and all the files I can find. I return home and drop the hard drive in the driveway and roll over it several times with the Land Cruiser. It's a vaguely satisfying feeling, the destruction. Then I gather the shattered pieces and all the files, throw petrol on and toss a match. There's a *whoomph* and the flames light up the Haitian night.

I wake up the landlord, pay my rent, pack ten pounds of toiletries and clothes, and give all the rest away to the weeping cook. I can't sleep, so I open another beer and wait for morning.

Over and over I replay in my head the implications of what we've just done. We told the Haitians that we couldn't physically stop their government from torturing and killing, but that if they told us in detail who was doing it and how, we'd bear witness and seek justice. Eventually the world would be outraged enough to send soldiers and reinstall democracy. We took notes, wrote reports, created summaries and a database of victims. I treated their wounds to give them comfort, an inducement to come forward.

They believed us, risked their lives to turn up at our offices all over the country, in full view of their attackers, to tell their stories. They exposed themselves, crawled in and spilled their guts, sometimes literally. They took off their clothes, told me exactly who stabbed them and how, and trusted me to treat them. I handed out aspirin and Band-Aids while the killers watched and waited. Now that they're at their most vulnerable, we're abandoning them, frozen in the headlights, roadkill for the *macoutes'* machine. And we're flying out, clutching our precious blue UN passports and bags full of Haitian art.

We just showed Haitians that our lives are more valuable than theirs. The logic of the mission was ours, not theirs, and so is the logic of our retreat. "Tell us the truth and we will seek justice" was our idea. "It's too dangerous and we must evacuate" is our privilege. Neither applies to the Haitians. A ship with soldiers arrives at the dock and exits the dock. Haitians have no exit.

The most basic principle they teach you at medical school, years before you even get to touch your first patient, is "First, do no harm." But harm is exactly what we've done, identifying the next victims for the assassins running Haiti. It was a vicious setup from the beginning.

Ken, October 15
Mogadishu

I go to India Base to see if Heidi's on duty. I'm on permanent CNN watch now. I want to see if they're covering the Black Hawk pilot

Michael Durant's release. I stick my head in, it's quiet, ceasefire style. Matt has his feet up on the desk, eating an MRE. He gets the good ones: combat rations from the Italian troops, they come with a little bottle of red wine.

Heidi's at her desk engrossed in a memo. I peer over her shoulder. Her memos usually have some interesting intel tidbits. She hates it when I do that, but I insist, c'mon woman, I gotta know. She says back off, you're not authorized. But I stay and read. It's not a memo, it's a letter home to her mom about life in the 'Dish. It reads like a short story, as good as those books in my dad's den.

CNN flashes to Port-au-Prince, Haiti, it's breaking news, something's happening. It's comforting that there's breaking news somewhere other than here. Until we get the actual newsbreaks. Young disheveled civilians are boarding a plane. They look somber. It's UN staff, they have those stupid blue UN baseball caps on. Their hands are full of bags and souvenirs. Where are they going? Oh shit, no. They're evacuating.

We look for people we know. A third of our colleagues from Cambodia came to the 'Dish, a third went to Bosnia, and a third to Haiti. We had high hopes and no clue. I'm looking intently for Dr. Andrew. I kneel right up next to the screen. If I look hard enough, I'll see him. Heidi leans back in her chair, crosses her legs and shakes the airborne foot fervently, narrows her eyes, smirks. She's in her wise and womanly and superior act. She's enjoying this. "Looking for your hero, Dr. Andrew? You're both so full of shit. Who do you boys think you are?"

But I can't help it. It's hard for me to imagine the doctor evacuating, defeated.

I was so intimidated by him when we first met in Cambodia, it took a long time for us to become friends. It's like he has one of those iron shackling rods he stole from the prison in Cambodia lodged directly down his back. He doesn't bend and his faith doesn't bend and that's precisely what I respect about him. He impressed and inspired me with that in Cambodia. I think I half came here to catch up with him.

But maybe I'm finally growing up, because that missionary shit scares me now. Look at how far it got us this week. Which runs out first, Doctor, evil or your ability to keep doing good works? And what if you're so convinced about your good works that in the meantime you fuck everything up and it all backfires and people die as a result? Like me and Danny did at the prison.

And now the good doctor's getting on a plane. They can't restore democracy without American soldiers. His mission is a failure. He's going to need another one. That rod will break before it bends.

Andrew, October 15
Port-au-Prince

At dawn a long evacuation convoy of white UN vehicles crawls down Delmas Boulevard, the main artery in this congested city. Normally chaotic traffic grinds to a halt as hundreds of Haitians drop what they're doing and stare. We're driving slowly enough for me to see the shock and abandonment on their faces, the last hope for change rolling past them down the hill. It's impossible to look back at them, to stare down that truth. I've never felt so much shame. I wish the car had curtains or reflective windows.

At an intersection a white Mercedes pulls up, its path blocked. A light-skinned woman in her fifties, one of those Haitians from the wealthy class that supports the coup, climbs out and waves. Doubtless we're interrupting a shopping trip. "Bye-bye!" she shouts, gold chains jingling at her wrist. The gesture is light, but the face behind the designer sunglasses is twisted with satisfaction and contempt. For her it must be sweet, the meddling foreigners finally on their way out, no more prying eyes.

There's an unreal calm at the airport. The *macoutes* are out in force, fingering their weapons, watching. It occurs to me as we assemble that this could be a trap; maybe they're just waiting for the signal to open fire. The journalists have the same idea, and are also here in strength, anticipating action.

"How do you feel about being evacuated?" one asks, sticking a camera in my face.

I feel like smashing your lens. "Why don't you piss off and go cover someone else getting shot?"

But it's a show, I'm no tough guy today. I'm slumped, dejected in a white plastic chair waiting to evacuate. Outside, the pink dawn is bleeding into a bright Haitian morning. The day promises to be full of violence, like the one before and the one before that. The charter jet that's to take us across the border is shining on the tarmac; the smell of jet fuel is making me sick. After four months I'm leaving just as clueless about Haiti as those tourists on the beach who left after four hours. I flip through my UN passport; they didn't even bother to stamp me out this time. We're irrelevant now.

On the other side of the barriers observers are arriving from all over the country. I can see several colleagues locked in tearful embraces with Haitian lovers, stolen moments as the clock ticks toward departure. Opposite me, a woman is clutching an oversized rag doll.

I just couldn't bear to leave her in this horrible country, she says, bursting into tears.

I hope CNN doesn't see this.

Outside the fence an overloaded Land Cruiser fishtails to a stop and four harried observers stumble out.

You're late, and there are supposed to be five of you, screams the personnel officer. The exasperated team leader ignores her and collapses into the plastic chair beside me, her face caked with dust and sweat and anxiety.

The fifth one's a nutcase so we left her behind, she says, shaking her head in disbelief. When we got the radio call to evacuate, that lunatic showed up at the office with her Haitian lover and his baby, insisting that we take them both with us.

She goes on breathlessly, When I told her no, she started to weep and wail and then tried to hit me. She just lost it. It went on for hours, despite all of us trying to reason with her. I told her that the UN won't help her kidnap a Haitian child and where was the child's mother anyway? There's no way we'd even get through immigration in the Dominican Republic. But she wouldn't accept it. So around midnight we just drove off and left her in the office clutching the baby.

Story over, she sags deeper into her chair, completely silent.

As more observers from the outer provinces arrive and gather in the departures lounge, everyone has an evacuation story. One guy refused to leave his house because he had just bought a banana tree, while another woman was in a panic because the weight of her cosmetics case alone, which she passionately refused to abandon, took up all of her ten-pound allowance. Several fights broke out when all debts had to be paid with just three hours' notice and no functioning banks. Lovers successfully kept their affairs secret until the emergency of evacuation precipitated a tearfully tender public embrace.

Across the crowd I catch the eye of one of our drivers. We both know that the moment the plane takes off, he's a target: I'm amazed he's come to the airport. We're fighting about money and banana trees and crying for ourselves and our rag dolls while he serves our mission to its sordid end.

It's a relief when the order finally comes to board the plane. CNN films a hundred of us walking single file across the tarmac. I turn my head away from the camera as we exit another bloody day in Haiti.

Ken, October 19
Mogadishu

The president's spokesperson, Dee Dee Myers, is on CNN. If I have to listen to Dee Dee Myers explain the military scenario in Mogadishu one more time, I'm going to projectile vomit on the screen. She sounds like the PR chick from a record label, describing why this year's album sales are, um, not down, but they're just not what we hoped for. The other one, Jamie Rubin, the spokesman for Madeleine Albright, is worse. He's the junior vice president for sales at the same record label, two years out of business school. We've got a really great new foreign policy idea, it's going to be a super-great way to defeat evil in the nineties, really. It's great. And it's new. And it's an idea. Really.

It's now an official ceasefire; we no longer intend to capture Aidid. Dee Dee calls it a "shift in focus," not a change, and adds her insight that, as a matter of fact, Aidid is a "clan leader with a substantial constituency in Somalia," and therefore we have to negotiate with him, not fight. Last week he was a war criminal the pursuit of whom was worthy of American lives; this week he's a corrupt but popular alderman from the south side of Chicago.

Dee Dee's taking questions from reporters now. I have a question, Dee Dee. Aidid was to be arrested for killing twenty-four Pakistanis in June, and then was pardoned for the crime and resurrected as a credible negotiating partner after killing eighteen Americans in October. What's the message if the policy of accountability for the crime of attacking peacekeepers is abandoned after a successful repetition of the same crime? How can the policy our soldiers died for reverse the next day, because of their death?

Dee Dee's not taking questions from Mogadishu today.

Heidi, October 25
Mogadishu

The tension in Mogadishu is electric. Everything you touch is charged with it, everything you say is alive with it. I find myself arguing with Ken constantly. When we were in Cambodia, he was a missionary for the American Way. Export democracy, the New World Order, never again, the bullshit was endless. It was funny to me then, because I thought it was just naïve Harvard drivel. Now it's not so funny and it's tearing him apart.

I feel bad for him; his illusions are shattered. But my patience is running thin. These boys need to grow up already. Andrew calling Ken and Ken calling Andrew and what did CNN say and Somalia and Haiti and Haiti and Somalia. They were both looking for trouble and they both found it, and now they need to shut up and stop crying. What did they expect? What were they trying to prove? No one cares except them that they had a plan to save the world and it didn't work.

I stop by the U.S. Army field hospital. It's part of my job to visit here every few days and get information on UN casualties, so the soldiers and doctors are used to seeing me around. I need a quiet place where I don't have to worry about being watched and listened to. I wish I worked here.

Waiting for the clerk to return from a break, I step outside to smoke a cigarette. A doctor stands smoking near me. She's shaking and sucking her cigarette hard. She keeps glancing over at me, like she wants to talk. She looks like bad news, so I try not to make eye contact with her, but she can't be stopped. "Do you know what they do to women here?" she asks me. She tells me what she just saw. I don't believe her. I can't. I want to stick my fingers in my ears and hum "Yankee Doodle," back away from her, get in my jeep, spray sand at her as I leave. I like the Somalis, and I don't want to believe it. Even in the ruins of Mogadishu, with the swarming machine guns, I still see them as cultured and civilized.

She says to me, Do you want to see? Can you go and look? I don't want to but I want to. I'm ashamed for the patient, but I want to see for myself. I want to come back out and laugh and say, No, no, you're wrong, that's not what it is at all.

The doctor says just pretend that you're a part of the medical team and I'll pull the sheet back. I'll hold it up so she can't see your face. We push the tent flap aside and enter. We pass through inflated tunnels, over rubber-coated ramps. The sound of air-conditioners and compressors mute everything, even thoughts. It's like being in the bowels of some creature, a twisting green snake in the middle of the Somali desert waiting to swallow the casualties of war. We enter the ward and the doctor stops in front of the bed of a woman in labor, her distended belly greeting me before I even see her face. The thing I am here to see has nothing to do with the reason she is here. The doctor asks me, Are you okay? I say, yes, go ahead. She pulls the sheet up at an angle that separates me from the woman lying on the bed.

By now the woman is used to being prodded and poked by the American doctors and, without a word, parts her legs for me. Her skin is very dark here around the opening to her vagina. At first I think she's been burned, her vulva has that running-wax appearance of burned flesh. But then I see it and I understand. There is no vulva. There's nothing there, it's all been sliced off and sewn shut. The doctors now have to reopen her so she can give birth to her child.

Maahatsaniid, I tell the woman. Thank you. The doctor lowers the sheet and we leave the room. The doctor looks somehow fortified, like she's passed her trauma on to me. I'm sorry, she tells me, I had to share it with someone, a woman. Yeah, *maahatsaniid,* Doctor. Thanks for sharing, but who do I share it with now?

After dropping the report off at my office, I come back to my room, drink a beer, and chain-smoke cigarettes and then fall asleep. There really isn't much else to do here but sleep. Late in the afternoon, a young girl sits on a stool near the foot of my bed. When she senses I am awake, she asks, "Where is your husband, Yusuf?" This is Anab. She cleans the rooms. In Arabic her name means grape, a symbol of purity.

Anab and I prepare to strip the room bare and air it out. It's a hundred degrees outside. Inside, the air-conditioner is permanently on and the one small window is sealed with plastic to keep the sand out. But in the dry season the wind never stops and the sand finds its way through and coats the sheets, my clothes, the floor.

We work silently together, grabbing the ends of my mattress and laying it in the sun to try to bake off the mildew smell. Anab puts in a CD, U2's *Achtung Baby.* She doesn't speak much English but she's learned enough about the West from me and the other UN staff.

Back inside my room, with the door closed, Anab removes the scarf that covers her head and shoulders and starts the afternoon nail polishing ritual. Choose a color, paint fingernails, toenails, several coats each, spend fifteen minutes admiring the nails, then remove it all to go home for the day. She's funny, this girl. I sometimes return home during the day and find her fully dressed in my clothes, the waist of the too-large jeans cinched in the back with a clothespin, her head scarves removed and her long hair combed out and bouncy. She doesn't try on the stuff I would go for—the sexier dresses I never get to wear here, the high heels. She goes for the same things a young American woman might—jeans and T-shirts, her version of hip-hop. When I find her like this, she doesn't even acknowledge me. No hello, no sorry, no oops, you caught me. She gives me a look like she's daring me to say something to her, but I don't. One day, if I have film in the camera, I'll take her picture playing dress-up.

I once bought her a pair of sunglasses in Nairobi, identical to the ones I wear. When I gave them to her, she tilted her head back sharply, looking down the length of her nose at me—her thanks, I guess—and promptly stuffed the glasses down into her bra without even trying them on and walked away.

We roll our eyes a lot, pretending to be irritated with each other, but we trust each other, I think. She calls me "sister," and when she speaks to me in confidence, she puts her hand squarely on my breast in the ritual manner of Somali women addressing each other. Each time this simple act, discomforting to me at first, renews the strong bond I feel with Anab. It crushes me to think that she too may have been mutilated.

At night I read and listen to the BBC, smoke, drink instant coffee, stand in front of my room looking up at the stars. I can't sleep, so I go for a walk. I come across an old boyfriend, a guy I dated from the UN in New York, sitting alone on a low wall, drinking a bottle of wine. He offers me the bottle and I sit next to him. I tell him what I saw today. I tell him everything from the doctor to the raised sheet. My words spill out and in between, I gulp from the bottle. I don't know if he understands my horror, but he must, because he takes my feet and begins to massage them, not saying a word and not really looking at me. I don't know, maybe he has seen it too.

When I finish talking, he tells me a story about working security for the return of property from Iraq to Kuwait after Desert Storm. He tells me that no sound could be heard in the room where the gold was weighed, that the helicopters hovering above with heavily armed soldiers had to keep their positions constant, to avoid upsetting the balance of the scales. I wonder what made him remember this story at this moment, what made him think to tell it to me now. And I wonder how I can ever date another regular civilian man, whose only stories are of petty crap at work and drunken weekends at the Jersey shore?

When Yusuf comes back to the room at midnight, I'm almost asleep. I hear him popping open a can of beer. He'll drink three before he'll come to bed and then he'll slide in behind me and I'll wake up and we'll make love. It's the same every night that he chews *khat* with the other Somalis. Without this ritual, he can't slow his heart down enough to sleep.

All through the day, I have been thinking about Anab, that maybe she's been mutilated too. I'm afraid to talk to Yusuf about it. What if he defends it? What would that mean for us? I couldn't go on with him if he reacted the wrong way. He's just lying there next to me with no idea that our relationship is at stake based on the tone of voice he uses when he answers me. As we lie in the dark, I hear helicopters landing on the pad outside; the sand gets kicked up and pelts my window. I wonder what they saw tonight.

Suddenly the questions fly out of my mouth. Why is this done? To all women? I'm praying the answer is that it's uncommon now and only a small group of peasants in the countryside still violate their daughters.

He tells me all Somali women are mutilated.

Probably no one has ever asked him about this. Maybe it's not even spoken of among Somalis. It seems that the look on my face tells him more than he has ever understood before. He tries to explain that he would never do this to a woman and believes it should never be done. And then just as I'm feeling better—at least better about him—I ask if his sisters have been circumcised. Yes, he says, but in educated families, the women only lose a small part of their vulva and are not sewn shut.

As if losing a small part of your vulva is a minor concession.

When the Norwegian Battalion left last month, they took several Somali women with them as wives. For weeks after, I would notice a cleaning woman or a laundry woman was gone. One woman I knew left with her two children, pregnant. Then we heard that her new husband had beaten her and she had disappeared somewhere in Norway.

Andrew on the Mekong River.

Andrew wilting in the
Cambodian heat.

Andrew in a Red Cross ambulance,
Cambodia.

Heidi sporting a peacekeeper's blue beret in Cambodia.

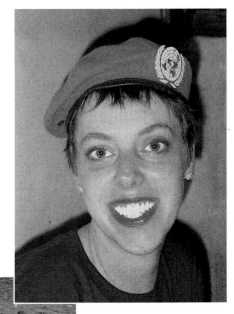

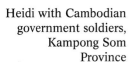

French soldiers guarding Heidi's polling site.

Heidi with Cambodian government soldiers, Kampong Som Province

Ken and Heidi on the Mekong River

Ken interviewed by NPR in Phnom Penh. Everyone wanted to know how to replicate the success of the election elsewhere in the world.

Ken, Heidi, and friend celebrating the success of the Cambodian election.

Phnom Penh street life

Ken and a Cambodian colleague observing a campaign rally in Phnom Penh.

Heidi, Somalia

Heidi in traditional
Somali dress, waiting
to board a helicopter.

Heidi and colleagues
in a UN Pakistani
Batalion commu-
nications transport
vehicle.

Ken, Heidi, and friends on a beach in Mogadishu. Swimming was banned after repeated shark attacks.

Ken and Heidi waiting with Nepalese Battalion troops for an escort out of the Embassy Compound in Mogadishu.

Ken with Somali police trainees. The United States, trying to exit Somalia quickly, left security in the hands of poorly trained and out-gunned local police.

Ken with Somali shooters waiting for the convoy to the prison.

Ken with Somali colleagues

Ken in Somalia

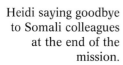

Somali prisoners seeking light and air.

Heidi saying goodbye to Somali colleagues at the end of the mission.

Ken, on a remote hilltop in Rwanda.

Rwandan kids rushing the UN helicopter.

Survivors struggle to recover the bodies of their lost loved ones. The Rwandan hillsides were dotted with thousands of mass graves.

Andrew and UN forensic experts, at the bottom of a grave, hauling out bodies.

Andrew during a break in the digging, Bosnia.

Ken and Heidi in the mountains above Port-au-Prince.

Ken with an international delegation of election observers in Haiti.

Marc

Ballots burning, Haiti.

Ken with Nigerian soldiers in Liberia.

Ken surveying
a massacre
site in Liberia

Andrew visiting Heidi in New Jersey.

Andrew outside UN Headquarters in New York.

In Brooklyn.

Suzanne and Andrew, just married. City Hall, Manhattan.

Full circle. Andrew on the partially completed structure of his new home
on the Mekong River.

November

Ken, November 13
Mogadishu

Deep sleep.

"India Base, I've been shot."
"This is India Base, identify yourself, over."
"I've been shot, India Base, I've been shot."
"This is India Base, if you don't identify yourself we can't help you, over."

Wide awake.
Silence.
I look at the clock. It's only seven. Who's operating outside the compound at this time? The convoy doesn't leave for another hour. The voice sounded American. There was something familiar about the way he said "India Base." Must have been a joke. Stupid joke.

I bring the radio in with me to the shower just in case. Then there's a panicked call. It's a new voice, not American, and it's for real. He's calling in an ambush. Men down. One Somali killed in action. Heart pounding, I step out of the shower. Nothing I can do, just listen and panic with them. Who is it?

The radio crackles now, security officers are calling security officers, transport to the hospital, everyone else off the net. Who was it? We all gather at breakfast. Did you hear the radio? Some did, some didn't. Did you hear someone say they were shot? Can you tell who it was?

It sounded like an American accent. Who's on the road that early? Oh my God, maybe it was the early run to India Base, the one Heidi hated. That's Matt's run. Fuck, that might have been Matt.

I get to the office, everyone on the compound already knows: it was Matt, his vehicle was ambushed by Somalis. He fired an AK-47 at them. Because he fired, he drew fire. He took four rounds in the chest. I go over to the Swedish field hospital. Matt's girlfriend, Liza, and her friend Sarah

185

are there waiting at a little picnic table outside the operating rooms. What do you say?

After a while a chaplain and a doctor emerge from the operating rooms. No.

Liza is a strikingly beautiful woman from Martinique. She is black and Matt is white and Sarah is white. The chaplain hugs and consoles Sarah, assuming the white girl is grieving for the white guy. We point at Liza. The chaplain is confused and embarrassed.

The doctor says, "We are still operating. Matt's young and strong and there's hope." The chaplain says, "I just came here from Sweden, I don't really know anything but I am here for you," smiles wanly, rings his hands, makes a small bow and stands there silent, smiles some more, and walks back to the hospital.

We're alone again at the picnic table. You always picture these moments in your mind with parents and family present. But we're eight thousand miles from home, no parents, no family, just one another. We wait for hours. Liza says that in the morning Matt came out of the shower while she was still in bed and caressed her shoulder, to say bye, have a nice day. His hand was cold from the shower and she pulled away. That was their last moment together. If she could have one more caress. Never pull away from a caress again. Matt's boss from India Base arrives. He's a competent, dedicated, tough marine, everyone respects him. It's like a parent finally showed up.

The doctor comes out slowly. He's in blue scrubs, young and handsome. Andrew's done this a hundred times. We all stand up. He says, "It's over. He fought and we tried, but four bullets did too much damage. It's over, I'm sorry." Liza doubles over, we all hug her. Matt's boss straightens himself up, clenches his jaw, blinks slowly, and says, "I'll go call Matt's dad."

Heidi, November 13
Mogadishu

I'm waiting in the office for news of Matt when the boss returns from the hospital. A stiff-necked marine, he's holding back his tears. "He didn't make it," he says to me and Marilyn, the other watch officer on duty. He didn't make it. Marilyn grabs a dust rag and says, "No. No. No," over and over again as she makes a circuit of the room, dragging the rag over already shiny surfaces, cleaning and cleaning and cleaning nonexistent dust, as though this will force everything back to normal. I put my face in my hands and let the information sink in.

I knew someone would get killed on that fucking convoy. They were ambushed on Dead Cow Road and Matt is dead. That road has been designated no-go for days.

The senior security officer responsible for the convoy lingers in the office dropping bits of information about what went wrong. The Somali shooters abandoned them, just disappeared, he says. Fuck you, I say, those shooters would never walk away from a fight. He says, Our shooters were in on the ambush. I look him right in the eye. He gets all red in the face and takes on his most intimidating pose, approaches me slowly and points his finger in my face. "You just back off on this," he says. The boss intervenes and they step out of the room together.

I flash back to the night I made the decision to move to the Embassy Compound. The security officer in charge of our convoy picked Matt and me up after work. As we pulled out of the gate, he lifted an AK-47 from the front floorboard and handed it back to Matt. You cover the rear, he told him. I could feel my ears burn bright red. Matt was not authorized or trained to carry that gun. This was an accident waiting to happen.

With a pistol clutched against the steering wheel, the security officer drove like it was the Mogadishu Grand Prix. Fun for him, he got to play cowboy and the guns were real. He made a bunch of quick turns and I lost my sense of direction. We were in a neighborhood I'd never seen before. There were Somalis all over the streets. They stopped and stared at us. You never feel safe driving on these streets, but for some reason that neighborhood was especially bad. I turned and looked for the shooters; they were gone. "Slow down," I pleaded, "we lost the shooters." He glanced in the rearview mirror and stepped on the gas. I kept turning and looking for the shooters' car, hoping they would find us. Suddenly he downshifted, came to a complete stop. The entire roadway for the next hundred yards was flooded. Too risky to pass through and stall out the engine. He threw it in reverse and backed up to the previous intersection. He looked both ways, and backed up again fast, our necks jerking in time together. We were lost, and my life was in the hands of this idiot cowboy. Matt and I looked at each other, helpless.

The security officer somehow found his way out of the maze of sandy back roads, and I vowed that would be the last time I'd ever ride in that vehicle. If I'm going to die here, it should be because of my own stupidity, not someone else's.

And now Matt's dead. I didn't even like him much. He was arrogant and self-centered, but for Christ's sake, he was only twenty-three years old. He didn't even get a chance to grow out of that. Just yesterday he was sitting at the desk, so proud to be writing out a big check for his last student loan payment. All his per diem money went into those loan payments. He was very disciplined about it for a twenty-three-year-old kid. Finally, he said, I can spend some money and take a nice trip with Liza.

He always carried this big, ugly green backpack around, must have weighed about thirty pounds. Said it was all the stuff he wouldn't want to leave behind if there was ever an emergency evacuation. I wonder where all that stuff is now.

Before CNN picks up the news that an American civilian was killed in Mogadishu, I call my mom. It wasn't me, I knew him, he was young.

Ken, November 13
Mogadishu

Liza insists on seeing Matt one last time. Not just his face but his body. He's wrapped up in sheets like a mummy. His head looks huge, swollen, gray. She tears the sheets away from his body screaming and crying, she's pulling the sheets off his legs and feet. They are white white. We can't do this. We pull her out of the room. It's the hardest thing I've ever seen.

Everyone leaves the hospital with Liza, but I can't go. I remember what Mr. Karim said to me about leaving his body, so I slump down against the wall and wait, I'm not sure what for. I can see the surgical team at the picnic table smoking and talking; they're tired. I believe the doctor, that they tried. But I wonder if Matt had been at an American hospital—fully stocked, good doctors—if he would have made it. Maybe a wheelchair, but alive. Four slugs in the chest. American doctors can handle that, can't they? The orderlies roll him away. I have to go now.

An American soldier passes and says, "I'm sorry, man." How did he know? It's a simple cliché thing to say but somehow the fact that a soldier, trained for this shit, cares about us—we shouldn't even be here—breaks me and I start sobbing and can't stop.

Heidi and I go to the Israeli PX and drink a full bottle of warm vodka. She asks why I stayed at the hospital so long. I say because of Mr. Karim. She cries desperately. It wasn't Matt so much as Mr. Karim and he's alive. It's funny what brings it on and what doesn't.

The next day there's a memorial service at the U.S. Army's Chapel of Hope. I walk in next to the UN chief administrative officer, the first thing he says to me is Matt shouldn't have fired the weapon, that's what went wrong. What is he talking about, and why is it so important for him to tell me that now?

A crew-cut American military chaplain with an eagle on his uniform gives a long speech about war and Jesus. Matt was neither a soldier nor a Christian. Liza goes to the podium after the chaplain is done. She's crying and can't speak but has something to say. Half the heads in the crowd are bowed, bobbing, sobbing. The sight of Liza at the podium unable to speak is unbearable for me and I have to look away. But she finds the courage and says Matt's parents are very far away, doubles over like there are shooting pains in her stomach, can't go on, then she does. They wanted me to ask his friends to write to them, she says, wincing, to tell them about his life here, about his last days.

A big, blond, confident, strapping American kid. No one close to me has ever died before. And Matt wasn't even close to me. He was the youngest American in the mission. He worked with Heidi at India Base, so I saw him a lot. He was at India Base when I called in from the ambush, he talked me through it. Two days ago he asked me if I thought he should go to law school.

I'm crying like an old grandmother. Maybe it's Liza. All those tears running down that smooth, round, beautiful brown face and Matt's parents in New York wanting to know what their son was doing here for the past six months and my parents are wondering too and it could have been me, and what if it was? Would a beautiful girl from Martinique read a message from my parents to my friends sobbing in the Chapel of Hope? No, but Heidi would. So Liza is Heidi and Matt is me and he's dead and what for? I can't take this.

Matt had big, blue luminescent eyes, full of youthful exuberance. Marilyn calls A-farts and dedicates that Peter Gabriel song, "In Your Eyes," to Matt's memory. I happen to walk by India Base when the song is playing. "In your eyes, the light, the heat, I am complete." Everyone is hunched over crying like babies. Grown men and women at the Intelligence and Operations Center doubled over weeping.

It could have been Heidi. I think about the time she came to me in

189

tears, afraid they were going to get killed on that convoy. And what did I tell her? "Relax, stop panicking, you're hysterical. Get it together." So she moved onto the Embassy Compound. If she had listened to me, she might be dead.

A UN Board of Inquiry is convened. I try to talk to the board. We'll call you if we need you. I send a letter to the board from a group calling myself "Friends of Matt" asking for minutes from the meetings. The board is stacked with UN officials who oversee security. I don't trust these fucks for a second to truly investigate and hold one of their own accountable. They tell me I have no standing to ask questions. I tell one of the senior security officers he should talk to Heidi, informally, at least. He says shut up and don't ask questions, you don't know anything about security.

Heidi knows everyone in the mission; she hears all the gossip about the board's proceedings. We are pretty sure about our version of what went wrong and who's at fault: we think the security officer was driving on an officially no-go road, didn't wait for the Somali security escort, and, the fatal mistake in our opinion, handed Matt—an untrained, unauthorized civilian—his AK-47. Like he did every time Heidi drove with them. But we hear the board is going to blame it on Matt: he shouldn't have grabbed and fired the weapon, he should have had his body armor and helmet on. Right. So that's why the chief of administration said to me too quickly that Matt shouldn't have opened fire. He must have thought the Justice Division might get involved. Motherfuckers. A kid is dead and no one is accountable. Blame the corpse.

Heidi, November 15
Mogadishu

I ask to speak before the Board of Inquiry. I want to tell them what it was like driving in that convoy twice a day. Only a handful of us know that and one of us is dead. Nothing is more important than ensuring that the board conducting this investigation understands the experience fully. I'm told that I wasn't in the car on that day and my past experiences are irrelevant. I send a letter to the board members asking that they hear me out. The letter goes unanswered.

I could say the hell with it, I was smart enough to get myself off that convoy, I made it alive. I could say I learned my lesson, now I know who to trust with my life and who not to and this is a good thing. I could let them shut me up, let them mutilate me and sew my vagina closed. Leave Somalia and never be heard from again.

But I can't because it's the UN's responsibility to protect civilians, not arm them. I believe with all my heart that if Matt wasn't already gripping the trigger on that AK-47 when they were attacked, he wouldn't have had the opportunity to open fire, and would be here irritating the shit out of me at this moment. I'm not blaming the dead, I'm blaming the living.

Ken, November 15
Mogadishu

People know how upset I am and how angry Heidi is and so someone leaks me excerpts from the confidential "code cable" document the Board of Inquiry sent to HQ in New York. It reads like a Soviet or Chinese Communist Party document from the seventies. It's a whitewash, no one is responsible, just murky policies and procedures. One of the concluding recommendations is to require that Somali shooters wear blue UN-marked baseball hats and T-shirts.

There's only one thing I can do. I'll go to New York to talk to Matt's dad. I'll tell him how I think his son died, how in my opinion it didn't have to happen, that the UN screwed up, and it's dangerous for us because they won't accept responsibility, admit a mistake, change anything. People are riding in that same godforsaken convoy with that asshole security officer right now. It's wrong and we owe it to ourselves and our colleagues and the mission to try to do the right thing. Somalia is a catastrophe, the mission's a failure, the U.S. is humiliated, I'm humiliated, that pussy of a president is humiliated. I can't do anything about that but, goddamnit, I'm gonna try to get something right.

Andrew, November 15
Santo Domingo, The Dominican Republic

After the evacuation, they dumped us in the Dominican Fiesta, a cheap resort hotel miles from anywhere on the outskirts of Santo Domingo with slot machines in reception and drunks slumped over the bar. I got a room with a balcony overlooking a large palm-fringed pool. It could have all been very pleasant, if you'd just arrived from minus ten degrees in Chicago.

My clothes still smelled of Haiti, but the room reeked of some call girl's stale perfume. I turned on the TV; footage showed us boarding the evacuation flight at Port-au-Prince airport. Scruffy, despondent foreigners, beaten dogs getting on a plane. We looked like Sasha and Alexi at Phnom Penh airport three years ago. I was relieved not to see myself.

We went to Haiti and walked unarmed into the offices of the men with guns and dark glasses and told them to their faces that they couldn't go on doing what they were doing, that it was unacceptable and had to stop. I played a high-stakes game with an empty hand and felt clearheaded and alive. We all assumed that sooner or later the assassins would be forced from power—by America, the only country that could do it. But after Mogadishu, the *macoutes* paid to see President Clinton's hand, called his bluff. Just a gang of thugs on a dock and he folded. I still can't quite believe it.

Then the UN yanked us out against our will into this catatonic tropical suburbia, this retirement home for failed humanitarians, leaving us sidelined with no way back in. I'm nauseated by the oiled-up tourists, defeat, and guilt. Hung over in a pastel pink hotel room.

In the afternoons I watch the pool from my balcony. Amid the scent of coconut suntan oil and piña coladas, I remember my gracious friend at the morgue, and the smell of corpses drifts in from across the border. But it's just an olfactory hallucination. As the days slide by, I become nocturnal. First I couldn't get up in time for the poolside brunch and now I have breakfast at 5 P.M. and barely see daylight. When I'm awake I have no desire. There's nothing to feel here, so I feel nothing. Except when someone calls me Dr. Andrew. Then I get a dull ache in the center of my chest and have to walk away.

Even the sunsets over the Caribbean don't bring me any pleasure. In the Dominican Republic you see them, while in Haiti you can feel them with your eyes closed.

I fall into a fuzzy sleep, a Latin sitcom flickering on the TV screen. I'm dreaming of bodies running around on a beach chasing their own heads when the phone rings. The clock reads a blurry 4 A.M. and I'm not sure where I am. A high-pitched voice says, "Hello, mister, are you lonely?"

"Sorry, but who's this?" I still don't know where I am, until I hear the sound of the casino in the background. She's in the lobby.

"You, mister, room 525, are you lonely?"

She doesn't have what I need. No one here does.

I need a ticket out to another mission. Give me Mozambique or Angola, Bosnia or Liberia. Or a package deal with a month of each. I don't need a salary or a job title; I'll even pay you to take me there. Just get me off the sidelines and let me redeem myself.

Ken, November 17
Mogadishu

The problem is that no matter how good your intentions, eventually you want to kill someone yourself. I lie in bed at night and listen to the exchange of automatic weapons. So much for the ceasefire. After a while you can tell the difference between Somalis firing and Americans firing. The Somalis use AK-47s, which have a high, explosive *crack* sound. The Americans use M-16s, which have a lower, duller, *pop* sound. The Somalis fire wildly. The Americans respond in more measured tones. *Crack crack crack crack crack pop crack crack crack pop pop crack crack crack crack*. They call it fire discipline. The Americans have it, the Somalis don't. Good thing too, or a lot more of us would be dead.

Deep sleep. Body at rest. Gunfire erupts outside the window. The moment the ears process the sound and the brain recognizes it, the body panics. You go from total rest to total panic in a fraction of a second. But you don't even realize you're awake yet. It's not clear who or where you are. You only know that your entire body is bursting with energy and fear.

And there's nothing you can do but lie there. Heart races, stomach churns, palms sweat. You're taught to roll to the ground away from the windows. Put on your helmet and flak jacket. Make yourself small and protect your head. But after the first week you start to feel ridiculous lying on your bedroom floor naked with a helmet and flak jacket on that don't fit; anyway, getting up from the bed to put on the equipment defeats the purpose of hitting the deck. If the air-conditioning is working and the room is cold, you just say fuck it and lie in bed panicking quietly.

And then you start to wait for it at night. You start to want to hear it. You don't want to sleep. You want them to fight. And you're disappointed when it subsides. It's like when it rains and then it thunders and you're scared, and then something inside you switches and you accept it, want it to rain harder, thunder more. Or you are in an argument and you try not to snap but you start yelling and suddenly you're happy to be angry. Or you're having sex and that moment comes when you lose your inhibition, stop posing, and you both let loose, claw at each other, howl at the moon. Miss Heidi calls it emergency sex. It must have something to do with re-membering you're an animal.

So that's what I'm thinking, just kill each other, you animals. And I'm jealous. And that causes me some significant confusion. Because I'm sup-posed to be a human rights lawyer and I signed up for a humanitarian mission. We were going to re-create Cambodia—keep the peace, export democracy, save lives. We just forgot to tell the Somalis that. So they am-bush and mortar and snipe and mine the shit out of us and now Matt's dead. And I lie in bed at night and want them to die too because they're animals and they're trying to kill me.

CONDITION DELTA
Bosnia, Rwanda, and Haiti, 1994–1996

Yugoslavia. At the end of the Cold War, Bosnia, home to Muslims, Serbs, and Croats, ignited. Bosnian Serb forces conducted a campaign of systematic expulsions, rapes, and executions, "ethnically cleansing" Muslims from their midst. UN peacekeepers were on the ground and NATO patrolled the skies, but fearing robust use of air power would endanger UN forces, the international community refused to act. The UN Security Council declared Sarajevo and four other towns in Bosnia "safe areas" for Muslim civilians fleeing Serb paramilitary attacks. In July 1995, Dutch UN peacekeepers watched as Serb forces overran the safe haven of Srebrenica. Serbs executed eight thousand civilian men and boys and bulldozed them into unmarked graves. Passive on the ground, the UN instead became aggressive in court, creating an International Criminal Tribunal— the first since Nuremberg after World War II—to prosecute war crimes throughout the former Yugoslavia.

Rwanda. Throughout the early nineties, Rwandan Tutsi rebels from the Rwandan Patriotic Front (RPF) conducted a series of attacks against the Hutu-dominated Rwandan government from rebel bases along the northern border. On April 6, 1994, one week after U.S. forces withdrew from Somalia, a plane carrying the president of Rwanda was shot down over Kigali and massacres of Tutsis and moderate Hutus began within half an hour. UN peacekeepers withdrew while a radical Hutu militia, the *interahamwe,* engaged in an orgy of killing over ninety days at a rate three times that of the Holocaust. In the meantime the RPF broke out of Uganda, defeated the Rwandan Army, as well as the *interahamwe,* and occupied the country. But they were too late to save most Tutsis, and when it was over, 800,000 had been slaughtered. Having failed to intervene in genocide on the ground for the second time in two years, the UN again chose to prosecute it in court instead, creating the second war crimes tribunal since Nuremberg.

Haiti. In September 1994 the U.S. finally sent twenty thousand troops to Haiti in Operation Uphold Democracy, and in October Jean-Bertrand

Aristide returned from Washington, reclaiming his presidency. Among the American Troops, twelve hundred U.S. Special Operations Forces operated out of twenty-seven towns and cities to maintain order and suppress paramilitary groups' antidemocratic activity in the run up to parliamentary elections in the summer of 1995.

Somalia. On March 28, 1994, the U.S. withdrew the last troops of Operation Restore Hope from Mogadishu. The UN stayed on but slowly began to dismantle its sprawling presence.

Heidi, March 1994
Departure of U.S. Forces from Somalia

U.S. troops are preparing to withdraw. As they break down their tents and pack their equipment into containers for redeployment, the Embassy Compound begins to feel barren and deserted. Busloads of silent soldiers pass by as they move out toward the gates on their way to the airport. Some nod solemnly or give a sad wave of good-bye to the scattered groups of UN staff watching helplessly alongside the road. There's an audible shift in the atmosphere as the clamor of the soldiers' daily habits dies down.

At the seaport longshoremen load containers and large artillery onto a ship bound for Mombasa. The U.S. Liaison Office advises all American UN staff to leave and offers us a free ride on the ship. They believe all hell will break loose minutes after their departure. They wind us up with images of armed Somali militia scaling the walls to loot and pillage. Luke's taking the ship and insists I leave with him. I know that standing there in his marine uniform, chest out, chin up, he wishes he could just order me to leave. If his blue eyes were the sky, there'd be a storm coming. As the day gets closer, he becomes more persistent, irate even, as I continue to decline under the pretext of loyalty to the UN. I don't know whether he's concerned for my safety or angry that I doubt his judgment. But it's much too exciting to leave now. I want to stay and see what happens.

Yusuf doesn't want to leave either, and when he hears there's a job opening in the UN spokesman's office, he rushes there to apply. I'd like to believe it's me he's staying for, but I know better. My presence is just a bonus.

The night before the last of the Americans are to leave, I give a farewell dinner party for Luke. I set up a table and chairs in the sand outside my room. I find an old metal drum and drag it back to use as a barbecue. We grill lobster and get good and drunk. The music is loud and we laugh and dance and argue. The night is clear and the stars drip down like a thousand crystal chandeliers. Yusuf accuses me of flirting with Luke. An Israeli woman from the PX I invited accuses me of using her as a beard to cover my attraction to Luke.

They're both right, but I can't help pushing it. There's something inside me now that feels almost violent, as though all the months of gunfire and incoming mortar rounds and snipers and all the hundreds of hours listening to radio transmissions and deciphering live rounds and spent rounds and stray rounds and projectile ratios and minefield calculations are ready to explode inside of me and I have two choices: I can smash someone in the head with a rock, or I can reach across the table and grab Luke's face in my hands and kiss him. One way or the other, it's not going to end well.

At the moment I reach my decision to kiss Luke, we hear a gunshot close by. We all roll to the sand and wait for another report. We creep single-file through the dark around the side of the building. A group of Pakistani soldiers stands on a low rise over a body lying on the ground. They're all speaking at once in Urdu. We approach and they become silent. A young Pakistani soldier, eighteen, maybe twenty, lies on the concrete. A pool of blood has already begun to congeal around his head. Streams of it flow into words inscribed in wet cement during construction here months ago— MAKE LOVE NOT WAR, KEN CAIN '93. One of the soldiers tries to explain what happened: they were playing at drawing their weapons on each other, and a round discharged. Just kids with loaded guns. Another boy is dead for nothing. The party's over.

I climb into my bed alone in the dark and try to sleep. Outside I can hear the voices of Luke and Yusuf. They talk together late into the night. The intel operative playing his role, digging for information from the Somali playing his role as informer.

Early the next morning, I hear a thud at my doorstep. Naked, I rise and peer through the blinds. A cardboard box sits outside, my name written in black marker on the top flap. I throw a blanket around me, reach out, and drag the box into my room. Inside are books, jars of peanut butter, boxes of hot cocoa mix and instant macaroni and cheese, gum, candy, magazines. And a note from Luke, written on old U.S. Embassy Somalia stationery, thanking me for everything and wishing me luck. I instantly regret not having left with him. I could have gone as far as Mombasa at least and then caught a flight back into Mogadishu.

I turn on my radio and within seconds I hear my call sign. It's Marilyn; she wants me to phone her from a landline. Urgently, she says. I run out the door to the nearest office and call her back. She's been trying to reach me for an hour. It's Luke, she says. He came into the office breathless, asked me to call you and tell you to get over to the helipad before he boards. Hurry, she says, he might already be gone.

This time I don't hesitate. I don't want to regret never knowing what was between us, if there might have been a chance for us. I'm sure that at the last minute he had the same thought. I run and don't slow down, through a hole in the wall, between buildings, around cars. As I come around a curve in the road, I see the last helicopter rising.

I'm too late. He's gone.

I sink down to the edge of the helipad. The *whoosh* of the helicopter blades fades away and the sand settles around me. I sit for a long time, just feeling empty, twirling a blade of desert grass around my finger. The compound is peaceful. Mogadishu is quiet. The UN will plod on without the U.S. In the evening I boil water for macaroni and cheese. I eat and then climb into bed. I find my hand between my legs. After, I cry myself to sleep.

Ken, May 1994
Leaving Mogadishu

I'm out. The American military has withdrawn. It's the end of the line at the end of the world. The U.S. mission in the 'Dish, once replete with pizza shops and the Israeli PX, buzzing with officials and helicopters, is slowly disappearing. The UN will linger on passively while the warlords of Mogadishu devour our naïve idea. I want no part of it. Miss Heidi finds it exciting—she wants to stay and watch—which I find interesting. I liked the beginning; she likes the end. I had high expectations that crashed; hers were low and surpassed.

My itinerary is Mogadishu, Nairobi, Amsterdam, New York. Three continents in five days. I take a Hercules C-130 supply plane out of the 'Dish with a company of Egyptian soldiers. We deplane and walk together across the tarmac, the UN has a special landing field in Nairobi just for us. But when I leave their company and cross the threshold of the main terminal alone, I'm a regular civilian again, a tourist.

I have a seventy-two-hour layover in Nairobi. I check into a hotel, turn on the TV, order room service. The hotel is run by Indians, the room service is good, hot oily curry with that long saffron rice you just can't stop eating. Fire going in, fire going out. But it tastes so good it's worth it. The TV plays a continuous loop of Hindi films from Bollywood. I lie on the bed and watch for hours and hours. Women with long, curly black hair, in flowing green and red saris, singing and spinning on Himalayan mountains, in front of Moghul castles, barefoot on white beaches. Ten hours, maybe twenty hours. *Acha acha hay chodi chodi chodi jah hay.* I just stare. I shovel in curry and gape at all that black hair and bare feet. The only time I hear my voice is to order room service. There's a thick wet gauze cloth wrapped around my brain, everything is fuzzy. I like to blink.

In between movies and eating, I stare at the ceiling fan. I can watch it rotate indefinitely. When I close my eyes there's a Hindi film playing on my eyelids, but it's Danny and Matt and Heidi and Abdi spinning around on top of dozens of Bradley Fighting Vehicles that don't fight lined up in a row at the airport. I think about where Heidi is and what she must be doing two or three times a minute.

I'm not depressed exactly. I just don't want to move or speak—just stare. I'm content watching the ceiling fan. I'd prefer not to leave this room. *Acha acha chodi acha hay.*

My next flight stops in Amsterdam. They have a sparkly new airport. The faucets in the bathroom are plated with polished brass. There's a sensor that knows when you reach for water. Hot to the right, cold to the left. It's miraculous, all you have to do is reach. And you can drink it. Reach. Hot water. Reach. Cold water.

JFK Airport in New York is packed. The whole world is here but in civilian clothes, everyone looks calm and fat and pale.

I stay in Manhattan with my old roommate from law school. He works late into the night, so I can watch MTV and VH1 and CNN in peace. This OJ shit is amazing, sure is a lot of energy and attention on one case, two victims. Big massacres in Rwanda, hundreds of thousands dead. The killing started a week after the Americans pulled out of Somalia.

I have to go see Matt's dad while I'm here. I want to and I need to, but I'm terrified; it's like running out into the line of fire to get to the APC. I have to talk myself into it. I spend blurry days wandering around the city before I get the courage up. My hazy thoughts cycle over and over and over. They don't move forward or backward. I tell myself to shut up, but the cycle is relentless.

I know that if it were me, my dad would want to know. Everything.

But what is the right way to talk to a man about his son's death? All Heidi's boss did was clench his jaw and do it. But he's been doing it since Vietnam.

My father is a psychologist who happens to specialize in bereavement. I drive all the way to Ann Arbor to get his advice in person, twelve hours on a smooth, well-graded, fully regulated American interstate, thinking about anarchy in Africa. We go to a movie, then sit together talking in his car before going inside the house. Fifteen years ago, this moment, in this driveway, was exactly the time and place he'd stop to console me, saying the things a father says to his son after a hockey game lost because of a mistake I'd made.

This is not just about Matt and his father, it's also about me and mine. I'm taking this all so hard because I can picture Heidi pulling up in this driveway, wiping away tears, taking a big breath, and then knocking on the door to talk to my mom and dad about my death in an ambush. But how much does a grown man reveal himself to his father? I think what I really want to say is, "Dad, I'm scared, I don't want to die. And if I do, I want you to know how much I love you and Mom." But all I can bring myself to say is that I need advice about talking to Matt's dad.

It's good advice; my dad's done this before. He says I need to separate what I need to talk about from what Matt's dad wants to hear. "Don't assume his way to grieve is your way. Be alert to how he wants to deal with this," he says. My dad's no dummy, he knows I'm on the warpath over the UN's lethal incompetence. "It's not about you, son."

I drive back to New York, another twelve hours to think.

Matt's dad also happens to be a psychologist and I sit in the patient's chair in his office. I struggle to keep it together. This is the hardest thing I've ever done.

I tell him about the song they dedicated to his son, about how everyone noticed his eyes. He winces as I speak.

He changes the subject to the humanitarian work we are doing and what a high calling it is to try to make peace and how proud we all are of the work and the courage it takes, the lives we've saved.

I don't add to that.

Heavy silence.

I'm trapped in the patient's chair, we are eye to eye. I have nowhere to go, these offices are designed to do that. Matt's here, my dad's here, the security officer's here, Liza's here. This office is full of people. They're all waiting, listening. I have to face all of them. But who the fuck am I? We weren't even close friends. Matt's father is trapped in the doctor's chair. He has no way out of this. Ever.

He's no dummy either. He can tell I'm torn up, that I'm sitting on a landmine, trying to lead him somewhere. He looks at me warily. It's time.

I say, "Are you interested in knowing more about what happened that day? I can talk with you about that, if you want."

The room empties and it's just Matt's dad and me again. He's tall, sturdy-looking, fills his chair. I can see Matt in his face. His eyes are alive, you'd want to have a drink with him.

He catches it right away. "Are you on some kind of agenda?"

I have to answer. He buried his boy. He nurtured twenty-three years of life, from what I could see, twenty-three good years. But he missed the last six months. What an empty chasm those six months must be. He doesn't know me. But I saw his boy smiling at the podium every morning at India Base. He can't even picture India Base.

He does have an idea though. His boy died in the service of peace. And that's true. My mind races as that idea fills the room. He shifts in his chair but his eyes don't leave mine. It's a good question: What is my agenda? It depends how I choose to understand it, render it. It's a conscious choice that I have to make here and now, Matt's dad is looking at me in pain.

I can complain and whine about everything that went wrong, everyone's mistakes. I could cry in righteous indignation the rest of my life. I could write scholarly article after article criticizing UN policy, make a fucking career of it. We could demand a board of inquiry at the UN in New York, contact the insurance company, collect leaked documents, fight. I'd love for those pricks to have to answer.

But where does that get Matt in the end? And where does that get Matt's dad?

It's not about you, son.

Okay. Yes. Right. Let it lie. Let it die. Maybe that's a choice Matt's dad and I silently made together.

No, no agenda, I say, just that it's true what you said about the work. We did deliver a lot of food, saved many injured Somalis, released dozens of dying prisoners. If I were a civilian in an African civil war, I tell him, I'd want a man in a white Land Cruiser under a UN flag to show up with a brief to protect me. I tell him a story from a week before Matt died: I picked up a bleeding Somali guy off the street who'd been shot. Matt talked me through all the checkpoints to the nearest UN field hospital. He had arranged for the doctors to meet us outside the last checkpoint. I saw the injured guy later with a big scar, a big smile, and big words for Matt and me: "You saved my life." Matt was young but he was so calm on the radio, you could always trust India 1's voice on the other end. That voice was your center of gravity when you got in trouble outside the compound. That's why it felt like they hit us all in the heart.

He nods, he's listening closely, every word. I'm learning from him what this means to me.

Danny called my parents in Michigan last week. He left a message with my mom that the UN is planning a new mission to Rwanda when the fighting there stops. At first my mom was reluctant to pass the message on to me. I can understand, she's proud of my work but hasn't had a full night's sleep since I left for Somalia. Danny's going to be the deputy and he told her he wants me to come work for him.

I make a conscious decision to continue to believe.

It's true, I say to Matt's dad, it is a privilege to do this work. In fact I'm going back to Africa as soon as I can. I think I'll serve in Rwanda next.

He's pleased, and I guess I am too. Now we can both stand down. He nods. Let's get out of this office, he says. Let's go have a drink. Tell me more about the work at India Base.

Heidi, December 1994
Mogadishu, as the UN Evacuates

As time goes by, Yusuf and I drift further apart. He spends most of his time with the elders of his clan and I am almost always working. I've been hearing rumors that his family is putting pressure on him now to go back to his wife. I ask him, but he denies it. He leaves the compound for a few days to visit with an uncle recently arrived from Saudi Arabia. When he returns, he hardly speaks to me. Something is going on but I can't figure out what.

Our problems are overshadowed by all the preparation for the UN's evacuation from Somalia. I get a fax from HQ saying I'm being transferred to the mission in Haiti, but I delay telling Yusuf. I'm holding on to hope that he will say to hell with everyone, let's pack up and move to Nairobi, find some work there. Stay together.

Somali staff are apprehensive about getting their final payments and helpless as the war rages and they lose their income. UN security officers, armed with pistols and taser guns, act panicked and worry me most of all. Small, scattered uprisings occur with increasing frequency. The company responsible for cleaning the septic tanks stages a demonstration, blocking the main intersections in the compound with their shit-sucker trucks. Another group manages to pass through the front gate fully armed and stages a showdown.

We clean and pack all the weapons in the office—an assortment of rifles, machine guns, and handguns. The room stinks of cleaning fluid and burns our eyes. Green metal containers are filled with ammunition to be counted and logged. I come across a small purple metallic orb so beautiful it evokes the essence of lavender. Soothing. Calming. In the palm of my hand, it's cool as ice. It's a grenade.

Sitting at the boss's desk, I slide open the top drawer. Among the forgotten papers lying creased and stained is a small plastic Ziploc bag. Inside is torn metal. I flip the bag over. Written on surgical tape is Matt's name. I puzzle over what this is but then recognize the splintered fragment of a bullet. The bullet. It sits in my hand, cleaned of the flesh and blood it ripped through. It's a terrible, secret thing that longs to be buried deep underground. I wonder if, when no one else is around, the boss takes this small plastic bag out and remembers, or if he has simply forgotten it's waiting there.

In the evening, there's a knock at my door and I open it to find Yusuf's friend Omar. He holds a bundle of bright green *khat* in his hand. I tell him Yusuf isn't here. It's you I want to see, he says, we need to have a conversation. There's something in his voice, in the look he gives me. I'm on guard immediately. Omar is thin, with narrow shoulders, and not taller than me. His salt-and-pepper hair makes him look older than his thirty-five years. There's something in his demeanor, both warm and cold, that makes people, if not nervous, then at least alert. I think it's the gold-filled tooth near the front of his mouth. Puts you in mind of a pirate.

I throw some cushions on the floor and set some tea to boil. I add a cup of sugar, a handful of cloves and cardamom, and a single tea bag and pour it all into a big thermos. I've become an expert at making the sweet tea to chew *khat* with. But I've never chewed without Yusuf. Somali women rarely chew, and then only in private with their husbands, using it as an aphrodisiac. It feels too intimate to be doing this alone with another man and I'm suddenly suspicious of Omar's intentions.

We sit together on the floor chewing the *khat* and waiting for the stimulant to take effect. We talk for a while about what's going on in Omar's neighborhood of North Mogadishu. The local warlord has instituted Sharia law, and punishment of the guilty has become a daily spectacle in the public square. Arms and feet dangle bodiless from a tree in front of the old courthouse with its pockmarked concrete façade.

We talk about everything but Yusuf, which tells me that's exactly what Omar's here to talk about. It can't be good; nobody waits this long to talk about good news. Each time I sense Omar is getting around to the reason for his visit, I veer off onto another topic. Anything to delay. I almost wish he would lean over and kiss me. I could deal more easily with that.

The room becomes quiet and we sit for a while in silence. I meet his eyes—I can't hide forever—and he understands I'm ready to listen. He sits tall and braces his hands on his knees. His face changes, becomes expressionless. He's here in an official capacity.

"I've long recommended to Yusuf that he end your relationship," he says. "It's nothing personal, this is business. Yusuf's wife's family is wealthy and powerful. The elders of her clan are involved in this decision also. Yusuf has caused a scandal for both his family and hers."

Although I expected it would be something like this, I find myself stunned to hear the words.

"No. You're wrong," I tell Omar. "Yusuf and I are adults; there's no one else involved in deciding our future." But even as I say this, I understand it's not true. "I want you to leave now," I say. "Maybe Yusuf can find his balls and come tell me this himself."

"Please," he says with authority, "I'm not finished. Take a seat."

I'd like to kick him. Instead, I take a few deep breaths and sit back down.

"Yusuf refuses to leave you," he tells me. "His uncle from Saudi Arabia has arrived," he continues. "He's counseled him that now he must marry you. There's no other choice. Yusuf asked that I speak with you, to help you to understand that you need to accept the role of second wife."

Okay, this I didn't expect. I've taken the game too far this time.

"Naturally," Omar goes on, "you will not have the same privileges as the first wife, but for all intents and purposes you will be left alone and can continue your relationship with Yusuf. It won't be much different than it is now.

"Look at it this way," he says, "you let him go to Toronto to see his wife two or three times a year, let him put in an appearance there, maybe he gives her another child, and then he returns to you in New York."

Surprisingly, my answer is not immediately within my grasp. I ask for a few days to think about it. Omar agrees and leaves me sitting alone on the floor, my thoughts racing both from the *khat* and from the ultimatum I've been given.

When Yusuf gets back to the room late in the evening, I mention that Omar came by to see me. He doesn't ask why, pretends not to be interested. I want to slap him. I decide in that moment that I need to get away from him. I tell him I'm going to Nairobi for a few days, I need to spend some time by myself, think about things. He doesn't ask what things. There's already distance between us. How different from my relationship with my former American husband, where marriage meant that nothing was left unrevealed.

In Nairobi I sit in a hotel room for three days. I chain-smoke and order room service. Flip through the channels. Nothing but Hindi films. Outside it's raining and chilly. I lie in a hot bath and for an hour, intrigued, I think, yes, what the hell, I'll do it. And then I lie on my bed for the next hour, cocooned in blankets, thinking, no way, this is absurd. I imagine calling my mother on the telephone from my smoky room in Nairobi. "Guess what, Mom? I'm going to be Yusuf's second wife."

Becoming Yusuf's second wife had always been a joke for us. My friends bring me newspaper articles describing the murders of second and third wives by first wives, telling me, "You see what will happen to you?" But it's not a joke anymore. The elders have sent this offer to me and expect an answer. Unknowingly I have become a player in this tradition. I was allowed to sit with the men, eat with them, and chew *khat* with them, deceived into believing we were all friends. I naïvely assumed I was a privileged insider.

If I reject his offer, I'll never see Yusuf again. If I agree, things won't continue the way they have been. My privileges will be revoked. As a wife I'll be accorded an unwanted respect, excluded from all the things that have made me long to be a part of this culture. I'll be the once-wild American girl who now in all her actions has to take into consideration the reputation of her extended family. So I have two choices: give up everything I've enjoyed, or give up everything I've enjoyed.

And if we marry, what will Yusuf do without that wild American girl? Replace her with another, of course. My surrogate will reap the benefits while I stand veiled on the sidelines.

When I return to Mogadishu, I still haven't come to a decision. I find Yusuf in his office behind his desk. The raspy voice of John Lee Hooker sings out from the portable CD player next to him. "Mama, talk to your daughter for me . . ." His big dark eyes look out at me from above the rim of his glasses and he smiles. I feel a little sorry for him. In sneakers, jeans, and a Nike T-shirt, he looks every bit as American as me. But it's a façade and this is the first time I can see behind it to the other man, the one who holds his traditions above all else. He doesn't ask, and I don't tell him, but I've just made my choice.

On the way back to my room, I start making a mental checklist of what I'll need for Haiti.

Ken, January 1995
Kigali, Rwanda

Monsieur Innocent is our houseboy, which isn't quite right because he's not a boy and he doesn't do any housework. When we agreed to rent this place in Kigali, we told the landlord we didn't need any help. But Innocent came with the house, he was in his little room out back when we moved in and wasn't going anywhere. He demanded a hundred dollars a month. It's three times the going rate and we didn't want him anyway, so we refused. But there was something about the way he insisted that made it clear he wasn't negotiating. We conceded and now he lives with us.

He's in his late twenties or early thirties, medium tall, mocha-colored skin, gentle smile, very skinny in the same nylon trousers and tattered dress shirt every day, an utterly nondescript African man—except for the alarmed, wounded look in his wide bloodshot eyes and his chin tucked into his neck in a permanent state of recoil.

One night we were having Mutzig beers in the living room. The Mutzig brewery was the first factory in Rwanda to open back up after the war. Monsieur Innocent walked by, saw the beers, and his face lit up. "Mutzigi, Mutzigi!" So we invited him to sit down and have a drink with us. He doesn't speak English and only speaks about thirty words of French, which works out fine because I only speak ninety if I'm lucky. It forces you to distill your idea down to its essentials and make your point directly, which is refreshing.

After the third Mutzigi, Monsieur Innocent started to open up and told us his story. There were three thousand Tutsis in this neighborhood before the war. Only five are left now; the *interahamwe* Hutu militia killed all the rest. They came looking for him on the first night of the massacres, they had lists of Tutsis to kill. They called out his name. He hid in the crawl-space of his house, listening to his neighbors beg and scream and die from machetes and studded sticks and hand grenades. He saw it through the crack in the wall. He heard his neighbors beg to be shot instead of hacked to death. Some paid the killers for a bullet. In the middle of the first night, when it got quiet, he ran to the neighborhood garbage dump and buried himself deep.

A Hutu neighbor saw him hide there, kept his secret, and sometimes left bananas by the side of the pit. In the middle of the night, when it was quiet, he'd crawl up and eat the bananas. He stayed there for three weeks. When the Tutsi rebels from the Rwandan Patriotic Front finally chased out the *interahamwe* and occupied his neighborhood, he heard them patrolling and he crawled out of the garbage pile alive. But his fiancée was dead. Every Tutsi he knew was dead. All but five. He named the survivors slowly. Over and over again. "Madame Chantal, Monsieur Didier, Mademoiselle Antoinette, Monsieur Jean-Baptiste, Madame Clementine."

Now every night, after the third or fourth Mutzigi, he reenacts the story, sometimes several times in a night. *"Monsieur Ken, interahamwe arrive, kwa kwa kwa"*: when the killers arrive he makes a chopping motion with the side of his hand against his neck, hard, and makes the hacking noise. *"Monsieur Innocent allez au garbage"*—he puts his arms in front of his head and makes a jumping motion when he hides in the garbage pit—*interahamwe demand, Innocent? Où est Monsieur Innocent? Monsieur Innocent dit, No!"* The *interahamwe* call out his name, he slams his hand on the table when he says, No! Monsieur Innocent is not here! *"Monsieur Innocent mange des bananes, interahamwe, kwa kwa kwa tout les Tutsis, eh la comment!?"* He makes a terrified face as he slowly peels back and eats the banana while everyone else dies, and then jumps back in the pit. *"L'Armee Tutsi arrive, Monsieur Innocent, oui!"* He jumps up and out of the pit when the Tutsi rebels arrive and save him. *"Mais tout le monde kwa kwa kwa,"* but everyone is dead. Except Madame Chantal, Monsieur Didier, Mademoiselle Antoinette, Monsieur Jean-Baptiste, Madame Clementine.

Sometimes he cries, sometimes he just sighs, but always he looks up into my face in panicked bewilderment and says, *"Monsieur Ken, eh la, comment?!"* I don't know exactly what the *eh la* means, but it punctuates everything; he says it in exasperation and passionate disbelief, exhaling, a low growl. But I understand *"Comment?"* How, Mr. Ken? How did you people let it happen?

The UN was here when the massacres started, twenty-five hundred troops. UN Headquarters in New York knew it was being planned, they had files and faxes and informants and they sat in their offices, consulted each other, and ate long lunches.

Most UN forces ran to the airport, they couldn't get out fast enough. This is not a case in which the UN failed to send troops to stop genocide. An armed, predeployed UN force evacuated as soon as it started. All those signatures on the Genocide Convention, dozens of rapturously celebrated human rights treaties, a mountain of documents at UNHQ on the subject of genocide, law professors all over the world making a living talking about this, and we *evacuated.* Tanks and supply planes and helicopters and soldiers sat useless and stationary for six months in Somalia, two hours away by C-130, and then drunk peasants armed with machetes and lists of names killed 800,000 civilians in Rwanda. And we evacuated. *Eh la, comment?*

So I'm here a little late. My job is to help collect evidence for the UN War Crimes Tribunal, the biggest genocide investigation since the Holocaust. There are 800,000 bodies rotting under the African sun. The entire country smells of decomposing flesh. The sickly sweet smell is nauseating and trips the gag reflex. It gets onto your clothes, into your hair, onto the bed sheets, the kitchen utensils.

I walk a field full of that evidence. A jaw here, a clavicle there, a femur here. Dead black skin wraps round skulls, except where the machete gash reveals white bone. I see a baby skeleton shrouded in a colorful shawl hanging from the mother skeleton's back. I wonder who died first. The baby skeleton still has tiny, clear, clipped fingernails.

We flew a special team of forensic pathologists in from Holland to help us number the dead at the site. The farther I go into the field, the farther I have to walk to return, and I start to panic. I freeze with one foot in the air, turning and turning on the other foot. I can't put the elevated foot down without stepping on human remains and I can't bear to break another bone. The hotshot chief investigator from Holland is back at the helicopter retching from the smell. I can hear him retch as I stand in the field with one foot in the air.

There is an old woman in my synagogue back home. Every year during the High Holy Days, she recites in Yiddish the names of neighbors from her village in Poland she lost during the Holocaust. The synagogue is always full with kids and noisy with ushers and whispering. No matter how hard the rabbi tries or how solemn the prayers, they never win the congregation's full attention. Except when this ghost-white, yellow-haired survivor recites the names. Her weak, Yiddish-inflected voice trembles but finds strength in those names. She's tiny and you can't see her in the crowd. But those names emanate from nowhere in the silent synagogue and find you in your seat, bring you to a village in Poland, show you an old lady's devastation.

My foot is in the air above a sea of skeletons and the hotshot is retching and that old lady is reciting names into my ear, but it's not Yiddish, she's whispering Chantal and Clementine and Jean-Baptiste and it's Africa and they're alive and it's now.

Andrew, February 1995
UN Headquarters, New York

The only things alive in this office are the African violet and me. But the violet's been overwatered and the UN is drowning me in thick patient files. The less life-threatening the case, the more words written. Five years ago in Cambodia, Sofany's file was a single sheet of paper on a clipboard.

It wasn't supposed to end this way, in an office pushing paper. After the debacle in Haiti I'd been desperate for a new mission. But the boss just expected me to idle in the Dominican Republic, waiting for the Americans to return President Aristide to power by force, after which we'd all go happily back and reinstall ourselves as if nothing had ever gone wrong. I couldn't accept that lie, so I resigned and took a three-month contract here at UN Headquarters in New York to tread water while I lined up the next mission. It was a means to an end, and the end was redemption.

That was fifteen months ago.

One of today's files is marked "Postlewait." My God, Heidi's finally out of Somalia. I hurry out into the waiting room and give her a big hug. The patients and the nurses stare at us. Let them wonder.

We go into my office and suddenly it's awkward. Maybe I should have had one of my colleagues examine her, but I say nothing, hand her a paper gown, and leave the room while she undresses.

As she lies back on my examining couch, the stiff paper creases and protrudes in the wrong places, distorting her shape. We're both unnerved by this forced intimacy. I take her pulse at the wrist. It's running fast and her hand is sweaty. Two minutes ago we were embracing, delighted to see each other, and now I'm Dr. Thomson, UN medical officer, part of the headquarters administration and she's vulnerable, body and future exposed before me. If I find anything physically wrong, I'm obligated to ground her in New York until it can be treated.

I wrap the blood pressure cuff around her slender arm, pump it up, and listen through the stethoscope for the systolic and diastolic readings. With most patients I'd be gossiping by now: asking about the kids, the boss; where did you get that winter tan; don't forget the mammogram, it's important; how was the last mission? I love this part of being a physician. Patients are endlessly original, varied, and surprising. What a strange privilege to examine another human.

But I'm not enjoying the privilege of examining Heidi. She's making me feel like a med student again. Now I'm the one that's sweating and my heart's racing and I'm sure she's noticing out the corner of her eye. I think back to the rooftop parties in Phnom Penh, where I wanted to be around her because she was forthright and insouciant and had nothing to prove. She fascinated me then, and since she's been at the nerve center of the U.S. military's fiercest battle since the Vietnam War, she fascinates me even more. She's everything but a patient, and that makes me feel anything but a doctor.

And it's not over: now I've got to listen to her heart. I slide the stethoscope under the crinkled paper and close my eyes, just need to hear those cardiac sounds and check for murmurs. It's all normal.

When I push my hands into the four corners of her abdomen to check her liver and spleen and intestines, she tenses up and squirms with pain and the paper rips. She says she's been having stomach cramps. I'm afraid I'm going to have to ask for a stool sample. How awkward for both of us. I get her to sit up and I listen to her chest at the back and it's easier, already less intimate. I skip the throat exam: she's already put up with more than enough.

"Okay, Heidi, we're done."

I escape to the corridor as she rips off that dehumanizing piece of paper. I've forgotten what her blood pressure was, but what the hell, I'm not taking it again. Two minutes later she's fully clothed once more. I toss my stethoscope on the desk and I'm Andrew and she's Heidi and we breathe again and grin at each other. She asks me whether she's going to live. She turns the office into her living room, her feet up on a chair, her right hand poised in mid-air cradling a nonexistent cigarette. Not if you keep smoking, I tell her. That's as far as I go; nobody has much luck telling Heidi what to do. She changes the subject and tells me I should escape to Haiti with her.

I never really failed at anything important in life before Haiti and that retreat still rocks me to the core. I need to find a mission where I can do more good than harm and get back to work. Heidi doesn't get that. She thinks that going back there is as easy as getting on a plane. But U.S. marines have landed in Haiti, Aristide is back in power, the *macoutes* are in hiding, and it's a tropical beach party there now. Haiti's at peace. What I need is a country at war.

Heidi, February 1995
Manhattan

I leave Andrew sitting in his little office overlooking the river, waiting for the next patient. And the next one after that and on and on. It's already late in the day, so I decide not to go back to work. After the job I did in Somalia, I feel like I'm a double agent, sitting around the office with three other secretaries, pretending to be one of them. They have no idea who I am now.

As I walk through the deserted streets of the Lower East Side to the apartment I've sublet, the wind cuts painfully through my thin coat. The cold gets in my bones and stays there. Only an African sun can warm me again. Hanging by its last thread from a fire escape above, a weather-beaten wind chime plays a mournful tune. If I collapsed on the street, no one would notice me until dawn when the garbage trucks pass by.

I used to have a lot of friends here in New York. Now most of them have moved on or are busy attending to their own lives. They go to work and come home and worry about paying the rent and how many years it will take them to save enough for a down payment on a house in Queens. I want to escape that for as long as I can. Ordinary life will always be here; I can come back to it any time.

In the mailbox I find a thick envelope with Yusuf's familiar handwriting. No return address. I hurry upstairs and settle in to read the letter. In page after page he beautifully describes his longing for me. But I know it's the memory of us that he's hanging on to, not the possibility of us. It's safe to say these things now, from wherever he is in East Africa.

Seven-thirty in the evening. Thirty-four degrees outside. Nothing to do, no one to call. If I could be anywhere right now, I'd be sitting at a table in the sand outside the Israeli PX, drinking a Macabee with Ken. Instead I crawl under the blankets fully clothed and try to stay warm.

After two years in Somalia, I became accustomed to sharing the bathroom in the mornings with a dozen other women and eating all my meals under the scrutiny of five hundred soldiers. I can't bear to be by myself here. I want to look in a mirror in the morning and see another woman's face inches from my own, as we both put our mascara on. I want to see my friend's shoes revealed under the toilet stall door and immediately break into a getting-ready-for-work conversation. I want to walk into the cavernous din of a mess hall and scan the room for friendly faces to share a meal with. What I don't want is to be here looking at fire escapes across the alley and crying into my Chinese takeout.

First thing in the morning I go to see Andrew for the verdict. Returning a stool sample to him yesterday was mortifying. He has a big smile on his face when he tells me the test results were negative. He shows me his handwriting in my file, "Fit for Haiti."

We go downstairs to the cafeteria for coffee. At a table near the window overlooking the East River, we watch tugboats endlessly push barges up and down the waterway. A few small motorboats sit patiently in the center near a tiny island, a good place to catch striped bass as they migrate from New England. I'm uneasy with Andrew, and the river is a good place to focus my attention. The illusion of who I thought he was started to break down yesterday as I sat there in that paper gown, swinging my feet back and forth at the edge of the examining table.

He looks so pale and thin, even under his many layers of sweaters. Like a detective, he grills me for information on other people we know, wants to know where everyone is, what they're doing. He's ravenous for information. It's obvious New York is killing him. He can sit here taking blood pressure readings and listening to coughs no more than I can work upstairs filing and copying and answering telephones. I wait for him to admit that but he doesn't.

I feel disconnected from him. He's a civilian now. By his own choice.

213

He left us out there and now he wants to know all about how we're doing. I try to be compassionate.

He asks what I've heard from Ken. I tell him about Michael, a guy we worked with in Somalia, a tough, hard-drinking Irish soldier who's spent twenty years of his life clearing some of the world's worst minefields. He met up with Ken in Rwanda. They went for a long walk together in the hills and, in a field, came upon dozens of bodies, feet cut cleanly off at the ankles.

Michael said he imagined what his wife was doing at that moment: cooking dinner, taking out the garbage, helping the kids with their homework. All he could think about was how much he needed to hear her voice. When they got back to town, he phoned her immediately. He said he broke down and wept for a full five minutes as soon as he heard her "hello." He lasted only a couple of weeks in Rwanda before he requested a transfer back to Mogadishu, traumatized. Couldn't even speak his first day back. All of his years of demining, he said, hadn't prepared him for that field of bodies.

But Ken's not a soldier. What could possibly have prepared him for that field of bodies? There's only so much he can take, I tell Andrew. I've seen him when he reaches his limit. It happened after he was ambushed, and again after Matt died. But I was with him and able to watch out for him. It was nothing that a bottle of vodka and a caress couldn't contain, but I don't think there's anyone in Rwanda to do that for him.

I should be there, Andrew says. I should be there with Ken. Yeah, no shit, I think to myself angrily. I want to tell him to buck up, stop thinking so much.

Come to Haiti, I tell him. I've been putting in applications for Ken in every office I can think of, trying to get him out of Rwanda. It's calm in Haiti now, different from when you were there. We can have a good life. He looks at me as though I'm inviting him to a massacre.

I feel guilty when we part at the elevator. He's embarrassed and wants to talk about it, explain himself. But I need to be back out in the field and I'm the one with medical clearance and a ticket and I've got to go now.

Ken, April 1995
Butare, Southern Rwanda

There are two rooms in the lockup. One is upstairs and has windows, a vinyl floor, and a light. It might have been a storeroom or the back office to a shop before the war. There are about a hundred prisoners here now, standing in each other's waste. At first you can't breathe, but you start to get used to it. The prisoners clap rhythmically when I come in. It sounds weird, like the Soviets applauding their figure skaters.

There's a hallway out and stairs down. Three men are sprawled out on the landing. It must be where they drag the sick ones. One guy's mouth is wide open and he's sticking his chin up like he's straining for more air, his eyes are staring and blinking a lot but not focusing. He's swimming in his pants. He has sparse sickly buds of black hair on his head and face. I step over him to get to the stairs. His eyes don't follow my foot as it crosses over his face, but he whispers in more air.

I go downstairs to the other lockup in the cellar. I want to see the cellar. Sergeant Jean-de-Dieu d'Amour, my escort from the Rwandan Patriotic Army's gendarmerie, told me I don't want to see it, but it's my job. He opens the steel door slowly and then backs off and shakes his head at me. A wall of stink the color of diarrhea and the taste of tequila puke slams into me. My head jerks down and away, I cough-sneeze, my mouth starts to water like right before you vomit, but I choke it down. I gotta go in there. If not I should have just stayed in New York.

It's pitch black inside, no lights, no windows, concrete floor. Before I went to Cambodia I bought one of those pencil flashlights cops and Con Ed guys use, but I always forget to bring it. This time I remembered and I step in with the pencil light ahead of me. I want to at least try to estimate the number of prisoners in here. I need to stomach this smell long enough to do that.

Men move back to accommodate me as I step forward. The flashlight catches shiny shadowed half glimpses of sweaty stubble-bearded men swaying and bobbing, dying eyes. They murmur as I move into the room. My little pen is the only source of light. As the door closes, the gap in back of me where I entered closes too. The men move toward me and swallow the light. I start to feel hands on me as they try to fit me into their rotting midst. They're chest-to-back, there's no spare space, the volume I occupy has to be replaced somewhere else in the room, and they need to feel me to orient their moves. Wet, bony, trembling hands gently find my arms and shoulders and neck and ears and head and back every time I shift. The temperature in the room is the temperature of the fevered human body. This must be what the hold of a slave ship was like. The penlight shines off glistening brown faces rimed in white and yellow crust. I say United Nations, United Nations. I'm not sure why.

215

I'm gonna puke. I'm ashamed to leave them I try to back out slowly the entire room has to shift again to accommodate the displaced space of me backing away they murmur and swim along the flashlight beam. I'm out. The door swings closed and Jean-de-Dieu d'Amour looks at me on the other side with sympathy. I was inside less than a minute that will never end.

We walk back upstairs. I step over the guy in the hallway. He's in the same position as before but he looks a little different. He's not blinking. That taut, stretched, gasping look is gone. There's no tension in the muscles or tendons. I grab Jean-de-Dieu d'Amour and say we need to get a doctor, I'll radio headquarters. He says no, he's dead. He's dead. I have to say it to myself a few times to believe it. He died while I was downstairs. He didn't move at all, he just turned off.

Okay, I know what I have to do.

We go back to the city. I drop Jean-de-Dieu d'Amour off at the gendarmerie and drive to the Senegalese UN Battalion HQ. The lockup I visited is in their Area of Responsibility. I jump out of the Land Cruiser and find the sergeant. I ask him how he is, praise Allah that he is well, ask how his parents are, his wife, kids, prime minister, everyone I can think of. Greetings with Muslim West Africans can take a full five minutes; they go through the whole list of important people in your life, and you have to reciprocate. Eventually you both run out of people to ask after, and only then can you move on.

I tell him the genocide suspects the RPA has arrested are dying in one of the remote lockups I just visited. I need some soldiers and a truck to help me transfer them to the official prison in town, where at least the Red Cross can register them, give them food and medicine. Some water. And soap. I raise my eyebrows and exhale through my nose hard. He knows the smell too. He's very sorry, he can't spare any soldiers or a truck, but he hopes my family stays well.

All right, I've played this game before. The first problem in a release or transfer negotiation is always logistics; you need a helicopter or truck more than you need the Geneva Conventions. So I find the battalion commander, pay respects, praise everyone he cares about at length, and then ask him if he has plans for dinner tonight. No plans. Good. It would be my honor to host you at my home tonight, sir.

I give a bunch of money to Monsieur Innocent and the cook. They'll use about half of it and pocket the rest. We make a feast. I fill the Senegalese commander with piles of chicken and goat, French wine and duty-free single-malt Scotch, fruit, and pie. I escort him to his jeep at the end of the night. His driver is asleep underneath, lying on his AK-47. The commander loved the single-malt Scotch and wants to reciprocate: if there's ever anything I can do for you Monsieur Ken, *s'il vous plaît*. Yes sir, thank you for asking. There is one thing, sir. I have an emergency at the lockup outside of town, I know how professional your soldiers are, I would trust them to accompany me on any mission. Could I request a small squad and a truck tomorrow? He'd never say yes if I asked him during the day in his office, but he can't say no here and now. See the sergeant in the morning, he says, I'll tell him to arrange everything.

The next step will be harder. In the morning I go see Jean-de-Dieu's boss, Lieutenant Alex, at the gendarmerie. The RPA officers hate us. I understand, I kind of hate us too. A drunk Hutu militia with machetes killed 800,000 humans in ninety days. The UN evacuated and the only action Clinton took was to block other countries from intervening. Don't cross the 'Mogadishu line.' Let them kill each other this time. So the Tutsis died a thousand deaths for our cowardice. Every three hours for ninety days.

But Rwanda is a tiny country with only a few paved highways. The Hutu militias were undisciplined, lightly armed, and they fought badly. It was the opposite of Somalia; it would have been easy to intercept them and stop the massacres, and everyone knows it. Lieutenant Alex knows it because the RPA did it. When the massacres started, they broke out of their enclaves in the north, smashing weak, drunken, undisciplined enemy positions everywhere they made contact. But they had no airlift, so it took three months to move overland all the way south and west, and by then it was too late.

What is the value of American power if we don't use it? We didn't stop genocide here because we failed in Somalia. They said it at the White House, they said it at the State Department, even the cooks and maids here know. To me, that means if we had succeeded in Somalia, we would have intervened here. Historians can write a mountain of books and politicians can give a thousand speeches disputing that, but a million civilian corpses are decomposing right now in unmarked graves in Bosnia and Rwanda. And the dead read our books and the dead listen to our speeches.

Hundreds of Somalis and eighteen Americans die in one firefight and we split. You think no one here noticed? The genocide started April 6, the week after the U.S. withdrew all that hardware from Somalia. The first thing the *interahamwe* did was to kill ten Belgian UN soldiers. They cut their dicks off and put them in their mouths, just like Aidid did to one of the Americans. They knew the UN would never fight, that we'd pull out right away. Which we did. If you are a dictator, terrorist, or rebel, and are still alive, it means you know how to assess the danger posed by your enemies. And in Somalia we just showed the world how dangerous we aren't.

So I have hat in hand when I go see Lieutenant Alex from the RPA. I like these guys and I respect them. They're disciplined and they're straight and they have an impossible task. It's as if Jews who survived the Holocaust formed a government after the war, not in Israel but in Germany. And then had to figure out how to arrest and prosecute the Nazis in their midst. So the RPA has arrested tens of thousands of Hutus on suspicion of genocide, and I come crying that some of them are dying in detention. Lieutenant Alex will be unimpressed by the tragedy and even less impressed by the hypocrisy of the messenger. I get it and I hope he can see that I get it: the UN passively watched his people die, and now that the fighting is over, we're back and we're whining about the well-being of the perpetrators. It doesn't make a hell of a lot of sense from where he sits.

Which is behind a huge desk with nothing on it except his gun. He never smiles and doesn't say much. I ask if he got a report from Jean-de-Dieu, that the prisoners are dying at the lockup, we need to transfer them to town. He says it's not a priority. I say I understand that, but I have to make a report, it's my job. It will go to headquarters, we'll both have to do a shitload of paperwork, let's just clean it up quickly now instead, between us. He says he has no transport to spare, you people need to give us trucks. Okay, Lieutenant, so that means if I can get transport, you'll authorize a transfer? He stares at me at length and doesn't say anything, then nods half an inch and flutters his long bony fingers, like he's sweeping me out of his office. Go. That's all he says, just, "Go."

I grab Jean-de-Dieu, he grabs four RPA soldiers for an armed escort, we pick up the Senegalese UN soldiers and their truck and we're off. I sit in the bed of the truck. Rwanda is made up of a thousand little mountains that push the air up, creating pillowy volcanoes of clouds, churning from white to black and every gray variation before your eyes. Under the light-show lies a riot of green vegetation over red clay soil. I lie down on an army rucksack, warm wind and light rain blow in my face.

I stare up into the mountains of clouds. I ask Jean-de-Dieu to teach me a song, I want to learn a Rwandan song. He teaches me the RPA victory song. He says he's been singing it since he was a little kid in Uganda: "Victory, the sons of Rwanda are victorious." We rise up, fists in the air, rocking back and forth on our heels on the flatbed of a Senegalese military truck en route to transfer dying genocide suspects to wait in a different prison to be executed. Jean-de-Dieu and I sing the victory song, do the dance. He's ecstatic. Victory to the sons of Rwanda.

I think I'm actually starting to understand. I was hell-bent on being an effective humanitarian in Cambodia and Somalia. But a naïve fog is finally lifting. Revealed is a train wreck of illusions, the depravity of someone else's war, the futility of a competence stillborn there. To understand this you have to become this.

The gendarmerie requires three elements to complete the dossier against the accused: a charge from the arresting officer, a witness testimonial, and a statement from the accused. In these remote lockups the soldiers arrest Hutus after a Tutsi in good standing denounces the suspect as a killer. We think that about a third of the accused are innocent, denounced on the basis of property disputes, family feuds, or fights over women. But the RPA is in a box. The other two-thirds of these guys killed, tortured, and raped sadistically. The result is that there are almost as many of these lockups dotting the countryside as there are mass graves.

When the RPA soldiers arrest suspects, they usually beat the shit out of them, execute a few of the worst among them, and hold the rest until more senior officers, like Jean-de-Dieu, come out from the city to transfer them to the official prison. But they don't take statements out here in the bush.

So Jean-de-Dieu has a big job today. There must be a hundred prisoners in the good room upstairs and another fifty in the bad cell downstairs. It's a two-hour drive back to the city and the Senegalese won't want to wait here long with their truck. So Jean-de-Dieu has two hours to conduct 150 genocide interrogations.

We walk into the well-lighted room upstairs. The prisoners applaud rhythmically again. I stand against the back wall with my translator. I'm just an observer, this is the Rwandan government's jurisdiction. Jean-de-

Dieu tells the prisoners he's here to transfer anyone with a complete file to the prison in the city. The prisoners clap heartily, some even smile, they look back at me and nod. Then Jean-de-Dieu says you have to confess to complete the file. Does anyone want to confess?

The prisoners are silent. The idea sinks in. For me too. If they confess to genocide, we will transfer them to an official prison, where they'll be registered, monitored by the Red Cross, get doctors, medicine, and food—and will be officially presumed guilty. If they don't, they stay here where they are sick, starved, and tortured and sometimes executed—but not yet officially charged. There's still a chance they can escape, bribe their way out, someone powerful can intervene. Big decision, bad dilemma, no time.

No one moves. Jean-de-Dieu asks again, does anyone confess? An old guy raises his hand. Yes, I killed. How many? Three, I killed three. With what weapon? A machete. But I was ordered to do it. Line up outside. He stands slowly and walks out to the truck. Just walks out. That was the interrogation and the confession. It took thirty seconds. Jean-de-Dieu notes it in the dossier. The old guy is officially guilty of genocide now. A middle-aged man raises his hand. I killed four. And my son killed three. He points across the room. A boy picks his head up expectantly. He must be ten. That can't be the son who killed. He killed three, the man repeats and points at the boy again. The boy looks at me, wide-eyed, smiles vaguely. He has the straightest, whitest teeth I've ever seen. Jean-de-Dieu takes their names and they line up outside. A young man rises and says, I killed five. With a grenade. But the *interahamwe* would have killed me if I didn't, I had no choice. I killed eight, I had a gun. It goes on like this for an hour. Half the room empties and they line up outside.

Jean-de-Dieu goes downstairs. I'm not going back down there. I go outside. I need air. The men who have confessed are lined up in neat rows squatting on the ground in each other's lap, one guy's knees at the other guy's armpits, elbows to shoulders, silent, immobile, passive. There are only two RPA soldiers outside; the other two are inside with Jean-de-Dieu. The prisoners could rush us and run. A few would get shot, the rest would make it into the bush. But they wait, stacked up in a row, so many genocide-suspect action figures waiting to be boxed up and shipped away.

Jean-de-Dieu appears with thirty more stunned-looking men from downstairs and we load them all up on the bed of the truck. The prisoners look from me to the armed guards and back at me. My presence must reassure them somehow. I wonder if they think they're going to be executed. So I get on the bed of the truck with them. The RPA escort soldiers look mean and scared and young. If anything happens on the road between the soldiers and the prisoners, I should be there to see it. If I stay close it will help keep everyone calm.

But maybe that's a lie, just a humanitarian cover. Would I have stood with captured Nazis on the flatbed of a truck after WWII to help them feel secure? Maybe I just want to be as close to their humiliation as I can get, and savor it, insert myself right into their transfer.

I count eighty-seven prisoners; the bed of the truck would only fit about thirty comfortably. They stand inside each other's contours again, like in the dark cell downstairs. The ones in the middle have nothing to hang on to, so each time the truck turns or hits a bump they sway deeply in unison, a ballet of the condemned. Jean-de-Dieu starts to sing a Rwandan song and claps. It's a call and answer: he sings a line and all the prisoners answer back with the same line. There's no tension; everyone falls quickly into a dominance-and-subjection pattern. Those prisoners with room to move their hands clap with Jean-de-Dieu's beat. It's a nice song, it sounds like a hymn. *Nkoze tsemba tsemba.* The clouds have opened up, there's a soft afternoon sun, and we've done a good day's work. These guys at least get a reprieve, they're alive for now. Jean-de-Dieu sings *tsemba tsemba,* claps and smiles, the prisoners clap and answer *tsemba tsemba.* The chorus is sung in a low bass. It's beautiful. The African lyrics have a melody and ring that somehow sound familiar. *Tsemba tsemba,* I feel like I've heard it before, it sounds like the name of an ancient god or magic spell.

We deposit the guys at the prison, where the Red Cross is waiting, Swiss nurses with clipboards and medicine. I owe Jean-de-Dieu a drink. We go to a very funky discotheque in town, full of armed RPA soldiers, UN staff, and HIV-positive prostitutes. They play a song that fills the dance floor every hour: "Fire in Somalia, fire in Rwanda, fire in Bosnia— *Stop it!*" The crowd, dripping in sweat, jumps and screams with fists in the air when the chorus repeats, *"Stop it!"*

I get home late. Monsieur Innocent is in the living room drinking a Mutzig. The *tsemba tsemba* song is still with me. I've been humming it all night. *"Innocent, tsemba tsemba? C'est quoi ça?"* What is *tsemba tsemba?* His eyes get huge. *"Eh la, pas bon, Monsieur Ken, tsemba tsemba—fini, complet, definitive, kwa kwa kwa,"* he chops his neck with the side of his hand again and again and again, *"fini, definitive, tous les Tutsis, eh la, tsemba tsemba—kwa kwa kwa Tutsis.*" Oh my Christ. It's genocide. *Tsemba tsemba* means genocide. Jean-de-Dieu made the prisoners sing their confession. I clapped and sang along. He was torturing them. With a genocide hymn. I thought it was a beautiful song about an ancient divinity. I was torturing those poor murderous condemned bastards too.

Heidi, April 1995
Port-au-Prince, Haiti
Operation Uphold Democracy

Outside my new office, a handsome young Haitian guy I've seen around the building sees me struggling with a box of files and rushes in to help me. He looks at me, smiling shyly. He tells me I look like Mia Farrow, embarrassed when it slips out of his mouth. Before he leaves, I ask his name. Marc, he tells me as he backs out the door.

Each time I pass him in the hallway, he lets out a nervous giggle. Lunch hours in a local restaurant, I feel his eyes on me the entire time. He doesn't leer; he just looks longingly out of big sweet, sad eyes. I've never had someone pay so much attention to me. Surely Yusuf, who kept me at arm's length, didn't.

I hesitate to pursue Marc. He's soft and young and innocent and might easily get attached. I have a feeling he's not the type of man who will allow himself to be treated as a temporary plaything, a lover when the need arises to help bide my time here. And I'm afraid to lose the woman I've become, absorbed into yet another man's world. In ten years of marriage I never learned how to be both a wife and a woman. Only when I stepped out of my husband's shadow was I fully able to see myself and realize it was me that was missing all those years.

But morning after morning, Marc and I manage to sit together on the shuttle bus. The lengths of our forearms touch and communicate messages. We pretend to ignore it, but neither of us moves away. I'm aware of Marc staring at my bare feet resting on the back of the seat in front of me. We talk about Port-au-Prince, what there is to do here and where to go out. I take a chance and ask him if he'd like to show me around some time.

The bus comes to a stop and people start getting off. Marc leans his body forward toward the door, but in the same motion, he turns back toward me, reaches down, and lays his hand on my bare foot. He doesn't grip it; it's not a caress. Oddly, the gesture is even more intimate than that.

I feel the energy pass up into my body. He holds my gaze and then says, sorry, I couldn't help myself. But our pact is sealed. I see us together in a hundred lifetimes.

Andrew, September 1995
Bihac Enclave, Bosnia

I needed a war and for my sins I got one. Last week I was examining a patient in my New York office when the phone rang. It was the prosecutor of the UN War Crimes Tribunal for the former Yugoslavia. Someone had given him my name, and he wanted to know whether I'd be willing to set up a forensic team to investigate massacres in Bosnia. I told him I'd have to think it over, but I'd made my decision before I put the receiver down.

The tribunal offered the first chance in nearly fifty years to bring to account men who destroy peace with crimes of war. It was the mission I'd been waiting for since leaving Haiti. So I subleased my apartment, packed away my stethoscope, and told the medical director that I'd be gone from New York indefinitely. Then I got on a plane for Sarajevo.

The tide of war here has just turned. The Serbs have met someone with a bigger stick at last: the Americans have finally weighed in on the side of the Muslims and are pounding the Bosnian Serb army with deadly accurate air strikes. Bosnian government troops have broken the siege around Bihac, shattering the myth of Serb military invincibility. They're racing east to grab back as much territory as possible before the Americans stop the advance and peace talks begin. The tribunal has indicted Bosnian Serb leaders for crimes against humanity and genocide, and with the Serbs now in retreat, the prosecutor wants me to find and exhume the mass graves they've left in their bloody wake.

I am being escorted around newly captured territory by a major from Bosnian Military Intelligence. There are credible reports that the Serbs massacred Muslim civilians around here, and the major is eager to show the world what they did to his people. But his information is vague in the extreme: go down this dirt road for a few kilometers, turn left at the T-shaped junction, continue until a clearing in the forest, and start digging in a depression in the ground. The problem is that there are X- and Y-shaped junctions where there should be Ts, clearings of all sizes between the trees, and depressions everywhere. It's a forest, for God's sake.

What we need is a witness. The priceless witness would be someone who fell down uninjured under the dead and dying, feigned death, crawled out after the killers left, and took a good look around before running off. Such people exist. If the killers are lazy or in a hurry, they sometimes neglect to finish off each victim with a shot to the head. This lapse in workmanship eventually brings us to the grave, and the grave in theory brings us to the killers.

But we are having no such luck here. Instead of a survivor, the major produces a hapless Serb prisoner who claims to know where the grave is. The prisoner leads us to the clearing in question and the Bosnian military gets to work with a backhoe, removing the topsoil. At one point there is a murmur of excitement from the soldiers when they uncover an old shovel, but that's the high point of our search. Beyond that we turn up only dirt. This prisoner has wasted valuable time and embarrassed his captors, so when the major slinks off into the forest with him, I follow along to make sure he's not executed.

I'm observing them when suddenly the sound of outgoing artillery booms from less than a hundred meters away. It's deafening. The major shouts into his radio, receives an agitated reply, and then orders his men to pack up.

"They attack us," he tells me curtly, "We leave now." Small arms fire crackles nearby as the Serb counterattack gathers pace. It's madness to be looking for corpses so close to such a fluid front line. I'm going to have to talk to the boss about it. Then I remember that I am the boss now.

We clear out back toward Bihac. On the way into town, some locals wave us down and insist we join them at a farmhouse beside the main road, on the route of the Muslim advance. They're roasting a whole sheep on a spit in the garden and passing around a bottle of clear plum brandy. The mood is festive and we don't say no.

As the ground rumbles with explosions to the east, we sit among wildflowers under fruit trees and eat strips of greasy meat and drink until we're quite drunk. It doesn't take long with this moonshine. The fields are a luminous green in the late afternoon sun. It could be a Saturday afternoon in New Zealand after the rugby match, except for the burned-out Serb tanks, their turrets lying at strange angles after direct hits by U.S. warplanes, and the fields dotted with dead pigs, feet in the air, killed by Muslims during the advance.

A stream of horse-drawn carts loaded with furniture and electrical appliances flows by, looted from overrun Serb houses. This Muslim advance was so rapid that kettles boiled dry in hastily abandoned houses and washing is still drying on clotheslines. On the other side of the front line, the original owners of these goods are also on the move in trucks and carts, fleeing for their lives, just as the Muslims have been doing all over Bosnia since the war broke out.

Our hosts offer us a newly vacated Serb house for the night, but we decline. Victory for them is sweet after having been on the losing side for so long. But we're little more than tourists here. This is not our victory and these are not our spoils of war. We withdraw to our five-dollar hotel rooms back in bombed-out Bihac, where stunned locals still scamper furtively from building to building.

I'm not looking forward to calling the prosecutor in The Hague to explain that we can't find the bodies. He won't be happy. He was blunt when he briefed me; he said he needed that forensic evidence urgently. But after today's scare, I'm going to have to be just as blunt with him; I won't risk the lives of my staff to dig up the dead.

This is strange work for a physician. There are more than three-quarters of a million bodies buried on two continents because we failed to prevent two genocides. We were supposed to be saving the living, but now we're setting up war crimes trials on behalf of the dead. This is turning into the largest forensic investigation in history, and if I wasn't frantically raising money and hiring experts, I'd be in a panic at how far in over my head I am.

The prosecutor cuts me off when I start to explain our difficulties here. "I know they're still fighting," he says, "so I've just signed your travel authorization for Rwanda. We need forensic evidence just as urgently there and I want you to dig it out for me while Bosnia quiets down. Hand in your return ticket to New York and go straight down to Africa."

Ken, November 1995
Butare, Southern Rwanda

There's a meeting at our office. It looks serious; they have pictures and maps out all over the table. They're discussing mass graves; I recognize some of the names of the sites. One guy stands up slowly and grins at me. He's tall and thin. Holy shit, it's Andrew! Big hug. Doctor, what are you doing here? I thought you were a prisoner of conscience in New York? I had no idea he was in-country. Usually we hear about each other's movements well before they happen via the UN's enormously effective global gossip network, but I've been deep in the field for months and lost track of him.

We start throwing Khmer phrases at each other like we used to. It's mostly nonsense, but no one else has any idea what we're saying and everyone is impressed. It feels good to flaunt it. Let's go drinking, he says. Give me a briefing, get me up to speed. And then we need to figure out how to get you assigned to my team. This is the most important mission yet; let's dig in our heels, get it right this time.

How am I going to break it to him, of all people? That I've conceded, caved, capitulated.

Sitting in Matt's dad's office, I managed to convince myself to believe in this work again. But I don't. It's a lie. We are the only beneficiaries of our righteousness.

Andrew and I do the only sensible thing in the circumstances, dinner at Hotel Ibis. It's the one real restaurant in town, here since Belgian colonial times. The steak au poivre is good, a dripping bloodred chunk of meat swimming in creamy white sauce with hard black peppercorns that sting magnificently by the end of the meal. Fresh French baguettes, Belgian fries, and the best red wine selection in Rwanda accompany a five-star meal. Lieutenant Alex and all the senior RPA officers eat here. So do the heads of the humanitarian aid groups. It's funny to see the humanitarians' Land Cruisers lined up next to RPA vehicles outside the Ibis. Everyone wants a good steak au poivre.

In the gift shop they sell T-shirts that say, *"Enterrons les morts mais pas la verité."* Bury the dead but not the truth. When the RPA chased them out of Kigali, the *interahamwe* set up camp here in Butare and used the Ibis as their headquarters. The *interahamwe* commanded genocide from this room.

I think I smell the scent of corpses on Andrew. I think I smell something else too. His shoulders sag. He tries mightily to appear upbeat, but this work must be killing him. He keeps it to himself, though, and we talk about everything else. Except that I'm quitting the mission.

The last I knew, Andrew was stuck in New York handing out Sudafed at headquarters. In the meantime there have been two genocides. He spent so much time in the morgue in Haiti, he accidentally became the closest thing the UN has on staff to a forensic expert, and now they've put him in charge of exhuming mass graves on two continents. Simultaneously. Jesus. The worse it gets, the more work for Andrew; the more work he does, the worse he gets. It's the Protestant work ethic in reverse.

It's painful to see him wrestle with his conscience. The God he was taught as a boy to serve is merciful and just, but there's no evidence of justice or mercy in Bosnia or Rwanda. Andrew's view of the world, and of himself, is rotting in those mass graves too. What an excruciating test of faith for a good man.

"If there is a God, Doctor, I want him prosecuted for crimes against humanity."

Andrew doesn't think it's funny. Easy for me to say, I'm outta here in nine days and a wake-up call.

"All right, let's figure out a way to get you on my team now," he says. "What do you think? I need a lawyer with dirt on his boots."

Oh Lord. I've got to do this now. Here goes. "Doctor, I can't take it anymore, I'm sorry to let you down. I'm afraid I'm going to grab an AK-47 and shoot someone. I dream about it. I'm going to Haiti, I need Heidi, I need a beach. Karim is there, I can't say no to them."

He suddenly looks thinner and more drawn than ever. With each excuse I've destroyed one more little piece of the illusion.

Heidi, November 1995
Port-au-Prince, Haiti
Operation Uphold Democracy

Marc has been teaching me to dance salsa. We go out several nights a week and take a lesson together early on Saturday mornings. After, we often drive to the coast for the weekend, sometimes north to Cap Haitien, sometimes south to Jacmel. Haiti has an abundance of coastline, some of it completely remote and pristine.

Once there we lie for hours and hours in the sand or floating in the water, talking, telling stories, getting to know each other. Marc wants to know all about the places I've traveled to. I ask him to tell me about life in Haiti during the coup d'état. I've heard Andrew's stories but now I want to know what it was like for the Haitians. For Marc.

Every night, he tells me, a different group of neighbors would stand guard. They'd go up on the roofs and listen and wait. In the silence he could hear his parents whispering in their bedroom, his sisters whispering in theirs. And Marc would lie in the darkness, staring at the ceiling. Everyone waiting.

And then they would come. The death squads crept down the dark street on foot or overflowed from pickup trucks. Cloaked in black hoods, in their pockets were scraps of paper carrying the names of the night's victims, innocents all. The first of the neighborhood watch group to see them would call the alarm, banging pots and pans together. Others took up the call until the entire neighborhood rose from its beds and joined in. Unwilling to face an angry mob, the would-be murderers scattered for at least another night.

I'm in awe of him and what he's lived through. There's this part of me that wants to know everything about people. To be immersed in the stories of their lives. When I look at Marc, I want his ancestors to be my own. I want the blood in my veins to be that of the rebelling slaves of Haiti of two hundred years ago, victors in a war for freedom.

I'm almost as proud of this history as Marc is. He won't leave Haiti, he tells me. He has an obligation here to his people. I want to have this obligation too. I want them to be my people. In a letter, he tells me he knows I could never live here, that our lives are on two different tracks, but he'd like me to think about it anyway. I don't have to. I've already decided Haiti will be my home. I belong here.

Early one night there's a bang on the balcony door. I open it to find Ken, sent here by my guardian angel. He still has the dust of Rwanda on his boots. I look around to see what he will remember of his first moments in Haiti.

Once Ken is showered and has a drink in hand, we start to catch up. I waste no time in telling him all about Marc. I tell him we're moving in together, we've already found a house. He holds back judgment, even though I know he's struggling to restrain himself. Eventually he'll get around to saying what's on his mind, but for now he lets me babble on.

The next morning Karim picks Ken, Marc, and me up to spend the weekend at his house. It's at the top of Montaigne Noire, as far up in the mountains above Port-au-Prince as you can go, over a slippery stone road carving a winding trail through the dense trees. This was Andrew's house only a couple years ago, but it's a different country now. Then the house was a refuge for him from the violence and fear of the city. Now, for us, it's a resort.

The house is built in the shape of a square, the center of which is almost entirely taken up with a swimming pool and a waterfall. There's an abundance of trees filled with tarantulas. It's disconcerting to have the hairy yellow creatures fall into your lap like autumn leaves while you're lounging poolside. I keep a dustpan handy to scoop them up and toss them outside.

Karim keeps the rum flowing and the music turned up. He's so house-proud and happy to host us that Ken says he's a young, stoned, Muslim version of an old Jewish lady. With his hands clasped skyward, Karim yells out prayers and blessings in Arabic. "Mr. Ken! Miss Heidi!" he bellows. "Our family is together again!" Marc smiles, happy to be a part of this family.

The rest of us are content to not move from our chairs the entire day except to occasionally slip into the pool to cool off, but Ken can't sit still. He needs something to happen. Suddenly, he decides it would be a good idea to challenge Karim to a diving competition. But that's not risky enough: he decides they should dive from the roof. They spring off, twenty feet above my head, as I beg them not to. They go back up and do it again and only stop when they realize I'm furious. You idiot, I tell Ken. I didn't work so hard to get you out of Rwanda only to have to call your mother and tell her you broke your neck in a fucking swimming pool.

Ken, November 1995
Port-au-Prince, Haiti

Mr. Karim brings the Barbancourt rum out to the pool in spotless tumblers, with neatly fractioned slices of lime. If you don't put too much ice or lime in, you can float the glass right in the sparkling pool water.

"Mr. Ken, Mr. Ken, Mr. Ken, any human rights violations today?" Mr. Karim asks with a grin.

When Marc goes inside for more drinks, I tell Heidi I like him a lot and never liked Yusuf. She throws ice at me and says, "Goddamn right, you like Marc. But only now you tell me you hated Yusuf all along? You prick, why didn't you tell me earlier?"

Cuz you'd never speak to me again if I did, you lunatic.

Dr. Andrew told me he could never get this pool clean. The pool was murky and green then. But Karim scraped all the algae off the sides with a toothbrush. It took weeks. The water is crystalline over azure tiles now.

He devotes himself to the pool daily; it's almost a religious thing. He tests the pH balance, flushes the filters, feeds the nutrients worshipfully.

Andrew's devotion took him elsewhere. And my lack of it brought me here. Heidi put my resumé on the top of the personnel inbox again and sent me a fax a week while I was in Rwanda, describing Karim's pool and the rum. Come to Haiti, she said, they even have good mangoes. It'll be just like Cambodia.

But after a week at the pool, no human rights violations to speak of, they sent me to a remote province a two-day drive from the capital over bone-breaking roads. Now I'm so far from Heidi and Karim, I might as well be in Phnom Penh.

The work is easy. It's hard to believe this is the same country Andrew evacuated two years ago. The prison I'm responsible for has only twenty-five inmates, most of them chicken thieves. They get plenty of food and water; they're not beaten. I have nothing to do, so I give English classes in the prison courtyard, which makes good use of their time and mine too. The grizzled, bony, bare-chested old guys are my favorite students. The young tough guys sulk in their cells, but the papas sit with me for hours and grin and make the same mistakes over and over again.

"My name is Ken, your name is LaPierre."

"Yes, yes, my name is Ken." Big toothless grin.

"No, no, *your* name is LaPierre, *my* name is Ken."

We finally did bring President Aristide back to power with full American force, which proves how effective we can be when we decide to. The team assigned to keep my sector secure is a small squad of U.S. Special Forces. There are only eleven of them, but they are the most effective eleven humans I've ever encountered. They have Humvees that travel to the next town in fifteen minutes over a bad road that takes a regular Land Cruiser an hour. When the rains wash everything out, they have Zodiacs to cut across the bay and skip the road altogether. They're older than regular army soldiers; they have kids and go to PTA meetings, so they know how to talk to a local mayor with respect and patience and negotiate without screaming or immediately flashing a weapon. Alleviate, not create, tension. But the most important thing they have is autonomy. They don't have to report to echelons above reality for daily operations. They just think it up and do it.

They're mobile, highly trained, fully armed American adults with autonomy. That's a hell of a combination. I'd like to travel from mission to mission with a squad of these men and see what we could accomplish.

Turn back time and set us loose in Rwanda during the massacres. I wonder how many lives we could have saved.

It's not dangerous now, but the *macoutes* haven't gone away, they're just hibernating until the Americans and the UN leave. We supervised the parliamentary election in my region recently and *macoutes* surrounded the electoral office where we'd collected all the ballots, rushed the building, threw the ballot boxes and furniture outside, made a bonfire, and burned it all. We just stood and watched. Then, to intimidate the voters, they did a voodoo ceremony, danced and sang and drank cane liquor, poured it on the fire, drank more.

Two weeks later the Haitian government announced election results from this region, with UN blessing: government wins 62 percent of the vote, opposition parties 38 percent. I watched all the ballots burn before anyone had counted them; they were still bound in boxes. I wrote a memo to UNHQ detailing the fraud. They answered that because my memo was transmitted without the signature of my boss, it was not an official communication, so therefore headquarters could not officially respond to my memo. Nor to the fact that the government made up the election results out of whole cloth. They just picked a number. That the UN then officially confirmed. The mission is called "Uphold Democracy."

But I don't care. It was just an election. People voted, they burned the ballots, faked the result, so what? We wanted Aristide in power and he's in power; no one cares about election fraud in my remote region. I was so naïve in Cambodia to believe we could export democracy with one election.

No one's getting shot, my prisoners are well fed and healthy, I have a nice little house all to myself, and I'm happy here. My cook makes fresh fish stew every day. I call her mama and she calls me *fils mwen*, "my son." I go spearfishing every weekend in a village behind a coral reef on a half-moon lagoon. A local fisherman waits for me at sunrise. We go out in a traditional wooden dugout canoe. I splash around for three hours and come back with two little reef fish, then he disappears for three minutes and comes back up with a monster that feeds his whole family and me for lunch.

The best thing about this mission is Geneviève. She's a French nurse who works for one of the charity groups at the hospital. She doesn't speak a word of English, but we talk nonstop about everything and my French is improving noticeably by the day. She wears faded denim overalls, braless, white tank top over dense brown skin. She has big red lips, green cat eyes, long auburn hair with wide looping curls that spill all the way down her back and along an astoundingly smooth and narrow neck. Tiny, delicate clavicles. All of which incites in me a sensation I can only describe as hunger.

I'd like to bring her to Port-au-Prince and introduce her to Heidi. I think she'd approve of this one. At least at first. It's risky though because I have a problem with Heidi's opprobrium. If she so much as frowns in the direction of a girlfriend, I'll never think of the girl the same way again. It's a decree issued from the Holiest of Holies that this woman is unworthy. I know it's not healthy and I try hard to resist.

I think Heidi may have a related problem with my judgments, so I make an effort to be studiously friendly around her boyfriends. But her problem is different: she's almost taunting me to disapprove. She pushes and pushes even the most unlikely relationship right to the edge; nothing else exists, it's life and death. It's like she's a performance artist and the performance is her relationships.

And she is devoted to her art.

I was never exactly sure what she saw in Yusuf, but with him came a clan to adopt, a culture to learn, a wife to hate, a scandal to withstand. I don't believe she would have ever agreed to be his second wife, but every time I underestimate her, I'm wrong. It's like she's daring the world to try to stop her, setting it up so her mom, her dad, me, anyone, will tell her don't do it. Then she can say fuck off, no one tells me what to do.

But it looks like she's come full circle. I think she's genuinely in love this time with Marc the person—not a country and not a conflict, but Marc.

Geneviève and I sleep on the roof of my house with the night breeze and the neighbor's voodoo drums. The Special Forces guys gave me one of their field cots. The webbing sags and springs just right and the aluminum frame provides grip and leverage. There is only enough room in the cot for our two bodies intertwined.

She angles herself perfectly, swaying gently, rhythmically. The field cot holds her in weightless poise above me. I don't have to move, she coils and uncoils in accelerating waves. Then she stops, arches her back, gathers handfuls of shadow curls in her hands and pulls them up off her soaking neck, wet strands bounce in rhythm with her hips. It's a writhing aerial dance now. Her raised arms form two luminescent triangles, clavicles and breasts protrude above me in a glistening silhouette under a riot of white Caribbean stars, a giant salt shaker spilled in the Haitian night sky. She whispers, *je je je jouis jouis jouis.*

232

What a beautiful word. The English word doesn't mean anything and is clunky, the Hebrew word means something else and is ugly, but *jouissance* sounds as beautiful as what I'm watching above me.

Maybe we should talk about getting married, starting a family. She's adorable with the kids at the hospital. All she wants on this earth is for those kids to be healthy.

But I'm leaving soon for Liberia. They called. They're trying to reassemble the team from Somalia. The fighting is bad, that's why they want experienced staff. I'm afraid I know what's waiting for me there. But I picture them under fire, cursing me, saying I was afraid to come. It's more important for me not to say no to them than to be happy here.

First I abandoned the mission in Rwanda and Andrew knee-deep in skulls for Heidi and a working vacation in the Caribbean. Now I leave the rapturous embrace of a tender woman I'm falling in love with for another African war.

I will have to look her in the eye tomorrow and tell her I'm leaving. We will probably never see each other again. This is going to hurt. It already does. It didn't when I left Tali—I was twenty-five with infinity ahead of me, and anyway I had to go home to graduate—but there's a cumulative effect. I have left too many women after too many "it's not your fault and it's not my choice, but I have to go" conversations. I'm almost thirty now; it's time for me to take responsibility for these decisions.

I watch Heidi play with fire everywhere she goes, and I guess I enjoy watching. But we all understand that one day the romantic adventure won't end well. And I watch Andrew twist his conscience and faith into a more and more intractable knot with each new impossible mission. They're both trapped inside their own illusions. It's all so clear to me. I wonder what's clear to them.

Andrew, November 1995
Kibuye, Rwanda

Lake Kivu. Dead center of Africa. It looks like Lake Geneva, spectacularly serene, with bougainvillea everywhere, growing wild to the water's edge. The Switzerland of Africa, they used to call this region. If you look west you can make out Zaire in the haze. The Hutu militias are there, just across the lake. They're pretending to be refugees, fattening up on humanitarian aid, some even earning good UN wages while they plot new massacres.

On this side of the lake, the newly dead outnumber the living. No matter how hot the African sun, I can't swim in water that had thousands of bloated corpses floating in it. The lake looks clear, but I keep thinking I see skeletons at the bottom and I'm worried I'll cut my feet on a sharp, infected bone. I can't go jogging, because I'm afraid of the packs of wild dogs. They've eaten too much human flesh and are hungry again. Every vulture in central Africa has congregated here, and if I lie motionless in the sun too long, they start to circle me, spiraling lower and lower.

A professor of surgery once told us in medical school that you don't need rubber gloves to do a rectal exam, just scrape some hard soap under your index fingernail and go straight in, and you won't get any shit under your nail at all. He was an old-school doctor and had probably done it himself for years. But I'm out of hard soap and the brown under my fingernails is not the product of a rectal exam but part of a corpse or, I guess, parts of corpses. It's nauseating to scrape it out with my Swiss Army knife, but it's worse if I don't.

The center of my world is a stone church and a mass grave. My team has been digging for weeks now, pulling out corpses under a screaming sun. The town is at high altitude, so it's dry heat at least. We all look fit and tanned, like a construction crew in summer. The forensic science is interesting, methodical, and slow. We found the first corpses a yard down under tons of compacted earth. We had to use a backhoe, taking care not to cut bodies with the blade. Each corpse on the pile is numbered, photographed, lifted onto a stretcher, and carried up to the church. Clothes are stripped off and washed, personal effects cleaned, and documents logged into evidence bags. The naked corpses are X-rayed, then autopsied under a gaily colored inflatable tent. The pathologists' bone saws cut through skulls and femurs, producing samples for DNA analysis. It reminds me of the sound of chainsaws clearing pine forest back home.

What we are trying to piece together is quite straightforward, just as in a murder investigation anywhere, only here it's multiplied by five hundred. We have to determine the age, sex, and stature of each victim, document the nature of the injuries and the manner and cause of death. We're hoping for as many identifications as possible to corroborate witness testimony.

Graves like this one are everywhere. My map of Rwanda is covered in red dots, one for each location with over five hundred corpses. It looks like a map of a cholera epidemic, starting with a handful of cases, then spreading unchecked in malevolent concentric circles through a nonimmune population. The epidemic was never contained and burned itself out only when it ran out of victims.

The forensics are clear already. These were unarmed civilians, mostly women and children, almost all of whom died of blunt or sharp-force trauma. They were hacked or clubbed to death, or both. The evidence will be devastating if it ever reaches court, which right now seems unlikely since the accused are living across the lake in Zaire, protected by President Mobutu.

This is an average massacre by Rwandan standards, unremarkable in scale or circumstance. Several thousand civilians had gathered in the church grounds, promised protection by the Hutu governor. Hutu militias went methodically through the crowd instructing other Hutus to leave, and government soldiers cut off the escape routes. Then the governor fired his weapon in the air as a kill-the-Tutsis signal and young men drunk on banana beer hacked them all to pieces. It's hard work killing that many people in a confined space with only machetes and clubs, so the killers returned home to their families each night to rest and drink before the next day's work. It took three days and so far we know of only two survivors.

About two dozen wounded did crawl out of the church the first night, down the hill to the lake. They must have been weak from blood loss and crazed with thirst. We have been mapping and collecting their skeletons from the steep slopes, where many of the skulls have come loose and rolled like stray soccer balls down toward the water. We've developed a special fondness for Surface Skeleton #23, whom we call "Banana Man." After he died, a healthy five-foot banana tree grew right up through the center of his chest. It was apparently well fertilized by his corpse, but you might think twice before eating the fruit. Banana Man had both his ankles broken with machetes by killers too lazy or tired or drunk to finish him off in the church itself. It would have been easy to track him down the following day: there's only so far you can crawl with bilateral ankle fractures. They killed him with what looks like a single machete blow to the head. He must have been lying on the banana seedling when they got him. I wonder what kind of a night he spent and what he was thinking as he lay there, waiting for his executioners.

Technically Banana Man was easy. Just photograph the bones, pick them up, and do the analysis. What's difficult now, five weeks and four hundred bodies into the dig, is the pile of entwined corpses several yards down in the grave. There's just no way to find the bottom, no matter how often the backhoe goes in. It's a wicked game of pick-up sticks, where I grab a leg or arm of what looks to be the easiest corpse to lift off, only to find that another part of the same body is buried under half a dozen others, all of which have the same problem. Sometimes I get obsessed over one that won't release and spend hours on it with a pick and trowel. This annoys my team, because they have to heave off other bodies just so I can extract mine, but I can't face the same body two days in a row.

In the end the body usually comes free with a pop and I collapse backward onto other corpses, hugging mine as it lands on top of me. Everyone laughs because we've all done it. It's horrible the first time you wrestle with dead weight, but after you've seen it a few times, you get used to it. There are just so many corpses that there's nothing else to land on. At any given time at least one of us has a leg stuck in the mud between the bodies. Once it happened to the youngest guy on the team just as we were quitting for the day. We pretended to leave without helping him out, stranding him for the night. It was only when we saw his eyes wide with terror that we realized we'd pushed it too far. He was shaking by the time we pulled him out.

The reason for all this slipping and sliding is that this was not a burial in the formal sense, but just bodies tossed fresh into a deep pit. One of the investigating lawyers introduced me to the local Hutu from the Rwandan Red Cross who organized the burial. He's now a prosecution witness. He says he returned here from the capital, Kigali, about a week after the killing and realized he had to do something about the thousands of corpses in town after his daughter asked him, "Daddy, why are all these people sleeping in the street in the middle of the day?"

So he got a bulldozer and some prison laborers, dug a hole fifty feet wide and seven feet deep in the banana grove behind the church, and worked for a week, tossing bodies off stretchers into the hole. It must have been difficult work with the bodies bloating, only a week old. The women and children and babies would have looked so much more human than they do now. The killers told him that if he buried the bodies before they had finished going through the pockets, they would put him in his own hole. No idle threat under the circumstances.

So that's why the bodies are so tough to pull out, entwined with layers of compacted earth between them. In one corner there were so many babies mixed together, we had to just estimate the number and put their limbs and torsos and heads all in a single body bag. It's disgusting work and we have all been getting infections. Even if I double-glove, I still cut my hands on fragments of bone, so I've put myself on high doses of antibiotics.

Following the afternoon rains, the hole fills up like a pond and needs pumping. Out of the pipe and down the slope flows a vile gray soup. Cremate me when I die. No one should have to end up like this.

We break at noon and eat lunch in the shadow of the church, a few feet from the piles of corpses stacked in white numbered body bags between the pews. Ham and cheese sandwiches, fruit, and Coke. Visiting journalists are appalled. We offer to share lunch with them and laugh when they cover their noses with handkerchiefs and vomit in the bushes. They want you to think that they're hard and unmoved, but it's difficult to maintain that world-weary pose when you're throwing up. In the end they ask if we might be able to hold the interview over a beer down at the lakeside guesthouse, if possible after we've showered.

The shower that our engineer has rigged on-site is the best part of my day. Piping hot water under pressure squirts out of a nozzle that I have come to worship. Pieces of strangers' flesh and bone are rinsed out of my hair, but I can't get the rotting stench out of my nose no matter how hard I blow, or the greasy feeling off my skin no matter how often I shower.

I've learned that it's easier to wash my skin than my clothes, so the less clothing I wear in the grave the better. I just have to get used to the feeling of human flesh sticking to me and drying on top of the sunburn. So I work in shorts, boots, and gloves when there are no visitors around, but dress up in an official-looking plastic surgical gown when I have to see outsiders. Some pharisee who hadn't been in this pit for five weeks once tried to tell me I should show more respect, but I figure the dead aren't as fussy about fashion as my righteous visitor. The living are easily offended on behalf of the dead.

Nearby, UN Ghanaian soldiers cook lunch over an open fire. They protect us and guard the site against intruders; one night last week they shot a wild dog as it was dragging an arm out of the grave. I ask these genial soldiers about the risk of attack from across the lake. One of them points to Zaire with contempt and spits on the red earth. They're not afraid of Hutu militias who kill women and children and then turn tail in the face of a real army.

But they ask me when we plan to rebury the bodies. I tell them that I don't know, we haven't even located the bottom of the grave yet. They keep asking the same question day after day and eventually I go see the lieutenant. I ask him to explain to his men that we're exhuming as fast as we can and that it's pointless for them to be impatient. He tells me it's not the speed of the work that's worrying his men but their fear of the spirits of the unburied dead. Especially at night.

I'm thinking about how many spirits must be haunting Rwanda when a dirty Land Cruiser with International Committee of the Red Cross markings pulls up from the direction of Zaire. It's the same model I used to drive in Cambodia. One of the soldiers drags back the rolls of concertina wire and a slim woman with shoulder-length blond hair climbs out. She's wearing a white linen shirt rolled up at the sleeves, cotton khakis, and boots and is covered in a fine layer of red Rwandan dust.

It's Suzanne. We met a few weeks ago at a party in Kigali. I try not to touch her with my stinking hands as I kiss her on the right cheek, the left, and then the right again. She says she's just back from reuniting Rwandan children with their parents in the refugee camps, and then she surprises me with an invitation to dinner.

As night falls I pull up to Suzanne's house. It looks like it was built for tourists before the war. We sit at the water's edge and stare out across the still, dark lake. We don't speak much. Each time I toss a stone, my thigh touches hers and I feel the warmth of her skin through the linen. I lean closer and breathe in her perfume. It's jasmine and vanilla.

A shout from Giuseppe pulls us back into time. He's a wry Sicilian who works with Suzanne. Inside the house it's warm and candlelit, and dinner's ready, steaming pasta with tomato and garlic sauce. He's braved the snakes to collect basil from the garden and the cook has baked bread. Red wine flows with the conversation and we're anywhere but Rwanda. For dessert we break off large slabs of bitter Swiss chocolate. Giuseppe goes to bed and Suzanne and I dance slow and close. Then she takes my hand and leads me to her bedroom.

I ask her to turn off the lamp as I undress; it's been a while and I feel suddenly shy. Suzanne pulls up the mosquito net to let me under. Her sheets smell sweet. We're tentative at first but our flesh is warm and we take each other with tenderness, and then abandon. Afterward, as the sweat cools, we lie close, shoulders touching. We're alive, we have breath and heartbeats.

The next morning she asks why I kept tugging on her arm during the night. I tell her that I'm not sure. I usually sleep alone, maybe it was just in the way. Then the dream comes back: I'm not in Suzanne's bed; I'm lying in the grave but can't get comfortable on top of the bodies; I curse them as I move limbs and skulls out of the way. I mistook her for a corpse.

Heidi, February 1996
Port-au-Prince, Haiti

I turn the dial to wash. There's a moment of anticipation and then water rushes through the pipes and into the machine. Grinning, Marc leans over the edge watching until it's full. It's the first washing machine he's ever seen, and we own a dozen of them, all imported from Miami, ready to be installed in Haiti's premier laundromat. When the machine begins to agitate, it jumps and dances in place and the workers run, scared but laughing, out the back door. They're excited, too.

Months earlier another shirt ruined by the housekeeper's hand washing made me wish out loud for a laundromat. "What's a laundromat?" Marc asked. An hour of explanation later, it was as if I had invented the wheel. I felt like an entrepreneurial genius. He couldn't have been more excited and immediately set off to draw up plans. We started with an informal survey of our female colleagues, who only wanted to know how soon we could open. Middle-class Haitian women are entering the workforce, just as their American counterparts did twenty years before, and no longer have time for housework. But their husbands still expect them to do it. A laundromat seems the most natural thing in the world; I can't believe no one here has thought of it already. For Marc it's as if a whole new world has opened. What other businesses are there in the U.S. to make women's lives easier? he asks me. He's caught on fast.

Early in our relationship we discovered we make a great team: I have the ideas and he has the ambition. And the best part is there's no competition in Haiti. Together we imagine a giant laundry monopoly employing hundreds of Haitians. Marc has so much faith in my ideas and in his ability to bring any project to fruition that he's quit his job at the UN and plans to run the laundry full time. I decide to stay with my job until the UN finishes its mission here and leaves.

After renting a building on a high-traffic street in town, we make alterations and renovations, order equipment and buy detergent, bleach, hangers, and receipts. We fly to Miami and buy a powerful new genera-tor so we won't have to worry about the lack of electricity. We place ads in newspapers and on the radio and hire people to hand out flyers in the markets.

Our grand opening is a week away and we still have to train twenty employees. We divide the group by function: Marc will train the customer service employees and I start with those operating the machines in the back.

In broken Creole I lurch through a speech fit for *Good Housekeeping* on sorting colors and water temperatures. I explain the use of net bags for delicates and point out suspect fabrics. In big block letters, I write "dry clean only" on a sheet of paper and tape it to the wall. I tell them they need to check the labels for these words. They've been working as laun-drywomen since adolescence and regard me with disdain. I'm afraid as soon as I leave, they'll throw everything into plastic buckets and do the job by hand, the way they always have.

At the front desk Marc is role-playing with the customer service group. "You ruined my shirt. What are you going to do about it?" he asks one of the women. She giggles and steps behind the group. Marc doesn't drop the character he's playing and continues to insist on an answer. One of the guys steps forward and says, "We didn't ruin the shirt. You brought it in like that." "No, no!" Marc tells them. "We're not trying to trick our cus-tomers. If they say we ruined the shirt, then we ruined it." He tries again. "I paid thirty dollars for this shirt. Are you going to reimburse me?" "Thirty dollars!" one of the women exclaims. "Are you crazy? That shirt didn't cost thirty dollars!" The others join in with their opinions. The mock problem-solving exercise has turned into a bitter debate. Exasper-ated, Marc says, "Okay, if a customer has any problem, just tell them to see me."

After all the employees leave for the day, Marc and I walk hand in hand through the building closing dryer doors, tightening the lids on bot-tles of bleach, picking up some lint that's drifted onto the floor. This is ours, he says. We did this together.

I head off to the market for food shopping. On the drive downtown, I go out of my way to pass through the old neighborhoods with their gin-gerbread houses. I carry a camera and take shots of a balcony I admire or a porch I'd like to duplicate. Marc and I can sit for hours putting these different details to the house we will build together as soon as the laun-dry is making a profit.

I'm the civilian now and I'm hoping Andrew and Ken won't notice I'm missing in action. I'm afraid to be called back into duty.

I set off on the mission to Haiti with the attitude of a marine, angry with Andrew for sitting behind a desk in New York. Is my derision responsible for his standing now among corpses in Rwanda, covered in their flesh and fallen hair? In turn, is Andrew responsible for Ken, running off to Liberia, ashamed that he too wasn't deep in bodies? Ken left Geneviève behind like all the others for the privilege of standing alone in yet another field, another country, another war.

I don't need that anymore. I just want to have an ordinary life.

Downtown, the Iron Market is a crush of hot sticky bodies and merchants pushing baskets of produce at potential buyers. It's intimidating but I've learned enough Creole to explain what I want and say no thank you for what I don't. There's always one guy who's learned some English from American soldiers and is at the side of any foreigner within minutes, hoping to be paid as a guide. Polite but aggressive, this one keeps pace with me through winding rows of stalls. He holds onto my arm at one point, attempting to guide me toward merchants who will slip him a few *gourdes* notes if I purchase their goods. I stop, look at him, look down at his hand on my arm, and he releases me and apologizes.

The sun beats down on the metal roof of the airless space and quickens the decomposing of the fruit and vegetables. But it's a good smell, like a pot of soup set to simmer. I head to the back of the market first, taking in the walls full of paintings for sale. The canvases are vibrant with color and pleasure and happiness; the poverty and direness of Haitian life don't exist in the artist's soul. Even if I have no intention of making a purchase, it's become my ritual to stand here surrounded by this contagious joyfulness.

By now word has spread through the market that there's a foreigner around and groups of children come running. *"Blanc! Blanc! Blanc!"* They giggle and hide behind each other, big smiles on their faces. A bold, older boy stands smiling at the front of the group. I'm like a grain of rice in a bag of coffee beans. I finally understand how that one African-American boy in my grade school class must have felt. They tag along as I go back and choose among the greens and roots for the makings of dinner.

At the house gate, I begin to unload my packages. The dog rushes out to greet me, barking and jumping and wagging her tail. We found her one morning after she had crawled into our yard near death from parasites and malnutrition. Many veterinary prescriptions later, she could finally stand. For weeks after, she would march in place in an attempt to not put her weight too long on any one leg. Now she's healthy and fattening up, although her legs are completely bowed.

A group of young schoolgirls passes by in their green gingham school uniforms, their arms laden with textbooks. They see me and begin whispering among themselves. Abruptly they all turn toward me and one yells out *"Gremelle."* The word hits me with such force, I step backward onto the dog's foot. A *gremelle!* They think I'm a *gremelle!* I want to kiss them. I've somehow graduated from a *blanc,* a foreigner, an outsider, to a *gremelle,* a mixed-race Haitian. Unaware of how happy they've made me, they laugh mischievously and run on down the road.

In the evening, out in the garden, my tutor has me close my eyes while he hides a book. When he's ready, he calls out words in Creole directing me to find it. Left, right, forward, back, hot, cold. Reinforced by my new status of *gremelle,* I try even harder. The late afternoon sun begins its slow descent behind the mountains. The cats have had their dinner and lie hot and sleepy under trees, ignoring the newly hatched chicks pecking the ground around them.

After my tutor leaves, the housekeeper prepares a table in the garden for dinner. The housekeeper's little girl watches TV in the living room and the sounds of American cartoons drift out. The cats stretch and scratch the coconut trees and a cool breeze blows through. It's an idyllic life. I never want to leave.

Andrew, February 1996
Kibuye, Rwanda,
The Skeleton Priest

I often sit in the church at dusk, staring at the stone altar, contemplating what it must have been like here, at night, during the massacre. Total darkness, hundreds of dead and dying women and children bleeding from machete wounds, knowing that their killers would return. I can still see the stains where their blood spurted, flowed across the floor, then tracked vertically up the stone walls and dried in the heat. There are tiny handprints smudged in blood under some of the pews. Who were these people whose corpses I now live with and how would their lives have unfolded?

I think of the operating rooms in the hospital where I trained, filled with teams of surgeons and nurses, stacked with sterile gauze, anesthetics, and clean white sheets. I wonder what these corpses who were once people would have given during those three nights for a soft pillow and a large dose of morphine. This is one church where a lot of prayers went unanswered.

There's a life-size plaster statue of the Virgin just behind the altar. She has a machete slash right across her breasts and someone has tried to glue her torso back together. She didn't get any more protection during the hacking orgy than anyone else, just got in the way, I guess. She'd make the perfect witness, but she's not talking. One witness who is says that some local Hutus returned to the church after the massacre, threw chlorine powder around, and made a feeble attempt to wash the blood off the floor, the altar, and the shattered stained glass windows. Then they began to worship. As if prayer and bleach could wipe away these stains.

When I can't take it any longer, I climb the rickety iron rungs to the top of the three-story bell tower, to be quiet and alone. Above is God, below are hundreds of cadavers stacked like cordwood between the pews and the altar. And the question that's haunted me since I first met Vary.

After many hours I decide God was here, maybe not far above where I'm sitting now, watching and listening. He heard all the desperate prayers, from the kids and the half-dead women, from the believers, the doubters, and the nonbelievers. Because everyone was praying for something, if only a quick death, facing a machete through the head.

And God just pissed all those prayers back down to earth, leaving everyone to die.

This can't be the God I prayed to as a missionary kid or at the communion rail as a medical student. This is a pitiless stranger and to pray to him up here in this bell tower would be absurd.

Ken told me that he grew up wondering what he'd have done if he'd been in Germany during the war. But I'm not Jewish and I didn't spend my childhood thinking about the Holocaust. What obsesses me is that genocide happened in Cambodia, and it's happened again here, right where I'm standing.

I wish that Ken could have been up here with me in this bell tower, with a heavy machine gun, a rocket-propelled grenade launcher, and boxes of ammunition. We could have cut those machete-wielding, blood-crazed drunken killers to pieces from here one by one. With insane joy. Put them all in a mass grave behind the church for the UN to exhume.

Even though Uncle Sam wouldn't and God couldn't and the UN just didn't, Ken and I might have stopped this. I know that's ridiculous—he's a lawyer and I'm a doctor—but the more time I spend thinking about it, the harder it is to escape the feeling that it's partly our fault. We should have been here to protect these people and we didn't show up. We should have been capable of changing just this tiny sliver of Rwandan history, but we didn't. People kill. The God I worship doesn't protect the weak, so only people can stop it. We're people and we didn't. All of us are guilty.

I'm fighting an overwhelming urge to throw myself headfirst off this tower, straight into the banana grove beside the grave. *Thud.* Just one more body for the pathologists to cut up. I'm shaking and sweating as I climb down the rungs to the safety and strange comfort of the corpses below.

Once I get back down, my faith all cut up and my knees turned to jelly, it doesn't seem so bad after all. My feet back on solid earth, more oxygen down here maybe. Fewer hallucinations, farther from God. I glove up and plunge back into the grave, where there's hard labor to be done, not the body and blood of Christ for my sins but ten more cadavers. It's salvation through exhumation, a new creed.

I make a mental note to avoid the bell tower.

A new priest has arrived, sent down by the archbishop to take control of what is left of church property. He's young, well-educated, and suspicious of the digging. I'm proud to introduce the team and explain the work; some of the world's top forensic experts are here and we have nothing to hide. Later he calls me up to his office, crucifixes on all the walls, and insists we pay rent, in cash to him will be just fine, because we have installed our equipment and mobile morgue on church property. It's to help the survivors, he adds, looking me in the eye.

I explain that we have written permission to be here from both the prime minister and the interior minister and want to return bodies to families for decent burials. He insists. The church's man on the spot asking for money to dig up corpses. I ask him how much rent he wants and on what terms, whether he'd like to be paid on a per corpse basis or on a daily rate; we could work under floodlights to keep our costs down. How about the per pound of flesh method, with a discount for the infants and children? I tell him to put his proposal on paper so I can send a copy to his archbishop.

From near the bottom of the grave, we pull out the body of a young male dressed in full priest's regalia. If this is the man we've heard about, he was with the people in the church, comforting the soon to be dead and refusing offers to be evacuated by boat at night to safety across the lake. Instead he chose to stay until the end. We treat him tenderly as we strip the body, wash the brilliantly colored robes, and dry them in the sun. Two priests, same church. One pays with his life, the other wants to be paid for the exhumation. The wrong man is in that body bag.

I'm down at the new governor's office later in the day discussing re-burial plans. This is no small issue, because of the sheer weight of corpses we now have on our hands. He is sitting at the same desk as his predecessor, the doctor who organized all this, whose name is still in gold lettering on a wooden plaque on the wall: Clement Kayishema. I've heard that he's now across the lake in Zaire, working with the UN in the refugee camps. He's got work to do to make up for the sixty thousand deaths he master-minded here. Where do you run as a Tutsi when Dr. Kayishema, Hutu governor, wants you dead? In this case to the local church, where the Virgin watches as you're slaughtered like an animal in the meatworks. With any luck he'll die before me so I can open a good bottle of wine and drink a toast on his grave.

The new governor is U.S.-educated and articulate, part of the new Tutsi ruling class. For some reason he doesn't like me or the work. He wasn't in Rwanda during the genocide, but each time we meet, he lectures me about our guilt. He's preaching to the converted, so I just listen and keep nodding.

He tells me that the people are angry with me because they're convinced thousands of civilians were killed at the church compound. They can't believe my experts have only found five hundred of them. They think my team is incompetent. I tell him we're well aware of all the other graves on the promontory and have already identified and mapped them, but that after nearly two months of digging, we now have the evidence the prosecutor needs, and are not able to dig up every corpse in town. That would take years.

"Then we won't let you leave," he threatens. I picture him and his soldiers holding us hostage in the church.

Then he tells me we have to give him money for the reburial. Anyone who's someone in this town wants cash for corpses. He has much more power than the priest, so I have to be careful. I show him the signed letter from the government in which they agree to take custody of the bodies after the investigation is over. I have to avoid taking legal responsibility for hundreds of corpses. I offer to lend him the forensic team, the backhoe, and our local laborers for as long as it takes to dig a decent grave and bury the bodies neatly in fresh white body bags. All he has to do is arrange the ceremony.

"No, they must be buried in the church where they were killed," he says. "I want you to dig a large hole in the floor, put the corpses in, and cover them over with thick glass so that people can walk on it and view the dead."

"But the floor is five-foot-thick concrete and the corpses are in no state to be displayed. It would be grotesque. And what about the relatives. Is that what they want?"

I have a vision of the church walls collapsing and the roof caving in on the engineer and his backhoe as he breaks ground for this crazy mortuary. I know it can happen because not so far from here a church with hundreds of people trapped inside was bulldozed onto the crowd. There was no need for machetes during that operation.

I suggest that he come up to the church to see for himself that his ideas make no sense. I drive him up there, because all he has is a motorcycle. We unzip a few body bags and he understands at once.

"Perhaps we could display a few of the skeletons, documenting their injuries," I suggest. "That would be much more decent."

"Yes," he enthuses. "What about a monument? You could raise funds in Europe and the U.S. from those Jewish groups."

I can't help picturing a hefty slice of that money going straight into his pocket. But I tell him that I'll pursue the idea when I get out of here. What else am I going to say?

I drive back down to the water's edge. It's peaceful here now. Some days I can look out across the lake and almost convince myself it is Switzerland and none of this ever happened. I have my UN passport and my air ticket out. But I don't smell so good, I have human flesh under my nails, and I spend my days arguing with priests and governors about corpses and money.

And there's no bougainvillea growing wild in Geneva.

CONDITION ECHO
Bosnia, Haiti, and Liberia, 1996–1998

ECOMOG: Liberia is a beautiful country on the West Coast of Africa founded by freed American slaves. Bereft of its U.S. patron at the end of the Cold War, it descended into a civil war characterized by total state collapse and a relentless campaign of sadistic, wanton violence. State authority was consigned to marauding rebels, many still in their teens. Still chastened from Somalia, Clinton and the UN refused to commit troops to Liberia. So peacekeeping responsibility was relegated to an African force not un- der UN command, known as the Economic Community of West African States Monitoring Group (ECOMOG), led by the regional superpower, Nigeria, and including small contingents from West African countries such as Ghana.

Andrew, July 1996
Near Srebrenica, Serb-Held Bosnia

I finally did take that flight out of Rwanda, retracing my path straight back to Bosnia. This time no one is shooting at us. The war is over; we've finally found the graves. It's now safe enough to exhume them because peace is being imposed by sixty thousand NATO troops. But NATO arrived too late for the eight thousand missing men of Srebrenica.

This gravesite would make a great picnic spot. It's a beautiful valley with a clear stream running through glades shaded from the harsh Balkan summer sun. It's just right for chilling the beer and bathing naked. Wildflowers grow abundantly, especially in the soil around the grave. No one comes by here; it's secluded from the main road, up a dead end dirt track. A perfect place for a massacre.

The guys on my team put another body into its bag, the remains of one of those eight thousand men, and stretcher it up the slope into the twenty-foot storage container. Serb militias brought their victims here at night by bus, lined them up in groups on the edge of the riverbank, and executed them with automatic weapons. Then they used a bulldozer to cover the bodies.

Young American GIs from the platoon detailed to protect us from the Serb military sweat freely under their helmets and body armor. Their cheeks bulge with tobacco as they spit out red juice at regular intervals onto the long grass. Their lieutenant climbs out of his Humvee and saunters over, his radio crackling. A truck has arrived down at his checkpoint on the main road and he wants to know if it's ours.

"Send it up," I tell him, "it's the body truck."

My deputy motions from down in the grave. I clamber down the slope to where he's kneeling beside a recently unearthed body. He lifts up its head to expose a strip of cloth bound tightly around the skull. It's a blindfold. Then he rolls the body onto its side to show me the hands tightly bound behind the back with thick wire.

Over my shoulder a large group of journalists is camped out forty meters away behind rolls of barbed wire. From the time we opened this grave, it's been a media frenzy; they all want footage of Europe's worst massacre since WWII. There are ten times more journalists here than in Rwanda, for ten times fewer victims. I ask my deputy whether they can see this blindfold through their telephoto lenses. No, he says, the body's covered in too much dirt.

We have a few hours before this news leaks out, so I tell him to get on the satellite phone to the prosecutor in The Hague to see how we should handle this evidence, and to use secure mode when he calls. He comes back a few minutes later, nodding. They want us to go public with the news at nine tomorrow morning.

This evidence is the reason we're digging. Eight thousand Muslim males from Srebrenica captured by the Bosnian Serb Army a year ago are still unaccounted for. The Serbs deny they have them. When the U.S. made public its satellite photos showing mass graves being dug in this area, Serb leaders said that these graves contained only battlefield casualties. We now have proof that they are lying.

It's a breakthrough for the prosecutor, but a tragedy for the relatives. Tomorrow my deputy will guide the journalists down into the grave itself and let them film the evidence up close. When the story breaks, it will send shockwaves through Bosnia and around the world. But I won't be here to see it; I have to transport another fifty bodies to the morgue.

The body truck backs up the narrow dirt road, lowers a metal hook, and winches the container up onto the flatbed. We have to get this evidence out of Serb territory, but NATO has refused us an escort. My driver crosses himself as we leave the safety of the Americans and set off with our macabre cargo.

An hour later we cross the Serb-Muslim front line, grinning at each other in relief. We pull up to our morgue, set up in a bombed-out clothing factory on the edge of a minefield. I hate it here. The pathologists' work, which I found interesting in Rwanda, is now a dreary, never-ending flow. It's like a production line. Inside, a radiologist positions a mobile X-ray machine over a corpse, guiding the pathologist's metal probe as she seeks bullet fragments. Here we find not Rwanda's machete wounds but anywhere from two to thirty bullets in each corpse. We burn large citronella candles under each autopsy table in a vain attempt to mask the stench, but now the smell of citronella nauseates me.

Our Bosnian translator sits at a table, wearing rubber surgical gloves and a face mask, examining personal effects from the victims' clothing.

I've grown to admire this taciturn young woman. These were her people, but she never complains about the work. I can't read the documents but I sit with her as she goes through them for me. There are simple love letters, faded family snapshots, bills and receipts, children's drawings. Each is a tiny part of the mosaic of tragedy, glimpses of a peaceful rural life before Serbs killed their Muslim neighbors and razed their houses.

I've seen thousands of cadavers over the years and ought to be inured to the sight by now. I try to hide the tears, but she sees. It's in these quiet moments that I realize it could be me and mine. I never met these people, but now I carry their pictures and letters and I'm surrounded by their absence.

This should never have happened. Srebrenica was a Muslim town that the UN declared a "safe haven" and promised to protect. But in July 1995, the Serbs, emboldened by years of American and European appeasement, attacked the town. The Dutch UN peacekeepers tasked to keep the safe haven safe got no air support, offered no resistance, and surrendered to save their skins. They then had a front-row seat as Serb soldiers rounded up the men and boys, herded them onto buses, and drove them away to their execution.

After Srebrenica, America and NATO went to war with the Serbs. Uncle Sam took the gloves off, called the Serb bluff for the first time, and almost four years of Serb ethnic cleansing ended in less than two weeks. If they'd done it sooner, I wouldn't be here filling up a UN morgue with Muslim corpses.

I pull myself away from the evidence table and walk outside to blow the stench out of my nose and clear my head. The women of Srebrenica are back, camped out in the car park on the other side of the fence. They're all dressed alike in wide ankle-length skirts, floral blouses, and paisley-patterned headscarves. I've tried to block their view into the morgue with blue plastic sheeting, but they still manage to peer through, hear the whine of the bone saws and smell the stench.

A year after Srebrenica fell, they still believe that their men are alive somewhere, in work camps in Serbia or in coal mines in Russia; they grasp at the flimsiest of rumors. But their denial, so desperately maintained, crumbles at this fence line, where the weight of the corpses crushes their resistance to the thought that their men, all eight thousand of them, are dead. All they'll get back, if they're lucky, are a few bones, some washed clothing, and a snapshot or ID card. Where the victims were made to undress before they were shot, they'll get even less than that.

I'm not on good terms with the women of Srebrenica. When they first turned up here, I took my interpreter and introduced myself. I wanted them to understand what we were doing and why. They listened briefly, but then something gave way and they began to weep and tear at their hair and bang their heads against the wall. Some of them even fainted. When I tried to comfort them, they turned on me screaming, spraying spittle into my face. The interpreter pulled me back inside the front gate, looking scared. I tried again the following day, with the same result. So I gave up. They hate me: they want their men back and I offer them nicely bagged remains.

They're right to spit. What happened here is obscene. Barely a year after the killings, we waltz back in under the same despised UN flag to clean up the cadavers. I was naïve to expect gratitude.

One day someone at UNHQ will commission an official report about this disaster, replete with mea culpas and lessons learned. But for me there's only one lesson and it's staring right at me every day as I eat lunch: If blue-helmeted UN peacekeepers show up in your town or village and offer to protect you, run. Or else get weapons. Your lives are worth so much less than theirs. I learned that the day we were evacuated from Haiti.

Everything about this work is contentious. I spend my time trying to shield the team from the politics, but it's impossible, especially with so many corpses and so much media. I'm tired of being responsible for others, and I know it's only a matter of time before one of them drives off the road, cracks up, or gets shot by an enraged Serb.

I drive fast out the gate toward the U.S. Army base that sits across the minefield, trying to pretend the women are not there. Out the corner of my eye, I see them converging on the Land Cruiser. If they get close enough, they'll bang on the windows and thump the hood. I can't take it, so I just accelerate away.

At the base I squat in a corner of the steam-shrouded shower block and let the water rinse away the stench and the fatigue. I stare at my feet, examine my hands, test each finger. My body seems fine, but my mind's in a daze. It's hard to make one thought follow another.

When I get out of the shower, my skin is pink and wrinkled. My watch says I was in there for ninety minutes, but it seemed like five. I wander over to the PX for more chocolate, which I've been eating in bulk as an antidepressant. Today they've got the dark, bitter kind, Suzanne's favorite, so I decide on the spot to take her some. To hell with the morgue and the dead dictating how I live. I'm taking a weekend off for a change. I want to be with her. The cadavers will still be here waiting when I get back.

Suzanne is based in Serb territory west of here. After Rwanda she got herself posted to Bosnia so we could be close. I pass through lush fields and forests and abandoned Muslim villages. Every twenty minutes there's a mosque with its minaret destroyed.

I drive at speed into the fading light, windows of the Land Cruiser down, stereo up, and balmy air smelling of freshly cut grass in my face. Each passing mile takes me farther from the corpses and closer to her. I want to make love to her without wondering whether I stink. She always has a good sniff before drawing her conclusion, an awkward moment. She says my Land Cruiser smells bad but I still smell sweet. She's a good liar.

I arrive just before midnight in Banja Luka, the Serb town where genocide was planned. Her front doorbell is broken, so I slip around the side of the house and peer through the bedroom curtains. I watch her as she sleeps, savoring the moment. Then I tap lightly on the windowpane.

The next day is bright and hot. Suzanne takes me for lunch at the medieval castle by the river—feta salad and roast lamb and local beer—then to the public swimming pool. Families barbecue under the trees, mothers nurse their newborns, and children frolic in the water. We could be anywhere in the world. It's just a short drive but a universe away from the morgue.

Monday morning I'm back to supervise the transfer of our first batch of remains to the Bosnian authorities. We spend hours preparing to make the handover as professional as possible. We rebag a hundred bodies in fresh white body bags, clean up the morgue, and put the whole team in new blue surgical gowns. Around midday the truck of local officials pulls up at the gate, pursued by a swarm of journalists. The Bosnians have ignored my request for discretion; they want to make an event of it.

It's a mob scene as part of the fence collapses and relatives and journalists surge forward through the gap. I'm not trained for anything I'm doing here, but controlling angry crowds is the skill I'm missing most acutely at the moment. It doesn't help to start shouting or getting aggressive, or you'll soon be on national TV as the UN asshole blocking access to the country's dead. So I just abandon the idea of controlling anyone and organize a human chain to pass the body bags hand to hand the twenty meters from the morgue to the truck. Two of our local workers station themselves inside the truck to organize placement of the heap of bodies, media all around. The whole gruesome process takes about two hours.

Bosnian officials sign for custody of each corpse and drive off with their burden, journalists and families in tow. I reward the team with the rest of the day off. A good morning's work, professionally done, without incident.

But job satisfaction never lasts here. There's outrage the next day, and calls from our Sarajevo office. The footage was shown on national television, the first glimpses for the Bosnian people of the eight thousand corpses of Srebrenica. No more denying the massacres. They must have been glued to their TVs. I didn't see it, but my translator told me it all looked professional, up until the moment when a close-up showed our local workers inside the truck tossing the corpses around like sacks of rice. You could hear the skulls crack as they hit the flatbed. It must have looked and sounded terrible, despite all our effort to get it right.

I set out to save lives and have ended up collecting the dead. Somewhere along the line, I lost sight of treating people and became obsessed with my own grandiose ideals of service. But there is no redemption in this. I've worked myself into the ground only to end up doing the very thing my parents begged me to avoid. I've ended up serving myself.

All that is left now is to hold on for that day, sometime after the first snowfall, when my deputy will radio me from the grave with the news that our backhoe has finally hit undisturbed earth at the bottom and the last of the dead are back above ground. When I receive that message, I'll drive out into the stubble of the cornfields, stand alone on the edge, and stare down into that gaping hole one last time. Then I'll let go of this millstone of belief and ideals that's breaking my neck, watch it tumble down and sink slowly into the mud at the bottom. I've had it with our humanitarian hubris. Let the dead bury the dead.

Afterward I'll give the final order of my brief but eventful forensic career, this time to the engineer. Bulldoze in this hole and bury my youthful illusions. Then I'll crack open a beer and drink a toast. Farewell death, you son of a bitch. Here's to the rest of my life.

Ken, 1996
Liberia

0700 HRS. This morning's task is to prepare a summary of human rights reports for UNHQ in New York. This one goes on top:

- There is an area in the south where a Nigerian ECOMOG contingent was deployed for several months this summer. They were in
the habit of encouraging very young Liberian girls from the nearby
displaced persons camp to visit and "seducing" them with rice and
a little money. The girls were nine or ten. Then a Ghanaian ECO-
MOG contingent established a camp nearby. The Ghanaians were
more gentle and generous with the girls. They would give them a
whole can full of rice as opposed to the more paltry handful from
the Nigerians. So the girls started frequenting the Ghanaian camp
more than the Nigerian. One day dead little girls started appearing
on the path from the displaced persons camp to the Ghanaian
camp—but not on the path to the Nigerians. The girls had been
decapitated and their heads inserted inside their nine-year-old
genitals. In the opinion of the investigating officer, this was a message to the girls from the Nigerians that it wouldn't be worth it to
frequent the Ghanaians for the sake of a little extra rice.

And these are the peacekeepers.

Clinton is so afraid to deploy troops now and Congress is so disgusted
by the incompetence of the UN that we have abdicated peacekeeping re-
sponsibilities in West Africa to the Republic of Nigeria, a government of
assassins. The UN is only here to monitor the African soldiers in ECO-
MOG. We have no troops of our own. It's peacekeeping by subcontract.

Thomas Friedman says Liberia has Bosnia envy. A cute phrase for an
ugly idea. What the UN pays for four days of peacekeeping in Bosnia
would pay for one year of peacekeeping here. But Liberia has no oil, no
strategic relevance, and the airport, hotels, and beaches offer neither rest
nor recreation. No one comes, no one cares. An orphaned little war at the
end of the earth.

It's like the capital punishment discrepancies we studied in law school:
the perpetrator of capital murder is three times more likely to be executed
in some states if the victim is white than if the victim is black. Two hundred
thousand humans died from war crimes in Yugoslavia, in the middle of
Europe, and 200,000 died from exactly the same crimes here, on the edge
of West Africa. For Yugoslavia the UN created the first formal war crimes
tribunal since Nuremberg and is deploying batteries of human rights officers, forensic pathologists, lawyers, and investigators, including Dr. Andrew.
For war crimes in Liberia, the UN sent, well, me.

I'm supposed to use sanitized diplomatic jargon in my report. "UN officials have accumulated evidence of twenty-three gross violations of human rights including the right to be protected from arbitrary and extrajudicial execution." But fuck it, I'm tired, and I don't care about protocol anymore. In Cambodia I believed passionately in work I didn't understand; now I understand it all too well but don't believe a word of it.

So this time I'm going to send the raw reports. I use the same form I used in Cambodia; it's a durable format: how many died, did they torture, were you raped? They'll ignore it all in New York, like they ignore everything else. General Roméo Dallaire, the commander of UN troops in Rwanda, sent a fax detailing imminent genocide and they ignored that. Kofi Annan, the head of UN Peacekeeping, ordered him to stand down and do nothing, other than share his information with a handful of diplomats who already knew, including the French, who at the time were arming their allies among the Hutu extremists, who then committed the genocide. I heard General Dallaire can't live with himself now and is deeply depressed back home in Canada.

If they could ignore an urgent fax on impending genocide from a general, they'll certainly ignore reports of torture from me. But I'm going to send a thorough compilation anyway; at least they'll have to read it and think about it before they file it away. Maybe it will keep someone else up at night.

- Fighters are moving among the displaced of various areas looking for pregnant women. When they find one, they gamble on the sex of the unborn baby. They then cut the mother's womb open and pull out the baby to see who won the bet. The mother and baby are then thrown to the side of the road, as the fighters go looking for their next victim. One woman was forced to watch as her pregnant sister's stomach was ripped open and her unborn baby thrown into a pit latrine. She was spared, made it to Monrovia, but for months refused to utter a word. She refused to eat, went to the toilet where she sat, and lost the will to live.

- A man reported, "I heard the NPFL rebels saying to a man, 'We want to buildar your engine.' Immediately I saw the fighters kill the man and remove his heart, kidneys, and liver for cooking and eating." (The translator's notation on the witness statement says, "'Buildar' means to cook for eating and 'engine' is the inside organs of the human.")

- The displaced attested to seeing a bandit cut off a woman's breast, roast it, then eat it, while leaving her to die of blood loss.

The Liberian human rights group that produced the last report added this note, a gratuitous insight for the reader to ponder: "Cannibalism adds a whole new dimension to human rights abuses. The right to life is threatened based on a perpetrator's appetite, and there is a fear of persecution based on one's fitness for consumption."

0730 HRS. Mr. Ignatius Peabody is here for our meeting, right on time as usual. It's already ninety degrees and ninety percent humidity, but he's got a tweed suit on, proud and official. He works his ass off for a Liberian human rights group I like to collaborate with; I have all the time in the world for this guy.

"Mr. Ken, how you keepin'?"

"Good to see you, Mr. Ignatius, thanks for coming in. How are you?"

"Ah keepin' fine tank gawd, anh-hen. But it not easy-oh. Fighteen small small outside."

I wonder how long it took him to get to my office, how many checkpoints he had to pass. Even our own guards harass these guys at the front gate.

"How da job?"

The job. The job. "The job is, is, well, okay, Ignatius, given some of the alternatives."

"I tank Gawd fa da United Nations enh-hen, I tank gawd fa ECO-MOG enh-hen, I tank Gawd fa you."

"Thanks, Ignatius. How's the family?"

"It not easy-oh, too much fighteen, but family keepin' fine. How da body?"

It's a beautiful West African custom, just like the Senegalese soldiers in Rwanda, but the greetings can go on like this forever. The twist here is that Liberia was founded by freed American slaves. Rich plantation owners, including Madison and Jefferson, paid for the passage of their freed slaves back to Africa to create a free republic—especially for the house slaves, many of whom were their offspring. So the spoken English among the educated elite in the capital is inherited directly from the upper crust of southern plantation slave culture. They have Baptist churches and plantation-style houses, and the president used to wear a top hat. Even the constitution was written at Harvard Law School by the guys whose portraits hang on the library walls. It's like one of those *Star Trek* episodes when you find yourself back in your own country one hundred years before you were born. Forced by the echoes of American slave English—which I've never heard before—to consider the worst crime my country ever committed, which I've never done before.

When the freed, repatriated slaves—who hadn't lived in Africa for generations—arrived on the coast, they re-created the only society they knew, the plantation. In the process they colonized the indigenous Africans living in the area; pressed them into labor; denied them access to justice, property, and wealth; and violently repressed the inevitable series of revolts, until all hell broke loose in one of the nastiest wars on the planet.

The most bloodcurdling aspect of which is systematic rape. I've asked Mr. Ignatius Peabody to have one of his female staff compile existing reports and take new witness statements from a refugee camp outside of town. I want to make a specific report to New York on rape. Every time I go on a helicopter mission across the rebel lines, I hear inconceivably sadistic rape stories. If they kill you, even if they eat you, at least you're dead. But I can't do this investigation myself; I'm a foreigner and I'm male. But mostly I'm not sure I can sit in that camp and look those women in the eye.

Ignatius has a stack of material. I pick up the first files:

- I was nine months pregnant. When the fighters came, they grabbed me and my husband and tied us up. The head of my husband was cut off in front of me. I was then raped by about fifteen young men. I delivered my baby a day after. Now my womb cannot stay in place.

- I was forcibly taken into the bush with my three children and husband. The rebels accused my husband of trying to kill General War Boss and General Kill the Bitch. My husband was tied to a thorny tree; black driver ants were put all over his body while I was raped as a pregnant woman in front of my three children by four fighters. Later an order was given that my husband should be beheaded in front of my children and me. My husband cried for mercy, but they did not listen and cut his esophagus and my husband finally died.

I don't need to read any more. I know what's in that stack. We estimate that a third of the women in displaced persons camps have been raped. Half the population of the country was displaced during the war, so if we're right, that means one in six women has been raped. We give questionnaires to demobilized fighters and ten percent of the fighters admit to having raped more than ten times during the war. Not a single prosecution, investigation, UN report, press exposé, nothing. It's as if 100,000 rapes never happened.

I shake Mr. Ignatius Peabody's hand. We shake our heads. He's going back out there, through the gates, through the checkpoints. I have to go to the morning staff meeting.

"Thank you, Mr. Ignatius. I can't promise that anything will happen with these reports but I will pass them on to New York."

"Ah say, ma people, what we have done-oh."

"Godspeed Ignatius."

"Tank Gawd for life, Mr. Ken."

0830 HRS. The UN head of mission, a retired ambassador, sits at the head of the conference table, not quite filling up his chair. He wears one of those short-sleeved safari shirts, with a thin gold pen dangling, clipped to the wrong side of his breast pocket. His face is expressive, sometimes glum, sometimes animated, but always a little stunned, disconcerted, the look of a grandfather startled from a nap by someone calling his name sharply.

Next to the ambassador at the head of the table is General Hassan, commander of UN military observers, an Egyptian general with a chest full of flags, pendants, and medals, a carved wooden walking staff, big gut and even bigger mustache, eyes, and smile. On the other side of the ambassador is the chief administrative officer, Vishnu Nodonwog, an Indian from Trinidad. Vishnu was called in to replace the last CAO, who was removed for taking a fifteen percent kickback on everything we purchased. In the name of cleaning up the old corruption, Vishnu tapped the phones, paid local staff to spy for him, and threatened to send anyone home who opposes him—including vulnerable young secretaries who have the temerity to refuse to sleep with him—all to facilitate his own quest for a fifteen percent kickback on everything we purchase. He has a full head of bright white hair and a trimmed white Fu Manchu mustache in a stunning pattern against very dark brown skin, a handsome sculpture of a man. Except for the fraudulent, leaden eyelids that close fully most of the briefing.

The rest of us fill the table in descending order of seniority. Next to me are a political affairs officer from Afghanistan, a humanitarian affairs officer from Ethiopia, a security officer from Iraq, and Billy, the ambassador's nephew, who is supposed to be the disarmament officer. Billy giggles a lot. Marilyn keeps the minutes. Marilyn worked with Heidi and me in the 'Dish.

But the reason I'm here is missing from his seat at this table. My boss's boss in Somalia was a man of enormous integrity. We worked together during some of the worst moments a UN mission has ever faced, and whenever I was in over my head, which was often, his advice and leadership were measured, humane, and incorruptible. I trusted him entirely, a precious commodity under the circumstances, especially given how dangerous my direct boss could be. When he called me in Haiti and asked me to come work for him, I thought it a matter of honor not to say no to a man like that. A month after I arrived, he called me to his office and said he couldn't take it anymore, he was leaving Liberia and the UN.

So now I'm an orphan. Which is a bad thing to be when they're fighting.

The ambassador clears his throat and the briefing begins. The ambassador tells the general we need more precise figures on the troop strength of one of the rebel factions. The general had told him 376 fighters, but when the ambassador used that number at a ceasefire meeting, everyone laughed at him, he was embarrassed. So what is the true number? General Hassan smiles and says, "No sir, Mr. Ambassador, I said you number is three sevens six, not 3-7-6." He writes it out on a pad and smiles broadly. "You see, 7-7-7-6, three sevens six."

The general has satisfied and amused himself. He has the floor and uses it to announce intelligence that the rebels are bringing weapons into the capital, Monrovia, and creating arms caches throughout the city—small arms, RPGs, high-caliber machine guns, mortars—stockpiling them in strategic locations. Fighters are streaming into the city, preparing for a major offensive.

Everyone at the table jumps on the intelligence report because everyone already knows. You can feel the tension at the checkpoints now. Harder, more disciplined fighters have taken over from child soldiers at key chokeholds in the city. There is more firing in the distance at night, people are stocking up on food at the markets. You can smell violence and fear approach. There's rhythm to an impending bloodletting and it's accelerating. The anxiety is contagious from the fighters at the checkpoints to the civilians on the streets to us at this table. The room is alive with the emergency.

Smack. The ambassador slams his hand on the desk. "I tell you, I want you people to stop spreading rumors about arms caches in this city," he says. "I plead with you to stop gossiping. This kind of talk *Is. Not. Helpful.*

To. The. Peace. Process." He slams his hand down to emphasize each word of his plaint and glares at us wide-eyed. The political affairs officer sitting next to me from Afghanistan has lived through generations of fighting, and he's not at all intimidated by the ambassador. He says, Yes sir, but what about the arms caches themselves, sir, are they helpful to the peace process? He kicks me under the table, raises his big, black, bushy Afghani eyebrows to the sky, nods a tiny little nod to himself and to me; a mischievous smile sneaks across one corner of his mouth.

I start to laugh quietly to myself. I try to stop but I meet his eyes again and it erupts—something about the startled look on the ambassador's face, the fever of fighting closing in on us, the Afghani guy's eyebrows. The room is silent, it's a big moment in the ambassador's hold on the reins of power, but I'm starting to shudder with laughter. I try to swallow it down, choke it back. I bite the inside of my cheek. But it doesn't work, the wall of my stomach relaxes, loosens, something else is releasing inside me, not mirth. It's a relief to let it go; it's a shade away from a sob.

The ambassador clears his throat again, his eyes dart around the room. He's preparing to reestablish control of his meeting, which is always dangerous. The next agenda item is something I want all of us to take seriously, he says, it's very sensitive, very serious. The *r* becomes a *d* and the two words sound funny together—"vedy sedious." "There's been a lot of confusion about my role in this conflict, our role," he says. "It is my intention to clear up the confusion."

There has been heavy fighting in the north on the highway to the border, he continues, between a Nigerian ECOMOG battalion and one of the rebel factions. The rebels are using civilians in the city as a human shield against Nigerian attacks. There are heavy casualties on both sides. The rebels have cut off the highway so no food can get into the city. The civilians are trapped. The rebels have taken a Nigerian officer hostage and have desecrated the bodies of fallen Nigerian soldiers who are lying on the highway.

Together with our Nigerian brothers, I intend to organize a ceasefire and a goodwill convoy mission, he says. I want us to go up that highway, retrieve the Nigerian bodies, negotiate the release of the hostage, and deliver food to the trapped civilians. My goal is to show that the road is open. This is a humanitarian emergency, and we have to be seen to be doing something.

The humanitarian affairs officer interrupts and says the rebels will just commandeer the food and the trucks. The food will never make it to the civilians. And even if it does, it will endanger them more than help; the

261

rebels will kill them for it. I'm not endangering my staff or the civilians, she says.

If a civilian is going to challenge the ambassador, General Hassan certainly isn't going to stay silent. So he says that if they are still fighting, then the highway is probably mined. First we have to ensure that road has been demined. Next to pile on is the political affairs officer. If we are traveling with the Nigerians on a goodwill mission to the rebels who are fighting the Nigerians, he says, the rebels may ambush the Nigerian convoy with us in it.

I have spoken with all concerned, the ambassador says, waving his hands, and I have assurances. They have promised me safe passage. He nods his head emphatically.

I've heard all this before. They used to tell us every morning at the briefing in Somalia that "General Aidid has assured us that he is restraining his boys; his desire for peace is sincere." Every morning they would assure us and every afternoon someone would get ambushed.

It's my turn to weigh in. Sir, if the rebel leaders here have assured you, how do we know that the orders have been passed to the boys at the checkpoints? These checkpoints are miles apart and they have no radios. What about the forces still fighting in the bush? We know that they don't follow orders from the capital. Do the leaders even know if the fighters mined the road or have any idea where the mines are?

I sound like Andrew in Cambodia when he was establishing how much I didn't understand about my work and he did.

The ambassador says it again: we are hopeful they won't attack the convoy. I am hopeful the road is safe.

I snap. I just don't care anymore. Fire me, send me home, I can't accept that answer.

"Sir, have you ever called the parents of someone on your staff to inform them their child is dead? What would you say to the mother you'd call tomorrow? We were hopeful? We had assurances? We wanted to be seen to be doing something?"

My only ally at this table is Marilyn. She was at India Base with Heidi when Matt died. I don't know if I could have said that without her here. She's sitting next to me; out of the corner of my eye, I can see her nodding. Marilyn was the one who called A-farts to dedicate "In Your Eyes" to Matt's memory. She puts her hand on my back and presses lightly into my flesh with her fingertips.

My hands are shaking, I'm expecting the ambassador to scream at me, send me home immediately. I've seen it happen before, these guys are so proud.

But it's okay. I want to go home.

The ambassador summons all of the authority that his sixty-five years can muster, inhales deeply, exhales slowly through his nose, frowns bitterly.

"We all knew the risks when we volunteered to come here, Mr. Cain. There are no guarantees of safety in a war. Are you saying you refuse to go? Are you afraid to travel on the convoy?"

Checkmate.

"No, no, sir. That's not it. I'll go. I wanna go."

1100 HRS. The highway is just a ragged, thin blacktop strip through dry scrub brush. We pass ten Nigerian checkpoints as we head north. Half the convoy is Nigerian military vehicles, so they just wave us through. It's calm and normal and safe; civilians milling along the side of the road with baskets of food and babies everywhere. We should stop and confer with the soldiers at the checkpoint to get intel about the road north, but it's hard to stop a twenty-vehicle convoy, so we just fly through.

Then we hit no-man's-land. No checkpoints, no civilians. The convoy slows, the vehicles bunch. The lead vehicle must see that we're about to hit the rebel front lines. Then we do. They're deployed on all sides of a desolate crossroads. Two mounted heavy machine guns face opposite directions in the middle of the intersection. The convoy makes an accordion, then we stop.

UN officials and Nigerian officers greet the boys at the checkpoint warily and slowly, and everyone dismounts. This convoy is supposed to be concrete evidence of an abstract ceasefire discussed in the capital. You never know until the two sides mingle, and even then you don't know. I linger in back at the periphery of the negotiation. No one will tell me anything useful at the center of attention.

There are bodies of fallen soldiers all along this highway. If we can find them and return them to loved ones in Nigeria, it should help calm things down, at least it's evidence of goodwill. I brought the skeleton crew from the Liberian Red Cross with me to collect the bodies. They were scared and didn't want to come. I had to call in a favor to convince them. I better find some bodies or I'm wasting their time.

But the rebels aren't going to just show us bodies they've desecrated. I need help. Little kids always surround us asking for candy and pens, and they usually know what's going on. I give one bright-looking kid a one-dollar bill and ask him where the Nigerian bodies are. He sprints up a hill into the bushes and points to two dogs digging at two decaying bodies in a heap. That was easy.

The men's bodies are mangled from the force of the automatic weapons fire that killed them and are crawling with maggots. I call for the skeleton crew. The two orderlies in white gloves, masks, and white lab coats look otherworldly against the green and brown of the bush. They clasp two green body bags and pick up one of the bodies, one orderly holding the wrists, the other holding the ankles, and swing it into a bag. The bag falls in a heap at their feet. The orderlies pick up the second body by the wrists and ankles and start to slide it into the other bag. As the body slumps in, a hand detaches and the orderly is left holding the hand. The body and the bag fall in a tangle with the first bag. The orderly holds up the hand and looks at it, at me, at the kid, at the dogs, at the other orderly, at the bags, at the hand. He's lost track of which bag held which body and which body is missing a hand. He's reluctant to bend over, with the hand in his hand, to look for the body missing a hand. So we stand on top of the hill immobile, staring at each other, frozen in time, the little kid looking at us quizzically, the detached hand poised in the hand of the orderly with the white lab coat.

I turn back down the hill to join the convoy, leaving the bodies and the bags and the orderlies and the hand and the boy and the dogs and the smell.

1400 HRS. The second rebel checkpoint is alive with the light and heat of Africa at midday. The rebels are drugged up, kids on crack with big guns. They snort gunpowder and amphetamines before they fight. It must be a hundred degrees, but one guy has on a winter coat with a furry hood. An oversized red-and-white American Airlines luggage tag dangles from his neck, alongside an African talisman to prevent bullets from hitting him. He's swinging a rocket-propelled grenade launcher like it's a baseball bat, a bulbous green grenade attached at the top.

They're wild, not in uniform or under any kind of command. Bags of stolen food and random household goods lie in piles on the side of the road. This is a failed state, reverting to anarchy. It's impossible to distinguish the conduct of war from a criminal gang on a looting rampage. Half the rebels are prepubescent. I see one kid holding an AK-47 almost as big as his eleven-year-old body. Another kid with bloodshot crazy eyes rushes up to me in a gyrating dance and a Toledo Youth Hockey T-shirt, right up into my face, voodoo fetishes dangling, bad breath and sweat, "Ah big commando killa here, ah big rebel guerrilla, ah gonna eat you, white man." He says it over and over in my face.

I backpedal toward a group of civilians gathered at the edge of the checkpoint. There's an old man crumpled in a wheelbarrow, and a young man, who must be his son, leaning over him resting on the handles. The old man's face and head are wrapped in a rag stained in old, dark blood. The son says he was shot in the face during the fighting, can I move him to a hospital? The old man cocks his head and looks up at me, wistfully amazed at my presence. "Ah dyin, ma son, ah dyin-oh."

I can't hold eye contact, so I look at the son. His dad is folded into a wheelbarrow, dying. Stuck at the edge of a rebel checkpoint. There is nothing he can do for his dad. There's a tattered burlap rice bag lying in the wheelbarrow next to the old man, probably all of the belongings they could grab when they ran. The rebel kids are singing and firing into the air thirty feet away. We're going north, the hospital is to the south. I can't bring them with us. We're impotent. All three of us.

I see a middle-aged man nearby, his face deeply furrowed by worry lines. He looks approachable. There are rumors that the battle here between Nigerian peacekeepers and the rebels was over plunder rights to a local diamond mine. So I ask the guy if he knows what sparked this round of fighting. "Minerals," he says without hesitation. "Minerals from de African soil. Very sorrowful to see how tings goin.' Gold and diamond business will carry plenty people from this world."

So that's why an old man gets his face blown off and dies in a wheelbarrow. Because Nigerian peacekeepers are stealing diamonds from a country whose peace they are supposed to keep.

I ask him if there is any way to move the injured man in the wheelbarrow down the road south toward the capital. He says no. When the fighting started in the north, civilians fled south, to this village, on the way to Monrovia. But Nigerian peacekeepers stopped them and held them here, saying "We are in charge of your protection, we will assure your security." When the fighting moved south to here, the civilians were trapped, as the rebels advanced and the Nigerians withdrew. When the rebels finally occupied the village, they executed dozens of civilians, accusing them of collaborating with the Nigerians. Why else would they have stayed here? The Nigerian front line is farther south now, but they still won't let civilians pass. So the old man in the wheelbarrow and his son are stuck.

I wonder how many civilians have died since Cambodia from spurious assurances of security by peacekeepers who offer protection but can't live up to their lethally empty promises? Will there ever be an accounting? Or will our failures and their civilian casualties just dissolve into unrecorded history—like 100,000 rape cases here—unexposed, anonymous, abandoned?

1600 HRS. We reach the last checkpoint in the north before the border, where the worst fighting was, where the hostage is supposed to be. Two Nigerian military vehicles lie overturned and burned at the gate to the city. I walk over to see if there are bodies. No bodies but piles of spent shell casings. Hundreds. The soldiers must have returned intense fire from the cover of their overturned vehicles. One of the vehicles has blood all over it, but it's not spilled blood, someone spread it around with their hands, in a pattern. They whitewashed the vehicle with blood.

The skeleton crew finds a body at the side of the road. He's shirtless, lying on his stomach with his legs resting straight and flat, ankles crossed in back. The way a teenager lies on the floor watching TV. They turn him over, he's as stiff as a wooden plank. Three AK-47 cartridges lie in the pool of blood where his body fell. He must have been executed at pointblank range right on this spot. There are so many maggots seething on his face, it looks like he's expressing an entire range of vibrant emotions.

I am supposed to work with a Nigerian officer, Colonel Kapelley, to locate the hostage and see if we can negotiate his release. UN officials, Nigerian officers, and rebels are all milling at the checkpoint, but no one is actually doing anything. Colonel Kapelley tells me he will be in charge of the negotiation, it's his countryman, his fellow officer.

Everyone follows us and then surrounds us when we get to rebel HQ. It's just a modest house they must have commandeered from a civilian family. Two rebel commanders stand on the steps of the porch above us. They're a little older and a little harder than the kids at the checkpoints. They have those vapid killer eyes you see a lot in the best soldiers. It's hot and we're surrounded and everyone is sweating. Our status is ambiguous, the ceasefire is a theory, and we could easily become the next hostages.

Colonel Kapelley says, We demand that you release the hostage. It is your obligation and your commanders at headquarters in Monrovia have assured us of cooperation.

Oh shit. He's doing it all wrong.

The rebel commander explodes, "Ah on da ground here, Ah on da

266

ground, no Monrovia commander nuttin'. No release, no way, you people still shooting."

Bad start. You have to show a little respect, ask for modest concessions first, let them make the decisions. It's going to embarrass Colonel Kapelley, but I've got to step in and try. I've been doing one version or another of this since Cambodia. I'm not exactly sure what the colonel does back in Nigeria, but not this.

I ask the rebels their names.

"General Snake and General One More War, on da ground, Alligator Base, no man fear nuttin'."

Colonel Kapelley laughs derisively. He's served twenty years to make colonel. These guys are only twenty years old and call themselves general.

Great, Colonel, pull rank, that'll help.

The rebels square up into the colonel's face and glare.

He leans over and whispers to me, Forget it, they're going to kill him anyway. Let's get out of here.

Bullshit. They always say no at first. We need to let them be defiant for the audience; they usually soften if you give them time. I was doing this once in Rwanda when the fighters said no in different shades of defiance for half an hour, but in the middle of the conversation, the prisoner just appeared from the barracks, free to go. They never agreed to release him, never said anything cooperative, but they must have sent a signal somehow. I wasn't even sure if I was free to put the guy in my vehicle. We drove away looking over our shoulders to see if anyone was chasing us.

It's sweaty and tense. I can smell the liquor on the rebels' breath. They're hostile and cocky and the crowd surrounding us is shuffling, restless. It's still hot but the day is getting old. We need to give this time and let the conversation unwind, but they can smell that Colonel Kapelley is scared and recalcitrant, which agitates everything.

I say, "Listen, General Snake"—I can't bring myself to say General One More War—"we're asking for something small, not something big. We just want to see the hostage, let him write a letter home to his wife and kids. You can read it to make sure there's no intel in it, just let him contact his loved ones."

I want them to think of their hostage as a human with a family. And if they let me in to see him to write the letter, I can also bring him some water and Cipro and gauze and antibacterial cream. I'm sure they beat him and he has infected cuts.

Colonel Kapelley says, "No, no, no," to me, audibly this time, "you don't understand Africa," and he backs away.

My arms go numb and I feel lightheaded. I have to put my head in my hands. If I were doing this alone, I think I could have gotten in to see the hostage. I scream at him inside my head. *I am willing to try to negotiate this out and you're not? Why am I risking my life on behalf of your fellow officer, and your soldiers, including dead ones?* I start to float up above myself. I'm looking down at our unhappy group of rebels, UN officials, Nigerian soldiers, Colonel Kapelley, General Snake, General One More War, and me. I watch from above as Colonel Kapelley reaches for my arm and pulls me out from the crowd and I pull back into the crowd. I slam back into my body. *WAIT. Why should I ask more of myself than the hostage's fellow officer does, for fucksake? Am I stupid? Has everything I've done for the past five missions been this stupid?*

I decide at that sweaty, dizzy, I-have-no-spit moment that this is insane, I am a naïve fool.

I leave their blessed assemblage and retreat back to the parked convoy. Two colleagues in blue UN baseball caps, who had been watching passively from the periphery, step forward to fill my empty place in the negotiation. They approach General One More War earnestly, expectantly.

0000 HRS. I stare at the shadows thrown by the ceiling fan in the middle of another sleepless night. My romantic ideas about peacekeeping are so obviously untenable now that I would be out of my mind to stay here, which forces me to realize that I was probably out of my mind to be here in the first place. Now what?

Time to go home. I've spent my youth.

Heidi, 1998
Port-au-Prince

Every day in Haiti, the sun shines and the sky is blue. From our bedroom window, I can see the ocean. The breeze blows off the sea and up the valley and through the mahogany shutters into our apartment, high up on the hillside in Bourdon. Even during the wet season, the rains come only after dark, and then just for an hour.

Every day in Haiti, we have no electricity until after dark. We are either at work or make do without our fans, without our refrigerator, without TV.

Every day in Haiti, late in the afternoon, at that moment when the day feels sad, when there's a stillness in the air, as if time isn't certain it will go on, and then it does, the plane leaves Port-au-Prince for New York.

On this one day in November, a week before my family in New Jersey will celebrate Thanksgiving, I'm on one of these flights to join them. Wary of being away from the business, Marc decides to wait and plans for a Christmas visit with my family.

On this one day in November, and not on any other day in the year before, the rain comes before dark, before the businesses shut down, before the laundry is shut down. On this one day in November, we have electricity late in the afternoon, before dark.

I don't find out until the next afternoon that Marc is dead. Rain and bad wiring and curiosity and impulsiveness ended the life of the man I've been in love with for three years. His phone line dead, he climbed to the roof to investigate, never suspecting a small electrical fire had severed the line. The invisible and deadly current met him halfway up the ladder and threw his body clear across to the roof next door.

It's been almost two years since Marc and I converted the building into a successful commercial laundry. But a few months ago, the landlord, under protest from Marc, began the haphazard construction of two additional stories above us. Truckloads of sand blocked exits, concrete blocks fell below to the sidewalk endangering passersby, and wobbly walls were erected on top of bundles of electrical wires. No building permits or city inspections were required, just the will and the money to do the job. Marc filed weekly complaints with the justice of the peace and with Electricité d'Haiti. The justice would come to the building and make a report, only to stamp and file it away somewhere. It was one of these bundles of wire that finally sparked the fire.

I return to Port-au-Prince from New York on the next flight to an apartment full of weeping, wailing women and men clutching rosary beads. On seeing me enter the family's home, Marc's sisters are at my side and I'm brought to a back bedroom for rest. Food and drink are brought to me almost hourly by one female neighbor or another who stands over me and insists, in Creole, that I swallow the offerings.

In the larger apartment, I can hear singing. It sounds like a hundred people are out there. They come at dawn from the Protestant church and don't leave until all the evening's chores are done, the food consumed, the buckets of water filled. After two days the UN sends over a radiotelephone for me to use. I call my mother in New Jersey. Standing at the back window, looking out over a concrete wasteland, I cry into the radio to her. She begs me to come home. She doesn't understand that I am home.

The day before the funeral, I'm driven to our house to choose Marc's burial clothes. I'm told that his brother will go that evening to bathe and dress Marc's body. Because I have visions of a big, soapy bath, with Marc's body lying cradled in my arms, while we each of us hold a soft sponge to his forehead, to his shoulders, to the places where he hurts most, I beg to join what seems a beautiful ritual. His brother is hesitant, but finally agrees.

That evening he asks me to wait in the car while he goes in and speaks with the mortician. I wait until he's out of sight and then, as if it's beckoning me, I'm drawn up a long drive toward a lighted garage. Through a slit in a dirty curtain nailed to the doorway, I see my first glimpse of Marc's body. It's just a couple of inches of his arm, a warm shade of brown, capped by the maroon T-shirt I bought him at the Gap the summer before. I stand still for a minute or two, trying to prepare myself before setting eyes on his face.

I step into a room not more than a shed, tiled entirely in white bathroom tile. Marc's body lies on a concrete table that takes up most of the small room. A man stands on top of the table between Marc's feet with a large knife in his hands, preparing to saw Marc's pants off through the crotch. Another man stands against the wall with a power sprayer in his hands. The room smells of chemicals, and my eyes, nose, and throat burn.

Marc's T-shirt looks almost clean; his jeans are unbuttoned and pulled down around his hips, exposing his pubic hair. His socks, stained from lying on the ground in the rain, are half pulled off his feet, hanging like limp windsocks. He wears an elastic band around his wrist like he was in the middle of some paperwork and put it there until he'd need it to bundle up his files again.

As I stand mute in this filthy room filled with the stench of chemicals, one of the men flips Marc's body over carelessly, pointing out to me the abrasions on his scalp where he slid down the wall and the long, dark burn mark left against his throat by the electric wire. I can't speak and for some reason I gesture down toward his feet. The man with the knife thinks I'm asking to see if there are injuries to his legs and slides the knife into the bottom of the zipper to cut the pants off. I shout no, no, don't, because I can't bear to see his clothes cut off of him and I can't understand why it would be any harder to just slide them off his legs. Like he did every night to walk around the house, sexy in his boxer shorts.

Marc's brother rushes in and holds me back, saying don't touch, don't touch. But touch is what I want to do and I put my hand out toward Marc's back as everyone holds his breath. What will the woman do? The woman merely puts her hand on the icy, icy cold shoulder that she slept curled against for three years. The woman wants to pinch and squeeze and slap this body into waking up, but instead she just moves away and out the door.

No soapy tub, no sponges, his clothing is stripped off, and the man with the power sprayer blasts the body with whatever chemicals are used to disinfect the dead.

We bury Marc in Jacmel, the small seaside town where his mother was born. The groundskeeper tolls the bell as we pass through the rusty gates. Three dozen of us, all dressed in white and each carrying a funeral wreath, silently weave our way between the headstones and *kavs*, the Creole version of a mausoleum. I walk in front of the coffin, on Marc's brother's arm, while the other mourners follow behind.

A group of children follow us from the gate and stand unabashedly among us. The coffin is placed on the ground at the feet of an old man. He removes several bottles from a paper sack and sprinkles oils over the coffin and into the dark *kav*. His soft, steady voice evokes *vodou loas*, praying for Marc's easy return to the spirit world.

I return to our house to live, alone except for our cats. The cat that Marc called Little Piggy begins to stalk me. I wander through the dark house at night and can see his shadow passing underneath furniture and against walls. He rushes me suddenly, wrapping his front legs around mine and giving me a quick, hard bite. All the cats stop bringing me their gifts of lizards, frogs, and mice. The old cat stops eating and dies in January.

Marc's rooftop garden becomes my refuge. I resign from my job, stop bathing and even dressing, and lie for hours in a lounge chair up here, staring at the sky or at the two towering palmiste trees, my mind completely numb. I concentrate on the flamboyant tree overhanging the roof, wishing it to suddenly bloom bright with its blood red flowers.

On the three-month anniversary of Marc's death, I dream of my mother coming to me, asking me to visit the graves of her parents with her. I'm awakened from the dream by the ringing of the telephone. It's my father. He tells me my mother died suddenly, early in the morning. She's been sick for a while, but we still didn't expect this.

Late one afternoon, at that moment when the day feels sad, when there's a stillness in the air, a lapse, as if time isn't certain it will go on, and

then it does, I board the plane for New York, leaving Port-au-Prince behind forever.

Andrew, 1998
Valledupar, Colombia

I've just touched down in Colombia, but this time I'm not on mission. I'm
here to visit Suzanne. I've taken early retirement from war zones, but
she's still at it, driving her Land Cruiser around in the mountains trying to
apply the Geneva Conventions to this interminable conflict. But neither
paramilitaries nor guerrillas nor drug dealers nor the army give a damn.
It's one of the most violent countries on the planet, her mission one of the
most quixotic.

My flight north from the capital, Bogotá, unexpectedly touches down
at some desolate village on the Caribbean coast. It's Riohacha, they tell
me. I don't see it written anywhere on my ticket, but I know I've heard
that name before. From the runway it could be Haiti—treeless, wind-
blown, and destitute. The turquoise ocean glimmers in the heat of the tarmac and images from the past start rolling in on the breeze. I'd thought at
the time that Haiti was as bad as it could get. How blind was that, with
genocide brewing in Rwanda and massacres being planned in Bosnia?

Valledupar, the last stop, is a definite improvement. I'm hit by a blast
of hot air as the plane door swings open to reveal a Red Cross Land
Cruiser waiting and Suzanne, tanned, fit, chic as ever.

"Hope you don't mind," she says, "but I've booked you into the only
hotel in town. Our Red Cross house is full."

It turns out to be a six-story concrete-block structure with plastic
flowers in the lobby and trashy art on the walls. It's the Hotel Dominican Fiesta all over again, minus the slot machines. The funk of despair
that's been hovering since Riohacha descends a little lower. We push
the beds together but our lovemaking feels cheap and wooden, like the
furniture.

"I'm sorry, it's my fault," I tell her. "You've seen me this way before. Remember how it was in Dubrovnik after Bosnia and in Nairobi after
Rwanda? Let's give it time; it always passes."

Suzanne's blue eyes fill with tears. She rolls away and I'm left staring
at the ceiling fan, cursing myself for not having brought sleeping tablets.
It's not one of my finer moments.

The morning dawns cloudless and humid, just the way I like it after New York in winter. We breakfast by the pool—papaya, mango, and fresh orange juice. The heaviness lifted during the night, so I figure the worst is over. She kisses me and leaves for a village in the mountains to deliver a family message to a hostage whom the guerrillas are threatening to execute. Something about the ransom not having been paid.

I'm alone by the pool. It's 9 A.M. I have a whole day to kill, and then a week. I have no transport, almost no Spanish, and I'm not really sure where I am.

What I am sure of is that I'm nobody here. A few laps of the pool followed by a vain attempt to decipher the local newspaper takes me to 10:30 A.M. Too early to start on frozen cocktails, too late for the daily flight out.

Suddenly I've got company. Two shiny new Land Cruisers with tinted windows pull up and out climbs a group of heavily armed paramilitaries with women who could be wives, mistresses, sisters, or daughters. The men deposit the women like hand luggage by the pool and cruise off to their next killing. The women are true bimbos, with too much gold and way too much plump flesh on show for midmorning on a weekday. God knows what they look like on Saturday nights. They're loudmouthed and stupid and have already terrorized the hapless waiter, who brought daiquiris instead of piña coladas.

I can feel the acid rising in my stomach and the taste of bile in the back of my throat. After a few minutes I've seen more than enough. I realize with unusual lucidity that I hate them for enjoying being with men who murder other women's husbands and lovers. Suzanne's Red Cross will cart the victims' bodies away, the fortunate ones shot through the head, blood congealing in the heat of macadam highways and dusty back alleys, the others indescribably mutilated.

I know when I'm beaten. I retreat to my room and gaze out the open window at the endless plain beyond the town limits. Out past desperate Riohacha, across the Caribbean to Port-au-Prince and farther still to Sarajevo and Phnom Penh and Kigali, each place grimmer than the last.

The women by the pool, those lovers of killers, have somehow hit my rewind button. Mass graves, amputees, emaciated prisoners, refugees. Backhoes and body bags. There's a meltdown going on inside. I can feel the heat in the middle of my chest. Ten years' despair unleashed on a heart gone numb. I'm empty, calm, unafraid. And wanting to die.

I switch on the TV. It's CNN Headline News, *en español.* I walk over to the window and look into the street below. In a sudden moment of pure clarity I know either I go out that window or I get out the dictionary and improve my Spanish. It's CNN or the pavement. There's no drama; those are the options. It's either the end, or it isn't. It's Russian roulette with half the chambers loaded, and the winner gets to watch TV.

The woman I love is somewhere in the mountains with the Marxist guerrillas and I'm standing by a fourth-floor window in Valledupar. I'm thirty-four years old. I've seen a lot of death and I've enjoyed my share of life. For the first time in ages, I'm at peace. I'm unshackled, floating, waiting for the next gust to gently blow me away.

I stand there for a minute, an hour, weight shifting between heels and toes. A lifetime passes; it's very still. There's not a breath of air to blow me anywhere.

And then it occurs to me that I'm not high enough up, that I could end up quadraplegic or a vegetable or both. Suzanne doesn't deserve that, incompetence for a final act, a lover who drools. The television's still on, and there's breaking news. Nigerian peacekeeping troops have broken rebel lines on the outskirts of Freetown and are set to enter Sierra Leone's capital. I love breaking news. History in real time pulls me away from the window ledge. My legs crumple underneath me and I slump onto the bed to watch other people's lives running out on the streets instead of my own. My shirt is drenched with sweat and I'm shaking. I daren't go near the window to close it. If I want to live, I've got to get to the ground floor.

I stumble back down four flights to the pool to find that the bimbos who triggered all this are gone. It's just past three, so I order a cocktail. The waiter is kind and patient with my poor Spanish. I smile at him, and then I begin to cry, a torrent of sobs that just won't stop. The drink sits there as the shadows lengthen, pineapple juice and alcohol separating out into layers. It's still there when Suzanne turns up hours later, worn out and dirty. I manage a smile.

"How was your day?" I ask.

"Well, we drove forever but at least the hostage is still alive. How was yours?"

"Well, it could have been better. I feel kind of useless being a tourist here, but at least you didn't check me into the top floor and turn on the Cooking Channel."

She stares at me, puzzled.

"Never mind," I tell her. "I was worried about you, out there alone."

RETURN TO NORMAL
New York, 1999–2003

The nineties end. War spreads from Rwanda into the Democratic Republic of Congo and from Bosnia into Kosovo; Haiti festers. Somalia hasn't had a government for over a decade. Meanwhile, in March 1999, the Dow Jones Industrial Average closed over ten thousand for the first time in history. Even more dramatic growth in the value of the NASDAQ and private investments in Internet and technology start-ups create trillions of dollars of new wealth. In contrast to the early Clinton years of grandiose plans to do good in the world, domestic concerns become paramount. The nation returns to conservative unilateralism with George W. Bush, a president who campaigned specifically promising to avoid nation building and "humanitarian intervention."

Heidi, July 1999
Home

I haven't lived at home since I was nineteen. My parents have moved since, into a three-hundred-year-old farmhouse in northwestern New Jersey. They bought it for a song and a promise to the centenarian owner that they wouldn't tear it down. Years of renovation followed. My father left the hand-hewn post and beam work exposed. My mother researched period décor and furnishings and filled the seventeen-room house with authentic details.

Everything remains exactly as it did on the morning my mother died; as if in memorial, my father refuses to remove even her coffee cup from the kitchen counter. I find myself performing similar rituals: I neatly line up Marc's old Doc Marten boots next to my bed and slide his toothbrush into the holder next to mine. This house has seen three centuries of births, weddings, and deaths; surely its walls can contain the grief of my father and me.

Living near the equator for so many years, I'd forgotten the pleasure the change of seasons brings. Summer now, the sun shines down at a sharp angle through trees heavy with leaves and makes the surface of the pool shimmer in silver.

Ken and Andrew have made the trip to New Jersey by bus to visit for the weekend. Having them here has been good for me. It's made me realize I need to be around people. But that won't be enough; I also need a routine, something to force me out of bed each day. I've had too much time off. I need to go back to work at headquarters.

Andrew asks me what's on my mind. Facedown on a raft in the center of the pool, Ken stops paddling and holds his breath. In the space of an hour, I can move from deep hopelessness to lacerating anger to joy at being alive. It's not easy for my friends to cope with, but they persevere, force me to keep putting one foot in front of the other, and occasionally ease me to the ground weeping in despair.

I scoop a struggling ant out of the water and smile.

I tell Andrew I want to go back to work. He tells me not to worry, he'll be there every day, just a few floors below my office. We can have lunch together all the time. To celebrate the moment, Ken does a belly flop off of the raft, soaking Andrew and me. I smile, and they relax.

Slowly, I'm coming back. I'll be okay.

Ken, December 1999
City Hall, New York

It's a bitter cold, clear winter morning in the Northern Hemisphere. Everything crunches and squeaks when you step on it, the cold stings everywhere it finds skin, reminding you that you are alive. There is a crystal clarity to the sky above the East River. The Brooklyn Bridge stands massive, brown, and inscrutable against the magnificent winter breach. The towers of Lower Manhattan sparkle in the sun, penetrating deeply into the explosion of blue.

Andrew is getting married to Suzanne at City Hall. I am the best man and it is my responsibility to bring the champagne, roses, and breakfast. I run block after block, eyes watering from the cold, searching for Kripsy Kremes, as the last moments of Andrew's unmarried life tick away.

We stand in the corner of the anteroom furtively drinking champagne from plastic cups and gorging on doughnuts under a no food or drink sign. Andrew and Suzanne have that lucky halo around them, the same one that surrounds the guy set to leave a violent mission. They haven't left yet but have already entered a new world, an unfamiliar, distant, and enviable place of permanence and commitment. It takes courage to go there too.

A courage I can't seem to conjure. It is always easier for me to leave women than to stay. The only relationship I've been able to sustain since law school is with Miss Heidi, and although we may be the only two people on earth who believe it, that relationship is unconsummated. We're like an old married couple, beyond sex. My girlfriends are always insanely jealous of Heidi; her presence somehow guarantees that I'm unreachable, unattainable, which gives me great comfort. But now Andrew is getting married. This is serious. Time is running out. Youth is gone.

Finally they call us into the judge's chambers. Suzanne's English is good but not perfect. The judge tells her to say "with this ring I thee wed." She smiles, laughs softly, and says slowly with her chin down, "wis zis wreeng I ze . . ." The sentence trails off, the judge didn't hear enough and is not quite satisfied. I try not to laugh and am not so good at that. Happy waves of laughter erupt from the center of me as I hand over gold rings Andrew bought at the central market in Cambodia ten years ago. He leans forward anxiously and repeats the words to her quietly, gently, and slowly with his perfect half-British accent. "With this ring I thee wed." Suzanne tries again. It's a bit better, good enough. We all exhale and smile and they are married.

We go outside into the brightest, bluest day I have ever seen. The pictures come out beautifully clear. I blow the happiest one up and now Andrew and Suzanne's wedding smiles greet me on the bed stand every morning. Their picture sits under one of Miss Heidi, Mr. Karim, and me celebrating at the Floating Bar in Phnom Penh right after the elections. I have a roomful of smiles to remember when I wake.

Andrew, September 2000
Rosh Hashanah in New York

Light from the candles in Ken's dining room hits the rotund dark wood Buddha statue, throwing a distorted shadow up the living room wall. Ken has carvings from every continent and snapshots from all his missions on these walls, and they always trigger cascades of memories. The ceiling fan turns as the best and worst of times wash over me.

This city's been the perfect place to find normality again. It's crazy enough to keep me feeling alive but benevolent enough to let me quietly heal. When I left for Rwanda five years ago, a friend bought me a subscription to the *New Yorker* magazine, and its arrival each week in the diplomatic pouch was a highlight, the intellectual free-for-all a lifeline. I read many an issue in that church. It was beside that African lake that my love affair with this city began.

This is my first Rosh Hashanah. Apart from Ken, I never had any Jewish friends before I came to New York, or if I did, I wasn't aware they were Jewish. I'm glad to celebrate here and eager to learn. When Ken invited Suzanne and me to share this festival, there was a tender insistence in his voice that caught me off balance, moved me. Somehow he knew it would do us good.

He sits at one end of the table with his Jewish skullcap on and leads us through the blessings with kindness and humility. He consults scribbled notes on the blotter pad on his knee; some of this might be new for him as well.

We dip apples in honey, that the coming year may be sweet. Next come pomegranate seeds, that our merits may multiply. They're mentioned all through the Old Testament, but I've never actually seen any, let alone eaten them. I put the tiny oval with its ruby red slippery translucent flesh in my mouth and crunch.

Then come the dates, that our enemies may be consumed. There's disagreement about the precise meaning of this passage, so we knock back more wine for inspiration. Someone thinks the idea is that the plans of those who wish to harm us should be destroyed. Ken demurs, says it's a play on the similarity of the Hebrew word *date* with the verb *to be consumed*. I have no idea, but I tell them I'm most comfortable with the idea that our enemies are within: pride and avarice and hatred. But getting it right seems less important than sharing this moment and listening to each other.

By now side conversations have ignited and Rabbi Ken loses his grip on the flock. There's irreverence here, clever levity that's strikingly different from anything I remember from my churchgoing days. God is present, we're praying, and at the same time people are joking and teasing each other.

I grab more honey and drift off again, this time into the future. That sweetness idea has hit the mark.

Heidi, October 2000
Fortieth Birthday

On Friday the thirteenth, a full moon rises under clear skies over the East River, as if invoked for the occasion. Guests arrive at my party at an uptown rooftop and gifts pile up in a corner. Marilyn flies in from Rome, where she's living now. She and I became close friends in Somalia, and she and Ken in Liberia. It's strange to be with her now in New York.

Waiters in bow ties pass through the crowd with trays of hors d'oeuvres and lavender margaritas. In a floor-length red velvet dress, I go downstairs to the apartment I left my ex-husband in ten years before. He long ago remarried, had kids, and moved on. His sister, Elizabeth, lives here now. She and I have remained close, and we see each other at work every day. I'm forever grateful to her for getting me the UN job when I needed it.

Here and there I spot a token of my marriage—a vase that held Easter lilies when my husband and I were in love, and a framed poster bought from a Soho gallery on a rainy Saturday afternoon soon after we started dating. Books and LPs too heavy to take with me when I left still line floor-to-ceiling bookshelves my husband and I built together. It's a time capsule of a life I no longer remember.

Elizabeth hurries around the kitchen directing preparations. This party is her gift to me. She hands me a big slice of cake. "Happy birthday," she says to me, smiling. I'm happy where life has found me at forty.

At midnight five long, black limousines arrive to transport the entire party to a club downtown. As guests run from limo to limo, looking for a free seat, my brother passes down the line handing in bottles of champagne. In our limo Ken pops the cork on a bottle even before we hit Central Park. We toast to the next forty years.

At the club we spill out of the limos into the fresh night air, which temporarily sobers me up. We wind behind the rope and past the doorman and into a low-ceilinged dark space where our group scatters, some to the bar, some to the dance floor, others off into corners of the room to watch the goings-on. My brother and his wife stand talking to a friend I worked with in Somalia. A high school classmate dances with Ken. The ex-girlfriend of the best man at my wedding laughs with a friend I worked with on the Bowery. And as usual, Andrew dodges people looking for free medical advice. All my favorite people are here and I'm enjoying watching them together.

But soon the room starts to spin. I realize I'm in trouble and I start searching the crowd for help. My brother and Ken both make eye contact with me and see the desperate expression on my face, but Ken is closer, so I reach for him and pull him toward the nearest exit. Outside, my red velvet dress dusts the gutter as I lean over between two parked cars, heaving. I puke down the front of my dress and all over Ken's new Bruno Magli shoes I bought him in Italy. My cell phone rings and Ken answers. He's close enough that I hear my brother's worried voice on the other end. "This is X-ray 4," Ken replies. "Be advised I have the package, I say again, I have the package. The package is secure, all is well, over."

Ken, October 2000
New York

I receive a fellowship at the Council on Foreign Relations, a foreign policy think tank on Park Avenue. I try to explain to Clintonites in striped pants what I saw of their "assertive multilateralism" policy on the ground. Military and intelligence officials listen closely to my stories and want to know more, in detail. Diplomats and policy specialists, in contrast, are dismissive. It's the opposite of what I expected. They already know everything. They don't need to hear about the field. It threatens their mastery of theory.

But within the council's supportive cocoon, I am finally able to think and write in peace, and my journal article on war crimes in Liberia is nominated for a national reporting award.

The ceremony at the Waldorf Astoria is very chic, a magazine writers' version of the Grammys or the Emmys. Everyone looks like they've just come back from the Hamptons. *Vanity Fair* and the *New Yorker* are nominated. Then they get to my article, published in an obscure academic journal, the *Human Rights Quarterly,* and the emcee's voice drops and she says, "This piece details the horrors of rape and torture in Liberia." They project excerpts up on a huge screen in big shiny black letters. Lots of flashbulbs popping, music in the background. It's all contrived to be dramatic as they read about cannibalism and I think of an old man dying in a wheelbarrow.

My article doesn't win the award, but after the ceremony a woman from the selection committee finds my table to introduce herself and ask what I plan to write next. I have no plans yet, I say. But I do have an interesting group of friends from the UN. Collectively we experienced— maybe represent—all the exultation and catastrophe of a decade spent trying and failing to do well by doing good in a new world. From faith to flesh and everything in between.

"Go home and write," she says. "You should be writing so hard your hair catches fire."

Andrew, June 2001
Hell's Kitchen, New York

Ken and I climb up the fire escape and onto the roof of the brownstone apartment building in Hell's Kitchen where Suzanne and I live. We've got ice and glasses and Barbancourt rum from Haiti, the Estate Reserve, aged fifteen years. Sunset off the Hudson River turns the sky a deep red. The brick wall has retained the heat of the day and feels good on our backs.

BBC has just announced that Slobodan Milosevic, the Serbian president who set Croatia and Bosnia and Kosovo on fire with his ethnic cleansing, has been flown into detention at the War Crimes Tribunal in The Hague.

Ken pours two shots and the amber smoothness of the rum takes us both back to the house on the hill above Port-au-Prince. The Barbancourt was so cheap there at the source. We clink glasses, knock it back.

"Here's to you, Doctor, to a job well done." He's always been proud of my forensic work. I think he might be even more proud of it than I am. Each time I hear his praise, I get a lump in my throat.

This is a moment of vindication for me, because at the time we were exhuming the graves in Bosnia, no arrests had been made and many of my UN colleagues thought the work was a waste of time. Tonight my long-shot investment has just paid an unexpected return.

But even if Milosevic gets multiple life sentences, it won't be enough. His arrest won't bring back the dead. As we climb down unsteadily, trying to not break our necks, words I haven't heard for a decade come back to me. "Vengeance is mine, says the Lord, and I will repay." Tonight, I wish it were true.

Heidi, August 2001
Three Civilians, Café Noir

Our favorite bar is Café Noir in Soho. During the day it's quiet and calm. We sit next to a large plate glass window, afternoon light pouring in from southern Manhattan. A large plate of glass survived intact only by a rare grace where we served in the field, and it's a marvel to be inside looking out, at New York, clearly, through clean glass. Sometimes we decide to take the day off, like we used to do at the Floating Bar on the Mekong in

Cambodia, and sit here for hours, everyone around us chatting, comfortable and shiny on their business lunches. And we just stare at each other in disbelief.

Mr. Karim is in town and there are a dozen of us meeting for dinner tonight. We're all friends from past missions, sitting at a long narrow table across from the bar. Some are still on mission and some of us have been back in New York long enough that we are craving the field. Sahra, our Somali friend who worked as a translator in the 'Dish, is now working for the UN in Sierra Leone. We've all tried to make new friends here in New York, and to reverse the alienation we feel from our peers. But the conversation doesn't usually go far once I say we lived in Somalia for two years, or Ken says that Andrew dug the graves of Srebrenica.

"He's double-checking my expense account receipts," a guy at the next table tells his friend. "You need to get yourself into Goldman Sachs, you get to seven figures if you stay long enough," the other guy says. From the end of our table, Sahra's voice becomes discernable amid the chatter. "You pass the Mammy Yoko Hotel and make a left at the amputee camp," she tells Andrew, describing where she lives in Freetown. Ken's head jerks toward me, "Make a left at the amputee camp," he says, eyes wide, eyebrows up.

After dinner our group disperses throughout the restaurant. Andrew sits on the patio, at the periphery of intense activity around the bar, engrossed in confidences with Suzanne. Ken stands nearby, accompanied by his new girlfriend.

After midnight, the wall between the staff and the patrons starts to crumble and it becomes a party. The bartender turns the volume up on an Afro-Cuban song and hands Mr. Karim a set of African drums that usually sits unused above the shot glasses. Mr. Karim goes into a trance when he plays the drums; he won't stop even when his hands bleed. The bartender turns over a metal champagne pail, sits it on a bar stool, and watches Karim for twenty seconds, nodding with his rhythm. Karim exaggerates the motion of his hands and arms so the bartender can synchronize. They nod and grimace at each other as they pummel their drums lovingly and nothing else exists on earth outside this bar.

The waitstaff are models and actors and dancers when they're not waiting tables. One emerges out of nowhere, establishes a space at the crowded bar. She's six feet tall and her hands and arms and legs start to gyrate in a kick-boxing, break-dancing frenzy, sometimes with Karim's rhythm, sometimes outside of it. The barrier between staff and patrons degenerates completely, free drinks appear on the table, the crowd at the bar erupts in rhythmic applause. Everyone is clapping or banging or drinking or kissing. No one is still or afraid.

Ken, September 14, 2001
Brooklyn, New York

I watch lower Manhattan smolder. It's like the field followed us home. New Yorkers say they're surprised the emergency has magnified friendship, ignited faith, incited urgent intimacy and other desperate measures to embrace life anew. Feels familiar.

The phones turn back on and I'm getting calls from Cambodia, Are you okay? My Haitian friends email, worried about me. The world is upside down: I worry about you, you don't worry about me. You are the victims, you are dependent and prone, I offer aid and succor. I am a witness to your tragedy, and a privileged witness at that. I am never a victim. The U.S. brings food, doctors, and soldiers to your shores to restore order to the mess you have made. I am not and New York is not and the U.S. is not a subject for your sympathy. The Somali Parliament offers its condolences. We created that fucking parliament.

I go to the Promenade in Brooklyn, directly overlooking Lower Manhattan from across the East River. I am, as the W. H. Auden poem tacked onto the fence over the river says,

> Uncertain and afraid
> As the clever hopes expire
> Of a low dishonest decade
> Waves of anger and fear
> Circulate over the bright
> And darkened lands of the earth

The Promenade has erupted in memorial: flowers, candles, personal pictures of missing beloved and heirloom pictures of missing towers, respects for lost firemen in schoolkids' scrawl, prayers for Muslims from Jews in the neighborhood and prayers for Jews from Muslims in the neighborhood. Humans crying and humans smiling.

I stroll up and down the Promenade with my neighbors under a golden September sun. I pass a fireman and overhear a fragment of his frustrated lamentations to his wife. "There is just no way, physically, to make it to all the funerals," he says. Below, across a desolate street in the lot of an abandoned warehouse, a man in a kilt plays the bagpipes. Alone amid cracked concrete, spindly tufts of grass, loose trash, and a rusting corrugated fence, the man in the kilt marches solemnly, proudly, his head bowed, up and down the lot, tirelessly blowing and squeezing, rendering the saddest song I've ever heard. No one speaks and he never looks up at his audience.

Andrew, June 2002
UN Headquarters, New York

The medical director has a mission for me. I'm sitting in her office staring at the traffic on First Avenue, thinking that I don't want to leave New York. She tells me that defense lawyers at the War Crimes Tribunal for Rwanda have complained that the UN is neglecting the medical needs of the accused. Someone has to travel to Arusha, Tanzania, and assess the prison; she thinks it should be me because I worked for the tribunal early on and I know the place.

Back in my own office, the first patient of the day is waiting. She's a brand-new recruit, just selected for the peacekeeping mission in Sierra Leone. I step into the hall and glance at her file quickly while she undresses. She's twenty-seven and was born in Rwanda.

As I pump up the blood pressure cuff around her arm, the morning sun glints through the blinds, throwing dappled orange light across her skin.

"How did you end up in the U.S.?" I ask.

She tells me she came here for her education in the early nineties.

"And your family, are they still in Rwanda?" There's a pause as the air hisses out of the cuff. The expression on her face changes ever so slightly.

"My family was killed," she says, staring at the ceiling.

I look back at the family history section of her form. She's marked five small crosses beside five names, and that year, 1994. They're all gone. In another age, it could be the chronicle of a plague.

I change the subject to Sierra Leone, amazed that she wants to work for us. "That's quite a choice for a first mission," I say. The rebels have amputated the limbs of thousands of civilians, terrorizing the population. But I can see she's eager. I examine many like her, off to some of our newer missions in places like Kosovo, East Timor, and Afghanistan.

"There's a lot to do there," she says, with a light in her eyes.

When I tell her she's cleared, her face creases into a wide smile. I wish her the best with her mission and hand her over to a nurse for vaccinations and malaria pills.

I'm rinsing my hands before the next patient when I catch a glimpse of my graying hair in the mirror above the washbasin. I'm thirty-nine, unsure how to weigh the past, uncertain of what I want from my future. What I am sure of is that I served as best I knew how, and that I was young. And that now it's time to hand over to others.

That's not how the medical director sees it. My phone's blinking; it's her again, wanting my decision about that mission. If I go, I'll have to contend with Clement Kayishema, Rwandan medical doctor, former governor of Kibuye and mass murderer. His was the first genocide indictment ever by an international tribunal and our forensic evidence helped convict him. He's been sentenced to life in prison on four counts of genocide, including one for the massacre at the church.

There was a time I'd have been curious to meet him, to learn how someone who's supposed to save life comes to believe he has the right to take it. No longer. I have as much interest in him and his well-being as he had for those terrified women and children in the church. The last thing I want to hear about now are his medical problems.

I pace back and forth, shuffle my papers, water the plants. Below me a seaplane banks gracefully over Queens and skids into a landing, leaving a dotted wake. I pull my expired UN *laissez passer* out of the desk where it's lain idle for almost five years. It's the color of a faded pair of jeans, the jumble of visas a montage of another life.

I toss it back in the drawer, my decision taken. I walk back to the director's office and slump into her sofa.

"You'll have to send someone else," I tell her, "I just can't do it. I'm a doctor, and this is a mission for a saint."

Ken, April 2003
Brooklyn, New York

I sit in comfort in my den in Brooklyn, watching another war in Iraq on TV, twelve years since Tali and I watched that Scud from her balcony. As the marines punch their way into the torture chamber of Baghdad, I am proud and in awe once again of the power of a great nation, my nation.

But I've learned enough over those twelve years to fear arrogance and imperial ambition: maybe this war is indeed an obligation of freedom, or maybe lives are sacrificed in the service of our leaders' hubris. It's taken me a decade to realize this, but no one will resolve the question for me, not embedded TV correspondents or Thomas Friedman or my parents. So I am left in my comfort, in Brooklyn, obsessed with the moral ambiguities, not just of another war in Iraq but of a decade of wars and our role in them.

When our human rights volunteer was killed in Cambodia, I went to Andrew to assuage my guilt. He said that the human rights groups live here, they know the risks, keep at it. But if instead he had informed UN leadership that my human rights training was responsible for the death of a Cambodian, that would have become the official conclusion. Responsibility can be rendered almost anywhere along the moral spectrum, depending who makes the definitive judgment and then tells the official story.

Or Matt. He died from negligent UN sloth, in which no one is accountable, nothing changes, and more will die too young. An outrage. Or not. He died a hero, stepping forward courageously to intervene in someone else's war, an honorable sacrifice. There is truth in both renderings. Who has the authority to resolve the dilemma, to place it on that moral spectrum? Who makes the conscious decision to bear witness, to tell the story? We need a volunteer.

Maybe it's not me, maybe I'm done volunteering. Perhaps I should just admit that I now understand the world is corrupt and brutal, that most nations look out only for their own interests, and people seldom rush to dangerous acts of selfless sacrifice. No shit. Where did I get the idea I would find otherwise?

We actually set out to save the world. That is what was insane—not ten-year-old warlords with bad breath and voodoo fetishes in Liberia, not Matt's assassin, not the boss in Somalia who set us up for an ambush in exchange for a fifteen percent kickback on the judges' salaries, not the Hutu militias who butchered a minority who had repressed them or the Tutsi survivors who executed the suspects—but me, for thinking I could enter a war and personally restore order.

So that's the easy answer: forswear idealism; resign myself to a sad maturity; put away the things of youth; be thankful I survived and move on.

But that's horseshit too, a craven capitulation. I'm not ready to let the youthful part of myself go yet. If maturity means becoming a cynic, if you have to kill the part of yourself that is naïve and romantic and idealistic—

the part of yourself you treasure most—to claim maturity, is it not better to die young but with your humanity intact? If everyone resigns themselves to cynicism, isn't that exactly how vulnerable millions end up dead?

When the Cold War ended, the power of freedom, democracy, and hope weren't abstract concepts; they were palpable in the Iraqi desert, across the Berlin Wall, in Tiananmen Square, atop Yeltsin's tank. That hope crescendoed for us in Cambodia. So we piled into Somalia, Haiti, and Bosnia—missionaries, mercenaries, and madmen with no understanding of the history, politics, or culture, but with Land Cruisers, military-issue radios, malaria pills, and the sure knowledge that we were on the right side of history.

What a feeling. Andrew wanted to bind the wounds of innocent war victims, hoping to find grace. Heidi embraced the freedom-born-of-emergency determined to liberate herself and, in the process, as many women as she could touch. I planned to harness the power of an ascendant America to personally undo the Holocaust. Don't laugh. We were young. We weren't the first, and won't be the last, to venture forth overseas with grand ideas.

Then eighteen Rangers fell in Somalia and suddenly history started moving in the wrong direction. Rwanda, Haiti, and Bosnia were all in flames, burning the remains of our innocence. One million civilians we promised to protect died on our watch. There are many competing versions of this story—U.S., UN, NATO, EU. But we were there and capital letters always lie and our version has no meaning if no one renders it.

So I make the conscious choice to believe again: we did not misspend our youth. At least we can bear witness. I did save lives and I did earn my way into Dr. Andrew's club. The act of rendering is therefore mine. I won the right, I am the owner of that privilege.

There is a plaque in the Garden of the Righteous at Yad Vashem, the Holocaust memorial museum in Jerusalem, which reads, "The Jewish people will never forget the righteous among the nations who endangered their lives in order to save Jews from the Nazi murderers and their collaborators. In their praiseworthy deeds they saved the honor of mankind." I have a copy of these words over my desk and I look at them every day on my way out. Who saved the honor of mankind in Rwanda? Or Bosnia? Or, God help us, Liberia? But I have another quote from the exit of Yad Vashem over my desk, which reads, "Son of man, keep not silent, forget not deeds of tyranny, cry out at the disaster of a people, recount it unto your children and they unto theirs from generation to generation."

I don't know who saved the honor of mankind during my time in the field, but I do know that an ancestral memory of tyranny commands me to keep not silent.

There is no ambiguity here. I am a witness. I have a voice. I have to write it down.

Andrew, April 2003
UN Headquarters, New York

I'm leaning back in my chair watching the computer screen as BBC streams war live into my office. On the other end of each pretty fluorescent flash, human beings are dying. Iraq's hospitals will soon be overflowing; there will be blood and chaos, never enough surgeons, lives running out onto the floors.

I'm about to shut it down when the screen pings with a message from Lumning in Cambodia. I click on the attached photos, a technology unimaginable ten years ago, when just faxing from the decrepit Phnom Penh Post Office could take half a day. There in front of me are the latest snapshots of my property beside the Mekong River.

Of all the places I served, Cambodia's the only one I've returned to. It's still a hard country, and our mission there didn't achieve even half of what it was supposed to. Those three days of election euphoria didn't lead to democracy, nor did we make the peace we thought we did; it took the next five years for Cambodians themselves to negotiate an end to their war. But regardless of the politics, the country is now at peace. It's always a homecoming to step off the plane into that tropical heat, to drive straight to the house to sit on the verandah with Lumning and the family and catch up. The following day we usually take the ferry over to the land, remove our shoes, and just stand there, glad to feel that earth under our feet. Each year the tropical vegetation has grown thicker and we now need machetes to cut our way down to the riverbank.

But toward the end of every visit, Lumning's youngest daughter, the heartbreaker who used to crawl around on the floor, asks me when I'm coming back to stay. Each time I look down into her dark eyes and tell her I have one last mission to do, and then I'll find a quiet job back in Phnom Penh. I've said that so often I think she's stopped believing me.

But this time I'm going to do it. I'm moving back to Phnom Penh to clear that land and put up a house there for Suzanne and me. We'll build it twelve feet up on stilts with a high tile roof and burnished floor planks and tall, wooden-louvered French doors opening onto wide balconies over the river. It'll be oriented to catch the prevailing breeze, so there won't be a pane of glass in the whole place.

Even with the Khmer Rouge gone, it won't be easy to live over there. There's not much on the far bank, just isolated farmers' houses in the rice fields and a small market at the ferry landing. There's no running water or power supply, no real road, and no bridge yet across the Mekong, so we'll have to ship all the materials across from the city and buy a boat to commute.

Lumning tells me there's fresh water about fifteen feet down, so we'll sink a well and buy a solar-powered pump. The one we used to have out at the hospital worked well enough, so maybe I'll take a visit back there to get the make and model number and find out whether anyone remembers who installed it. And if anyone still remembers me. I don't think I've been happier than when I worked at that hospital.

I should never have joined the UN thinking we could make peace everywhere. I ought to have known better. On the day Sofany sat up from her coma and started eating, I didn't conclude that I could save all my patients. Doctors are not omnipotent. To practice medicine you have to accept that there will always be disease. But because of what I saw on that operating table, I couldn't accept that there will always be war.

Heidi was never taken in by that. She'd figured out from her time on the Bowery that if you want to change anything in this world, you should start by attending to those around you. Which is what she did, one person at a time, through her cooks and drivers and the people she worked with. And the men she loved. While for me, with each successive mission, individuals somehow got lost; they became Haitians, Rwandans, Bosnians— populations, not people. It's taken me ten years to arrive back at that point from which she began.

I'm not sure what I'll do for work in Phnom Penh. I could always set up a small clinic or go into business with Lumning. But I'll worry about that once the house is built. For now, after years in the concrete canyons of Manhattan, all I want to do is plant again, get calluses on these soft physician's hands and red earth under my nails. The soil is astonishingly fertile: centuries of silt from the turbid Mekong have been deposited there with each successive flood. We should have fruit within a couple of seasons.

I'm going to invite my parents. I didn't spend nearly enough time with them during those peripatetic years, and I want to put that right. They're both keen gardeners and know what grows well in the tropics from their years spent in the Pacific.

At the end of the day, we'll sit on the verandah in sarongs and sip our drinks and swat at mosquitoes while the sun goes down orange over the river and the monks chant off in the distance. Grateful for muscles that ache, for breath and heartbeat. And as the moon rises slowly over the pagoda spires and the night jasmine tree releases her perfume on the warm breeze, there will be no more pink tracer rounds floating across the indigo sky. But there just might be a bedraggled ghost who's traded in his Kalashnikov for a banged-up windsurfer and is out where the current is strongest, carving silver wakes across tranquil water.

Heidi, April 2003
New York

With Marc's death I both lost and gained my life in one tragic stroke. The pure beauty of death is as impossible to describe as the birth of a child, the betrayal of a lover, the moment of orgasm. You can't know it until it's touched you, moved inside you, awakened every nerve in your body and made you feel with complete clarity things you never thought bearable. You make it through the long weeping nights when the ravens come to scratch at your eyes and you open a drawer and a scrap of paper with your beloved's handwriting floats silently to the floor and you're struck with the realization that you weren't wrong. He did exist but he's gone now.

And then one morning, after a very long time, you hear a rose bloom and the sun no longer makes you sad and you feel clear and privileged to have shared a life. You take each moment and hold it on your tongue and taste the bitter and the sweet and the sour and know that life is beautiful and you're grateful for the gift.

I think of all the women I've met over the last decade in other people's wars and the things they knew in their hearts. I remember how they continued to love and laugh, and to bring new life into the world with all the hope and courage to imagine a future. I remember a warm brown hand on my breast and a soft voice naming me sister. It was my great fortune to have known these women. Before leaving Somalia, I was honored to be asked by a Somali friend to name his newborn daughter. I pray now for that young girl in Mogadishu, whom I blessed with the hope-filled name of Aayaan. Aayaan. Daybreak. The moment of the day pregnant with promise. The long night over, life starts anew.

Posthumous Rehabilitation

The dead have remembered
our indifference
The dead have remembered
our silence
The dead have remembered
our words

The dead see our snouts
laughing from ear to ear
The dead see
our bodies rubbing against each other
The dead hear
clucking tongues

The dead read our books
listen to our speeches
delivered so long ago

The dead scrutinize our lectures
join in previously terminated
discussions
The dead see our hands
poised for applause

The dead see stadiums
ensembles and choirs declaiming rhythmically

all the living are guilty

little children
who offered bouquets of flowers
are guilty
lovers are guilty
guilty are poets

guilty are those who ran away
and those that stayed

AFTERWORD

When we sat down to write, we were convinced no one would ever read, let alone care about, our scratchings. So the empassioned, cacophonous response to the book—and the media firestorm after the UN fired Andrew—came as something of a surprise.

We thought our book was a coming-of-age story, told in the context of 90s war zones: Somalia, Rwanda, Haiti, Liberia and Bosnia. But it functioned as a Rorschach. Readers projected their own preoccupations onto it. According to Fox News, its most salient feature is a "sex scandal"; to the *New York Times,* Andrew's dismissal for criticizing the UN's capitulation to genocide; to the *New Yorker,* our whistleblower lawsuit; to CNN, the title; to many Amazon.com reviewers, Heidi's sexually frank passages; to one young Hollywood studio executive (who had only read the first two chapters), our (nonexistent) love triangle; to the UN spokesman, our betrayal of his bosses; to some UN staff, an inspiration to blow more whistles. And on it goes.

During long, hot, mosquito-riddled down hours in a hooch, or a bomb shelter, or transport plane, we fantasized about coming home and sitting with thoughtful readers at a university or bookstore to discuss genocide, U.S. and UN policy, dilemmas in humanitarian relief operations, the role of women in conflict, career choices, moral choices, writing choices. We've been lucky to live out that fantasy and discuss in detail what the book means—according to *us* this time—at talks nationwide. Readers ask us a remarkably consistent set of questions. Here they are with some brief answers. For more, we are happy to communicate with readers by email: *Thomsonad@yahoo.com; hpostlewait@gmail.com; kcain22@yahoo.com.*

1). *Why the title?* The title, and the story behind it, illustrates the intensity of what we felt in the field. In Somalia, for instance, two or three mortar rounds were fired into our compound many nights. You never knew if you would be alive the next morning, you never knew who wouldn't make it through the night. What do you do with all that fear and toxic adrenalin that builds up in your body? Sex becomes the antidote. You don't just want to be close to someone, to be intimate with them—you want to crawl under their skin. It's like climbing up on a rooftop and screaming out that you're alive. The phrase "emergency sex" is a metaphor for those feelings. Humans have sex, and writers write about what humans do. In the intensity of the moments we experienced, the walls separating consenting adults crumbled. (We got a taste of this in New York after 9/11.) That's interesting terrain for writers to inhabit, because it implies those walls need not necessarily be there in the first place.

2). *What was the UN's response to the book?* The UN decided the book wasn't "in the Organisation's interests" (it never said why) and responded like an authoritarian government. UN leaders mistook dissent for disloyalty and threatened Heidi and Andrew with dismissal if we published. As is tragically predictable at the UN, it miscalculated badly: after ten years of living it together and three years of writing together, there was no chance we'd pull the book. We decided it was worth losing our jobs. We said, publicly, that if we deserved to lose our jobs, then how much more so our bosses at the most senior levels of the UN—who did nothing, *nothing*, to stop the catastrophes about which we wrote.

The more UN spokesmen attacked us, the more the media covered the story and the more exposure the book—and its critique of the UN—received. Their attempt to bury the book backfired. Book burnings usually do. The UN's position became increasingly untenable. Suppression of freedom of expression by an organization created to protect such freedoms is a hypocrisy too rich even for the UN.

Events on the ground caught up with the UN's attack on the book's credibility. Our allegations that senior UN officials in the field often take kickbacks—denied with great hurrumphing by the UN spokesmen—hit a nerve during the Iraq Oil for Food scandal in which billions of petrol dollars designated for humanitarian relief disappeared under UN supervision. Our allegations of the lethal incompetence in Mogadishu that led to our colleague Matt's death were, sadly, borne out in 2003 when a suicide truck bomb killed twenty-three of our colleagues in Baghdad—because UN security failed again.

We refused to shut up. The bureaucratic stupidity was limitless. The UN compounded its initial mistake: it dismissed Andrew first; Heidi was next in line. We took our cases to Washington and enlisted the counsel of a public interest whistleblower law firm, the Government Accountability Project. GAP began a global media and legal campaign for Andrew's reinstatement. The book made international headlines again. Under pressure

from Congress, the UN rehired Andrew, withdrew its threat against Heidi—
and then passed whistleblower protection rules. More UN staff are now
coming forward with the inside information necessary to investigate corruption. And none of them has yet been fired.

3). *There are several sexually frank passages in the book, which have
received a lot of attention. Why did you include them?* When we took this
project on, we committed ourselves to writing honestly about what happens in the field—not only about the incompetence and corruption of our
bosses and the moral catastrophes of UN peacekeeping but also our own
foibles and the way we lived our lives. We were surprised that there was so
much controversy over three adults having a handful of consensual sexual
encounters over a ten-year period. Not so surprisingly, most of the controversy focused on Heidi's stories even though she and Ken have the same
number of sex scenes in the book. Curiously, some readers found the tales
of Heidi's sex life more objectionable than the mutilated genitals of Somali
women or the rape of thousands of Liberian women.

4). *Knowing now what you didn't know then, even after everything—
the joy and triumph of Cambodia, the thrill of Haiti and Somalia at first
and then genocide in Rwanda and Bosnia—would you do it all over
again? Regrets?*
This is how we spent our youth. So, as in any story of youthful indiscre-
tions—in our case the indiscretion of naive illusions—we regret everything. And we wouldn't change a thing. We came home disillusioned,
certainly, and perhaps a little traumatized. We regret the tragedies and the
failures, God knows. And the deaths of friends and lovers. And the damage
we did. But there is honor in the attempt. Was it a life well lived? It was a
life worth risking for illusions worth having.

5). *You're three very different people. The book clearly illustrates your
distinct personalities and backgrounds. How did you become friends? Is
your strange friendship the real subject of the book?*
Most media attention to the book concerns the politics of the UN and
the US involvement in wars we witnessed—topics of interest and import, of
course. Most responses from readers, in contrast, concern more universal
themes, chief among them friendship. As different as we are—we'd never
have been friends had we met at a cocktail party in New York—together we
were exposed to an outer edge of human experience most people will never

know. That was a crucible. We became a triangle; the alternate angles from which we see the world strengthened the whole. We can sense, without words, when one of us needs help. From three continents away. Because we've seen each other weep at the bottom of a mass grave; scream in glee at new love; walk away from responsibility in fear; volunteer for the line of fire. When the UN threatened to fire Andrew and Heidi if we didn't stop publication and stop speaking to the media, Andrew warned it to be careful: "We've been threatened by experts." Then we publicly called the Secretary-General, our boss, a coward in a series of global TV, print, and radio stories. We could not have done that separately. Without our friendship we would be different people, and there would be no book.

6). *Most war books are "boys'" books. Women are usually relegated to the status of victims, or cast in supporting roles. Through Heidi's stories,* Emergency Sex *also emphasizes a woman's central role—which raised a lot of eyebrows in the media. Why?* Women are expected to be nurturing caretakers; anything else is an aberration. A good example is all the attention paid to Lindy England's involvement in the Abu Ghraib scandal. Do we even remember the names of the men involved? When the media turned to portraying England as the not-so-bright victim of a masochistic male superior, we breathed a collective sigh of relief. That, we could deal with: woman as victim. But woman as protagonist? With the wars in Iraq and Afghanistan, female soldiers inevitably will turn to writing to share their experiences. Get ready for it: women aren't really made of "sugar and spice."

7). *None of you had published before—what compelled you to write?* We witnessed carnage of biblical proportions; we heard individual stories of resilience and faith almost too harrowing to be believed. The facts before our eyes were so much more dramatic than any fiction we'd ever read. What do you do with that? You have to share it, or at least try. We told each other our stories, we wrote vignettes home, even our memos to our bosses took on a literary edge. (Ken says, only half joking, that he wrote hundreds of memos from the field to his bosses, but this is the first one they actually read.) Eventually our stories took on a life of their own. The literature of first-person testimonials from the war in Vietnam affected us when we were young, and we began to realize that the power of bearing witness starts from, well, ordinary individual witnesses—there is no aristocracy for holding the rights to tell a war story. We had as much a right as anyone. All we needed was the courage—and each other—to do it, because none of us was ready to start writing alone.

8). *Weren't you concerned your criticisms of the UN would weaken its mission and be used by its enemies on the right wing for their own purposes?*
This was thorny for us, and, yes, we lost sleep over it. We published soon after 9/11 and the start of the Iraq war; suddenly the UN was a red-hot political issue. Our critique of UN corruption and cowardice is scathing. The right loved it. Conservative media promoted the book aggressively, but only the elements they wanted to promote, calling it a "UN sex scandal tell-all"—a total distortion. It was an eye-opening lesson in how unethical—and effective—the right-wing scream machine is.

Our critique actually comes from the left. But what were we supposed to do, muzzle our critique just because Fox News agrees with ten percent of the book? A lot of liberals thought so and told us so. But we concluded that the truth of what we saw and did must stand for itself, politics be damned.

Liberals are too skittish critiquing the UN: if anyone's values have been betrayed over the past decade it is those of us who believe most deeply in the organization's ideals. It's similar to the Catholic Church's scandals: church hierarchy thinks it's more important to protect the esteem in which the institution is held than to protect the humans the institution exists to serve. We disagree. Passionately.

9). *Is there hope for the UN?* Not until there is accountability and change at the top. Senior UN leaders did nothing while almost a million people they promised to protect were killed in genocides in Rwanda and Bosnia. To save their jobs, they then choreographed a campaign of denial and blame-shifting so effective that even a decade later the closest any came to accepting personal responsibility was a duplicitous "I thought at the time I was doing everything I could but realized later I could have done more" from our Secretary-General. No one was investigated, reprimanded, or fired, and no one had the decency to resign. All took refuge in their diplomatic UN safe haven, far above individual accountability and far from the suffering of victims.

The same people are still in charge. None of them was made to pay any price for inaction in the face of genocide, so it stands to reason that a decade later, none of them has done anything effective about genocide in Darfur. Rwanda and Srebrenica taught them well: at the UN, saving face—and your job—comes before saving lives.

10). *Where are you now? What do you do?* Andrew lives in Cambodia. He, Suzanne, and daughter Clara live in the house he built beside the

Mekong River. Three decades after the Killing Fields, Khmer Rouge genocide trials are finally beginning. Full circle. But he's busy planting bougainvillea and harvesting mangoes on his land. Ken writes full time, focusing on "dispatches from the homefront"—magazine articles, film, and TV projects about American forces returning home from Iraq. He lives in Brooklyn with his girlfriend Susie, also a writer. Heidi moved to Walla Walla, Washington, where she bought and restored a rambling old house. She works at an art gallery and has developed a taste for the fine wines of her adopted rolling hills and valleys of Washington State.

ENDNOTES

1. The human rights reports quoted in Echo on pages [255, 256–57, and 258] appeared in Kenneth Cain, "The Rape of Dinah: Human Rights, Civil War in Liberia, and Evil Triumphant," *Human Rights Quarterly* 21.2 (1999), 265–307. Three of those reports originally appeared elsewhere, as quoted in "The Rape of Dinah": p. [256]: "pit latrine," Peter Da Costa, "Counselling Victims of the Civil War," *Africa Report Newsmagazine,* March–April 1994, at 30, 31; [p. 257]: "breast," Justice and Peace Commission of the National Catholic Secretariat of Liberia, *Report on Fact-Finding Mission to Gbarnga* 3 (14–17 July 1994); and [p. 258]: "womb," "Rape: A Silent Scourge of the Liberian Conflict," *World Health Organization Newsletter* (WHO Office, Monrovia, Liberia), April–June 1995, at 1, 4.

2. Estimation of casualties is an enormously unscientific enterprise. For example, the U.S. Department of State estimates as many as 263,000 casualties in the former Yugoslavia; see U.S. Department of State, "Bosnia and Herzegovina," in *Country Reports on Human Rights Practices for 1995,* 15 791 (1996). But the International Committee of the Red Cross, among others, has challenged this figure and estimates casualties at a fraction of the State Department's number. See Peter Cary, "Bosnia by the Numbers," *U.S. News & World Report,* 10 April 1995, at 53. We have generally referred to media-derived "consensus" casualty numbers for each of the relevant conflicts we address, but our use of numbers varies depending on our understanding of estimates current at the moment recounted herein.

3. The Rwandan Patriotic Front (RPF) refers to the rebel group fighting the Rwandan government before and during the genocide, while the Rwandan Patriotic Army (RPA) refers to the government army formed by the RPF when it took power after the war. Pages [215–222].

4. During the military coup in Haiti (1991–94), the Haitian army and police used thousands of armed civilians as paramilitary auxiliaries to terrorize the population and eliminate any remaining political activity by Aris-

tide supporters. These plainclothes agents operated with impunity and were associated with a violent political organization known as the Front for Advancement and Progress of Haiti or FRAPH. Haitians sometimes referred to these auxiliaries as *attachés,* but they were also known in the vernacular as *macoutes* to indicate the reemergence of the Tontons Macoute, the feared Duvalier-era secret police network. We have generally used the term *macoute* throughout Condition Charlie as a catchall.

ACKNOWLEDGMENTS

Sloan Harris, our agent at ICM, had the courage to embrace this project in its earliest, inchoate form, then skillfully shepherded us through three grueling but exhilarating years. We are deeply grateful. Thank you to Amanda Urban for personally responding to our first query with enthusiasm. Katharine Cluverius has been a constant, and intensely appreciated, source of intelligent guidance. We are lucky to have the consummate professionals of ICM represent us.

JillEllyn Riley, editorial director of Miramax Books, has gone so far beyond the call of duty, including house calls, she redefined the concept of in-house champion; thank you JillEllyn for the loving care. Thank you to Jonathan Burnham, president of Miramax Books, for your faith in three unknowns on an unusual project. We are grateful to Peter Guzzardi for a masterful editorial hand and to Joe Veltre for early and crucial support at Miramax. Hilary Bass is as good at her job as it gets; Kristin Powers has been magnificently patient with us. We are lucky to work with the smart, warm, and talented folks at Miramax.

Thank you to Marlene Adelstein, Heather Bourbeau, Erin Sax, Rebecca Segall, and Lisa Shactman for indispensable editorial assistance. Bill Lychak offered us the single most important piece of editorial advice in three years of needing it. Thank you to Kim Busi for keeping us sane and to Dr. Allen Keller of the Bellevue/NYU Program for Survivors of Torture for providing the worthiest of causes to support.

Andrew, January 2004
Brooklyn

I am indebted to Eric Stover and Gilles Peress, who encouraged me to write when I would have preferred to forget. Christine Crevoisier, Andre Sirois and Gary Whitlock read different stages of the manuscript, and I'm grateful for their sharp eyes and clever suggestions. Steve Cain hit the nail on the head repeatedly with his keen advice, and Al and Bobbie Cain were faithful supporters, in life as well as in writing.

I met many kindred spirits while on mission, but among those who taught me much and whose kindness means the world to me are Jose Pablo Baraybar, Igor Begovic, Nick Birnback, Luc Côté, Mary Fisk, Anne Fosty, Anne Guillou, Bill Haglund, Bruce Henry, Patrick Hughes, Salvatore Lombardo, Fabienne Luco, Peter Mutch, Stephanie O'Connor, Patrick Peillod, Giuseppe Pogliari, Michel Thieren and Brenda Sue Thornton.

For their dedication in the field, my former UN colleagues in the human rights component in Cambodia, the medical doctors of the Haiti mission and the forensic teams of the Tribunals for Rwanda and Yugoslavia have all my admiration.

Thanks to the Medical Service of UN Headquarters in New York for having me back after each mission.

To Kenneth Cain: who is passionate and persistent about everything that matters, remains the most effective humanitarian I know, and who edited my writing with skill and care from the beginning, thank you. Ken, you're the brother I never had.

To Heidi Postlewait: who is unafraid to speak her mind (and is almost always right), bore her losses with grace, whose intelligence is as wicked as her humor, and whose compassion continues to inspire me, thank you. Heidi, they broke the mold when they made you.

I'm deeply indebted to my mum and dad, Carole and David Thomson, for four decades of prayers and devotion. We don't get to choose our parents, but some of us do get extraordinarily lucky. I'm one of them. Thanks also to my sisters Jane and Sarah, who provided comfort and a listening ear between missions, and for whom I have the deepest affection.

Suzanne Blanc-Thomson is a fleeting presence in these pages, but a constant one in my life. I asked much from her during the writing of this book, and she never failed to give generously. Suzie, for your sensibility, your wisdom, and your love, *merci infiniment*.

Heidi, January 2004
Brooklyn

Thanks to my colleagues in the Communications and Information Technology Service: those in UNHQ, for your camaraderie, and those in the field—the unsung heroes and backbone of any peacekeeping mission—I am privileged to be counted among you. Rudy Sanchez showed patience and forbearance, for which I am deeply grateful.

ACKNOWLEDGMENTS

I am grateful to the following friends from my years on mission, who gave me skills to survive, each in their own way: Denise Glasser taught me to cross the street in Phnom Penh; Hinda Mohamed coached me in "massaging the system"; Ali Farah Anshor kept me laughing; Peggy Pedre was always my co-conspirator and often my alibi; Jim Abelee taught me how to treat a sucking chest wound and other ways to stay alive; and Almaz Ghanem and Rana Istwani gave me knitting lessons when all else was lost. To Sandro and Claudia Calavalle—thank you for being at the end of that plane ramp with arms open wide. Ons Ben Zakour is never far from my heart. Jp Pueshel sustained me with an inspiring exchange of letters in which hundreds of stories found their voices.

I am indebted to Jerry Morrone (Cinnamon Toast, a long time coming), Margaret Kotarba, Katherine Kent Watkowski, Jeff Kaplan, Katie Orenstein, Susie Devenyi, Scott Vradelis, Catherine Montgomery, Suzanne Blanc-Thomson, Barbara and Albert Cain, Thomas Kotarba, Andrew Kotarba, Yitzchak El Hadad, Elizabeth Ricceri, and Cindy Postlewait for their ceaseless encouragement and support, in many cases, over a lifetime. Helen Vradelis was a whirlwind of grace and animation. Joey Postlewait was always by my side. To Yvette Blanco, a generous friend who graciously shares an office and a hallway with me, thank you for repeatedly dropping everything to hold my hand and contain my meltdowns. Franca Vinci believed in me enough to take on the work of five in order that I could find time to write this book. *Grazie, Schifezza.* Love and thanks to my brother, Troy Postlewait, for being the rock in my turbulent waters. Thanks to Amy Correia for letting me steal her line, and to Edwidge Danticat for wise editorial guidance.

Thanks to Tim O'Brien's Mary Anne Bell, who may or may not exist, but who understands what I'm talking about.

To Andrew Thomson, who was tasked with forensic work of historical significance in the graves of Srebrenica and Rwanda, a job no one should be expected to bear—your courage, strength and perseverance gave voice to people who could no longer speak for themselves. I am honored to be a part of your life.

Since the night we met over a decade ago, Ken Cain has been my friend and confidante. The idea for this book was his, and armed with determination of spirit, his winning ability to charm, and no small amount of angst, he pushed this project through to completion. Kenneth, I thank you from the bottom of my heart for cajoling, begging, and threatening me to keep moving.

My father, Calvin "Pete" Postlewait, made the mistake of sharing with me his stories of growing up a migrant farm worker, hopping boxcars across the American mid-west. The stories were thrilling and somehow glamorous, against the backdrop of suburban New Jersey. Thank you, daddy, for imparting those sometimes painful memories. They made all the difference.

My foremothers, Marie Ibbott, Elsie Spehr, Mabel Postlewait and Betty Wales, taught me by example what women are made of. My nieces, Hannah, Madison and Athena Postlewait, let me see life in a whole new way.

And with love and thanks to my mother, Linda Ibbott Postlewait, on whose shoulders I stand.

Ken, January 2004
Brooklyn

Scott Vradelis' fellowship was a small, daily miracle of inspiration and talent. Jeff Kaplan's unstinting support and inspired guidance were a godsend. Dan Braun read manuscripts early and often, bigheartedly and brilliantly. Responsibility for the contents of my share of the book is mine alone, but I was blessed with good friends who cared about the attempt to get it right.

Thank you to Mr. Leslie Gelb for wise counsel at the Council over many years and to Elise Carlson Lewis for encouragement and support. Pascal Soto and Luc Côté are two of the most courageous *militants des droits de l'homme* ever to do the work; I was lucky to have seen them in action. I thank Ken Petersen for sharing his love of telling stories. Mr. Ons Ben Zakour, Jim Scally, Hinda Mohamed, Ali Farah Anshor and the Mendises were family when family was far away: I love you.

Sloan, you said we'd need someone with *cojones* to pull this off. We did. It was you. Thank you to Naomi Wolf for constant inspiration and the example of fighting fire with fire. I was privileged to receive valuable guidance at a crucial moment from Mr. Nicholas Delbanco. Katie Orenstein and Ruti Teitel are two of the sharpest writers and thinkers I've ever met; I am grateful for their fellowship.

This book is about the sustenance of friendship. Old and good friends who do not appear in these pages have long sustained me in no less dramatic ways—apologies for being distant and gratitude for understanding to: Matt Schaefer; Steve, Daphne, Ethan and Rebecca Genyk; Keith Helber; Chris White; Andrew Ayre; Brad Vogt; David Carnoy, Frank Barrett; Ashan Abeyesundere; Priyan Attygalle; Mark Clark; Howard Sackstein; Rebecca Spence; Fabienne Hara; and Susan Paley.

Thank you to: Christina Capone for getting us started at ICM; Kate Farrell for the inspired referral to Christina; Alison Zarecki for the soundtrack; Amy Correia for the fresh take and humor; Dan Nelson and Charles Mixon for keeping me sane on Wall Street; Paolo Grassi for mentorship in the office and friendship in the air; Joe Monaco for generosity, expertise and patience on the water; Jill Bach for selfless help; Aviv Carmel and Sharoni Guesthalter for the decade-long tutorial; Nomika, Amram and Kibbutz Migvan for the inspiration; Mitchell Horowitz for introducing me to a propitious path, and to my sister-in-law, Gina Champion Cain, for the warmth, hospitality and support. Yvette Blanco has been as generous a friend as one could hope to find. "Liza," I am infinitely in debt to you.

I've been honored to work with dedicated American officials—in the field and back home, in uniform and out—whom I will refrain from acknowledging by name. I am unapologetically critical in this book of American peacekeeping policy in the nineties. But if any disrespect is inadvertently implied to you, your mission or the uniform, the weakness is my skill as a writer, not my respect for the job you do.

My brother, Steve Cain, was among the original proponents of this book—well before I had the confidence to consider the idea seriously. But his advocacy was so emphatic and sure, it was destined to capture the imagination of a younger brother. He has been providing ferociously intelligent guidance on every draft since. Thank you, Steve.

To Suzanne Blanc-Thomson: apologies for kidnapping your husband and gratitude for your gentle and important support. To Andrew Thomson: thank you for your courage in writing this book and living its subject. Writing with you has been the highlight of my UN career. In acknowledgement of my sister Miss Heidi, who prefers minimalism in such matters: it has been my great fortune to know this extraordinary woman.

To Susie Devenyi, with love and stunned delight: in your passionate grace and unassuming genius, you've written a happier end to my Return to Normal than I ever dreamt possible.

How to fit an ocean of esteem held, gratitude owed, and love felt for my parents into the thimble of these few words—at the end of a book called *Emergency Sex*? Albert and Barbara Cain are my favorite professors, smartest editors and, ultimately, the audience that matters most. They suffered the events herein, with painfully tender patience, as acutely as I did. For that I am sorry. But in their lifelong fidelity to an ancient obligation, they propelled me—imperfectly but inexorably—onward. For that I am grateful.